Leap into Learning

TEACHING CURRICULUM THROUGH CREATIVE DRAMATICS AND DANCE

by Kristen Bissinger
and Nancy Renfro

photographs by:
Anne Jackson

illustrated by:
Cara Grauer

FOREWORD

It seems that destiny brought Kristen Bissinger and I together. The vision of a book such as this one had been incubating in the back of my mind for some time, but I knew that I lacked the necessary skills to hatch it into reality. Puppetry was my stronghold and main avenue in introducing creative concepts into the classroom.

Six years ago, Kristen attended one of my puppetry workshops in Pennsylvania. Afterwards, she introduced herself, and began sharing her drama/dance ideas with me. Within five minutes, I knew that I had met the co-author of this book. The storm of her unbounded enthusaism and animation, original ideas and obvious dedication to the education of children swept me along, and a deluge of idea-sharing began. We also shared similar experiences as learning disabled students.

It took six years of hard work for this book to come to fruition. Many of the ideas were new and needed to be fine-tuned in Kristen's classrooms. The end results is this book; a melding of ideas by two people who, after struggling painfully as young children in the process of learning, have developed alternative methods of education.

The authors, through personal search, determination and pure tenacity, with the assistance of certain perceptive teachers who introduced alternative methods of learning, were indeed fortunate to emerge as successful students, sharing a mutual zest for learning that knows no bounds. Most of all, they believe in each child's uniqueness and capacity to excel, and in the teacher's role as a powerful and positive guiding force in the classroom.

I am greatly indebted to Kristen Bissinger for her hard work, and for the many hours she devoted to creating, researching, piloting , and consolidating ideas into making this book a reality.

* * * *

I have been partially deaf all of my life. Cut off from the seemingly effortless communciation that is so much a part of everyday life, I was unwilling to consider myself handicapped. My personal survival hinged on a deep commitment of creative endeavors, especially in the realm of the visual arts. I was eager to try out all the media and like a sponge have, throughout my life, absorbed one applied art form after another — crayons, paint, paper, clay, and wood; and later, with career orientation in mind — graphics, architectural design, puppetry and fine arts.

My early education was centered around a system that was purely verbal. Most teachers made a special effort to give me the best advantage in their classroom by strategically located seating and repeating things when necessary. Despite attempts by considerate teachers to include me, most of the eight years in elementary school were passive ones spent daydreaming, window staring or clock watching. It was simply too much of a strain for this hearing impaired person to try to listen for long periods of time. The immediate result was poor academic grades. Fortunately, my behavior was excellent, but I can readily empathize today, with children with behavioral problems which often stem from a disability. It takes incredible discipline and patience to sit for five or six successive periods in a totally *passive* capacity.

Thus I am an advocate of a multi-media form of education, one that incorporates art, music, dance and drama in exciting ways, expanding the opportunities for *all* children to learn. It is my fervent hope that the efforts put forth in this book will help to pave the way towards alternate methods of teaching.

Nancy Renfro

As a young student I often felt a sense of humiliation when asked to present material in front of the class. I failed miserably at spelling bees or math problems on the board and would probably have been diagnosed as dyslexic or learning disabled had I been born in this era.

It was not until fifth grade that my experience with education took a positive turn due to a perceptive and adventuresome teacher. One afternoon the class was asked to push back the desks and curl up on the floor like seeds in the soil. Mrs. Short played music and asked us to close our eyes, imagine ourselves plants and grow up toward the sunlight. I remember profoundly enjoying this experiential break from our ordinary routine of learning. I felt centered and totally refreshed. It was a wonderful new experience in the classroom!

With simple bits of encouragement and inventive teaching such as this, I began to make strides in my educational process in the fifth grade. As I matured, I gradually built new self-confidences and overcame my difficulties fitting into the educational system. Since then, I always delighted in experiential learning activities as they were introduced.

My failures and successes within the educational system have had a poignant effect upon me. I know the rapture and satisfaction that come with drama and dance activities; in the last ten years I have sought new ways of merging these medias with education. The drama/dance approach to education has done wonders in my life and is devoured eagerly by those I teach. I receive great joy in seeing my students' faces light up as I enter the room. They know we are going to participate in a unique and creative experience, one that will bring newfound discoveries and self-esteem. It is in this situation that learning can truly begin.

Kristen Bissinger

Acknowledgements

I would like to express my heartfelt gratitude to my co-author, Nancy Renfro. Through her intuition and inspiration we started this venture. Her positive and persistent spirit has been a guiding factor throughout our efforts together.

Anne Jackson, our photographer, has been wonderful to work with. Her superb professional approach and good sense of humor have companioned this project.

Cara Graver's delightful illustrations have matched our wishes that she express the magic of children in motion.

Lucy McIlvaine's encouraging support and enthusiasm as typist, editor and friend has been invaluable.

Special thanks goes to my husband, Tom Bissinger, for his steady support and excellent editing; my children Zachary and Esther for their understanding; to Betty Jane Dittmar, who has inspired me by her creative and versatile approach to dance and the arts; to Jean McMillen for introducing me to Creative Dramatics and for the loving support of her and her husband, William McMillen, during my college years; to my Re-evaluation Co-counseling support group - Karen Laughman, Barbara Faison, Connie Rainis, Holly Smith, Kathy Wilson and Marina Gresham for helping me hurdle writing blocks; to Carole B. Rozewski for her years of faith in me as a person and a teacher; to my parents-in-law Robert and Marjorie Seller for their insightful assistance; to my sister Cheryl Cutler for her ongoing spiritual support.

Gratitude goes out to a number of teachers and students whose work and play in drama/dance classes helped form this book:

- Caryl Ann Cooper and the children attending the Children's House of Northern Chester County, Pottstown, PA.
- Nancy Etter, Karen Clemente and the dancers of Feet First, a Center for Contemporary and Classical Dance, Phoenixville, PA.
- Mary Louise Lloyd, Lynn Morris and the childen attending Copeland Run Learning Center, Downingtown, PA.
- Carol Kulp and the participants of the Green Valleys Association Summer Camps, Birchrunville, PA.
- Kevin Hughes, Philip Graham and the Kimberton Waldorf School classes of 1994 and 2000, Kimberton, PA.
- Amy Faga and her Academically Talented Program classes in the Owen J. Roberts School District, Pottstown, PA.
- Phyllis La Drew and the children attending Brandywine Academy, Downingtown and Glenmoore, PA.

Finally, I would like to acknowledge my parents, Howard and Enid Cutler, who have expressed trust in me throughout my life. By their zestful example they continue to teach me the joys of the learning process.

Kristen Bissinger

TABLE OF CONTENTS
SECTION ONE – THE PRIMARY TOOLS

SECTION TWO – CURRICULUM CLASS PLANS

Section One

MAIN INTRODUCTION

Leap Into Learning! is a guide to creating exciting and topical learning situations based on skills developed through creative dramatics and dance games. The classroom becomes an energized and well organized arena in which creative intelligence is activated and curriculmum material is brought to life.

A quick glance at the table of contents will convey an overview of the multitude of Language Arts, Social Studies, Science, and Math activities which are geared for teaching K-7th graders. To highlight some examples:

• Prepositions are experienced through the enactment of a story adventure that takes a bear family through a berry patch, under and over obstacles.
• Enactments of folktales, such as the Russian tale "The Little Snow Maiden", give insight into other cultures during social studies units.
• A contact dance game, "Push and Pull", centered around pushing a partner, prepares the participants to enact the formation of metamorphic rock in a science lesson.
• Calling out numbers while stamping and clapping in a circle formation teaches participants the multiplication tables in a math oriented activity.

Full involvement in drama/dance enactments allows participants to assimilate important factual information while enhancing understanding of that information.

By guiding children through a *creative learning adventure*, one in which they have input and take an active part, we are able to provoke thinking — and motivate interest and research.

In a study of Christopher Columbus, for example, we might provoke thinking and motivate research through enacting the answers to questions such as: "What were the prevailing beliefs about the ocean and the world in Columbus' time?" "What hardships were faced in soliciting funds to finance such an adventure?" or "How did Columbus and his crew feel when they sighted land?" By putting themselves in the shoes of the great explorer and his crew, the students are given an opportunity to assimilate far more than dates, locations and names of the ships used in the voyage.

The classroom material presented in this book is beautifully suited for all types of students, whether they learn auditorially, visually, or kinesthetically; whether they are accelerated learners or those who learn more slowly.

The drama/dance teaching method proposed in this book affirms the student as a wellspring, one who contributes to the learning process, rather than a receptacle to be filled with information. This method utilizes rather than suppresses the student's needs to move, socialize, discuss and become intrinsically involved with what is being learned.

What is Meant by "Dance" and "Creative Dramatics"?

For many teachers the inclusion of dance will be a new wrinkle. The aspect of dance utilized in *Leap Into Learning!* is *creative dance*. It involves the basic elements of dance: space, time, force, body movement, and body parts. This approach is very different from teaching a traditional dance *form* such as ballet, modern, jazz, social, or folk dance. Neither teacher nor participant need be familiar with any of the above dance forms to participate fully in the creative dance activities found throughout this book.

Because of pre-conceived notions it is advised that, at the outset, the teacher be judicious in using the term "dance". Occasionally, boys are reluctant to dance because they envision ballet or social dance forms. But it will be discovered that most students participate with enthusiasm when challenged to develop their own movement within a class structure. It is suggested that the leader wait until the group is fully involved in drama/dance activities before revealing to the participants that they are indeed exploring aspects of dance. (Refer to "How to Use Basic Dance Elements" that follows for a more in-depth look at this approach.)

Creative dramatics is a *process* rather than a product form of drama. Through this process themes are brought to life through thoughts, actions, and dialogue. Participants are initially warmed up with movement, mime, and characterization exercises. They are thus prepared to enact a scenario. For instance: The class members might be divided into smaller groups and each group given the theme of fire to explore. The leader may set the scene by saying, "You are cave men and women. One half of each group has fire, the other half does not." The groups must develop action and dialogue around that given scenario. The solutions may be diverse: One group might stage a fight to capture the fire, one group roast an animal, and another barter for a few coals. *It is important that enactments are practiced simultaneously so that everyone remains involved and interested.* At the conclusion of practice time, all the groups may share enactments for the others to watch.

The Value of Drama/Dance Techniques

In a momentous way, drama and dance have been closely combined in this book. The term "drama/dance" will be used hereafter to identify the proposed teaching medium.

Teaching through drama/dance might be seen as a new form in educational circles, but it is one of the oldest forms of instruction known to humanity. The cycle of educational methods, originating in drama/dance, has evolved through oral history to written history, and into the current computer age.

Why include drama/dance in the existing classroom structure? How can it enhance the prevailing teaching methods? It has not proved wholly effective to take the young and active student and attempt to confine him or her to a seated classroom environment with focus on cognitive development through audio/visual methods of teaching. Such an approach is more appropriate for teen and adult level teaching. In contrast, a drama/dance teaching method involves the whole human being: the physical, intellectual, emotional, social, and spiritual. Here is a method that reaches the young learner, the concrete and kinesthetic learners, and provides a welcome break to sit-down activities. A growing number of educators, both public and private, are coming to recognize that children learn best through active, hands-on teaching techniques which incorporate games and dramatic play.

This type of teaching is called "developmentally appropriate practice". It is based on principles which Piaget and other knowledgeable educators have discovered about the way children learn.

Not only will a drama/dance method of teaching energize existing methods, through active involvement of participants, but other benefits will be realized as well. The objectives of drama/dance activities are to:

- *Develop self-esteem* by providing each child with an avenue of self-expression. Self-esteem is built upon creative expression.
- *Encourage and guide the child's imagination* which becomes dormant and inactive unless exercised.
- *Encourage group-esteem* by giving young people opportunities to grow in social understanding and cooperation. Learning to understand and/or empathize with others through character portrayal, as well as learning to interact socially with other children, are highly important experiences that help students form a supportive learning environment.
- *Provide an emotional outlet* – Among the arts, all of which offer constructive opportunities for channeling emotions, drama/ dance is unique in its concrete use of people and social situations.

- *Build skills in "thinking on one's feet"* – Poise comes from being both physically and verbally articulate. Because the dialogue and movements in drama/dance are improvised and not memorized, there are many opportunities to "think on one's feet".
- *Encourage freedom of expression* – Both teacher and participants gain new confidence and satisfaction from this physically inventive medium.
- *Increase involvement and enjoyment* of literature and the subjects taught through this medium.

The authors of this book view drama/dance in the classroom as an Aladdin's Magical Lamp. As we hone and polish our drama/dance skills the magic in each and every one of us comes forth. We all contain within us special powers and potentials: the ability to imagine, to blossom, and to express our thoughts and feelings in a unique way. By setting the stage for these magical qualities to come forth, adventures in learning take flight. So be fearless, take wing and be willing to venture into the new!

Teaching Tips

For many teachers the concept of using creative dramatics and dance as mediums for teaching may be totally new. Others may already be well acquainted with the use of dramatic and movement techniques for enlivening the classroom. However, it is not at all necessary for the teacher or students to have previous drama and dance training for a drama/dance method of teaching to be successful. *Leap Into Learning!* aims to be useful to both the novice and the experienced teacher, offering a wide selection of ideas that can be adapted not only to the classroom but for recreational purposes as well, such as summer camps, youth groups, church and after school programs, and drama and dance classes.

The following are guidelines to enhance the use of this book.

- *Be confident* – The children are going to enjoy being involved. Select activities from the curriculum class plans in Section Two that you feel confident with and appeal to you personally. Go over the curriculum material thoroughly. Practice reading or explaining the material to yourself before presenting the activity to the class. The more this drama/dance method is used the easier and less time-consuming the preparation will become and a lifetime skill will be acquired.
- *Explain the activity clearly and concisely to the participants* – Be sure that everyone involved understands what they are going to do before they

begin. Explain to the group members that they will be doing exercises to become limber and strong, learning dramatic, dance, and pantomime skills, and acting out a story or lesson. Ask the members to define the terms *pantomime* and *drama* and explain these terms, if necessary.

• *Have a clear class structure* – The class plans in this book have been structured under the headings: Objective, Getting Started, Warm-up and Activity. These headings with accompanying text become the components that help the teacher to prepare for the class activity.

It can be helpful to highlight key words in this book or write simplified notes for easy reference in the middle of a session.

Keep the participants motivated and involved by alternating between the livelier and quieter exercises. For example, a class may start with a locomotion exercise, proceed to stretches, followed by an active movement game, a reading of the story or explanation of the material, then finally a full enactment. This pacing guards against physical exhaustion, overexcitement, or boredom.

• *Introduce a control mechanism right away* – The exercise "Jump/Freeze" has great appeal, gets the participants moving, and introduces the ideas of freezing both action and talking on cue. Later on this game can be adapted for use during any part of a class activity. Use a hand clap, a word signal such as "freeze", or a drum beat to cue freezing. If participants become overexcited regain control by having them freeze, then proceed in a new direction or have a seated discussion to refocus their attention.

If one or several participants become disruptive, speak to those involved about unacceptable behavior and/or interject a practice session of the desired behavior through a warm-up. (See Introduction to Primary Tools - Discipline.) If the undesired behavior continues ask any unruly participants to leave the group.

• *Begin with group activities in which all can participate simultaneously* – Most of the Primary Tools are geared toward simultaneous participation. Only a few exercises in the "Create and Copy;" category single out participants for individual performance and these exercises can be introduced after several sessions of group work. It is important to note that activities found in the Primary Tools and curriculum class plans are to be enacted, for the most part, simultaneously. Simultaneous enactment keeps everyone involved and diminishes the possibility of initial embarrassment of the individual in front of peers.

• *Never force a child to participate* – Some children may be reluctant at first; let these children be non-participating members of the group until they are ready to fully join in the activity. On the other hand, do not allow a child who is not involved to spoil the activity for others through disruptive behavior.

Other than keeping these beginning tips in mind, the factors of *time, space* and *age level* need to be considered before overall planning.

Space

The success of a large motor activity such as drama/dance is directly affected by the space in which it is conducted. Too small a space tends to increase the sensation of confusion, too large a space makes control and concentration on the task more difficult. If you think your group is too wild or noisy or find the group members are highly distracted, don't give up! It may simply be that the space is not right.

On a whole, a larger space is easier to deal with than a smaller one. A gym or all-purpose room is ideal for these activities. If a very large space, such as a gym, parking lot, or playground is available, define the space you wish the participants to use with sports cones, a line of chairs, shoes, rope, or other boundaries. If working in an outdoor space expect more distractions and therefore difficulty in concentration, though some activities such as "Shadow Sleuthing" and "Animals and Their Habitats" work best outdoors.

If a classroom is the available space, push back desks and all obstructions to maximize the space available. If necessary, the group members can take turns for large motor exercises. Divide the group in half. Have one half watch while the other half moves. Keep the movement happening quickly from one half of the class to the other.

The following is an activity approach to preparing the room for drama/dance activities:

If a classroom is the availabla space, push back desks and all obstructions to maximize the space available. If necessary, the group members can take turns for large motor exercises. Divide the group in half. Have one half watch while the other half moves imaginary items. Keep the movement happening quickly from one half of the class to the other.

The following is an activity approach for preparing the room for drama/dance enactments:

Move That Museum Piece!

Objective: To clear the classroom quickly and quietly in preparation for creative drama/dance activities.

Getting Started: Design a floor plan with your class to achieve maximum open space in the room. For example: desks can be arranged around all the sides of the room or lined up on one or two sides. The aim is to make the open space in the middle of the room as large and free of obstructions as possible. Discuss hazardous elements in the room such as objects having sharp edges, glass (aquariums, windows and mirrors) and electrical cords. Also keep all exits free of obstructions.

Activity: The participants are to imagine that they are museum curators moving priceless objects of art to moving vans for transport to another museum. In this case each desk can represent a priceless object such as the "Mona Lisa", an Egyptian mummy, or dinosaur bones. Establish that the sides of the room or the designated location are to represent moving vans for transporting the art to its next exhibit location.

Set the scene by explaining, "We must quietly remove all the art in this exhibit and pack it in the moving vans to send it on to the next showing." Continue by saying, "Choose a partner to be your assistant. You will help each other lift your desks and chairs out of the center of the room then fit them neatly into the trucks without making a sound. Quietly drive your truck away, then regroup in a circle in the center of the room." Once the circle is completed, the warm-ups for the drama/dance class can begin.

Themes under study in the classroom can also provide opportunities in which desks become props. In this way, moving the desks becomes a game and provides a pantomime warm-up which leads into the curriculum activity. For example:

Social Studies – construction materials for architectural monuments (Eiffel Tower, a pyramid, World Trade Center); objects involved in a historic event (such as supplies for Columbus' voyage).

Music – instruments being trucked for a road tour (grand piano, guitar, synthesizer, violin).

Language Arts – material related to a story to be enacted (in "Robin Hood" desks could become valuable furniture, trunks of gold, etc.)

Time

Age level as well as schedule will determine the time alloted for an activity. In general the class plans in this book are geared to a one-hour session. Simpler activities can be done in forty-five minutes and in some cases a warm-up or two can be deleted to save time, although, in general, this is not advised. If time is restricted it is possible divide warm-ups into two segments, and present the same curriculum material over two sessions using different warm-ups each time. Or, when time is limited, the teacher may wish to cover the warm-ups fully in one session, review the warm-ups briefly, and perform the main activity in another session.

Morning hours are generally recommended for drama/dance activities, for physical energy is high at this time of day. However, it may be preferred at times to conduct these activities in the afternoon when a break is needed from seated academic studies.

Age Level

The material in this book is centered around preschool through seventh grade curriculum. In each titled section or category throughout the book the activities are presented in order of difficulty. Many of the activities are appropriate for all the age levels and many can be tailored to suit any age level. In most cases the curriculum content will clue the teacher as to the appropriateness of an activity. In many cases a warm-up or activity can be adapted to suit an age level, for instance, an activity such as "Dictionary Wisdom" can be easily adapted by utilizing simpler or more advanced vocabulary accordingly. A stretch like "Twinkle, Twinkle Little Star", which may appear "childish" to an older group, can be done without the song or to a more advanced poem or song. If middle school students hang back or appear embarrassed, encourage self-esteem and present the exercises with open enthusiasm. Most important in approaching older groups is to break down inhibitions. Once inhibitions are melted with the introduction of game-like contact dance structures, such as "Body Sculpting" and "Action/Reaction" as found in the Primary Tools, middle school and high school students as well as adults, delight in this playful approach to learning.

On the other hand, more advanced material may be streamlined for younger groups by omitting more complicated aspects and terminology. For example, when conducting "Photosynthesis" with a younger group, the advanced vocabulary included in the activity can be de-emphasized and focus placed instead on the gestures and the basic concept.

Choosing a Beginning Activity

Each section and category of *Leap Into Learning!* is organized according to skill level, the simpler activities placed first.

Choose an activity near the beginning of a section or category that inspires you personally and is age-appropriate for the group. Read it through, stopping to study and refer to the suggested warm-ups located in the Primary Tools section before proceeding to the main curriculum activity. If the activity is centered around a story or poem, it is advisable for the teacher to read that literature before reading the class plan so as to understand the choice of warm-ups and the activity itself.

If one is working with an ongoing group it may prove useful to begin the study of drama/dance by exploring a few sessions of Primary Tools, establishing the rules and gaining familiarity with the beginning activities method, before attempting a curriculum study. The enthusiasm with which most groups receive these activities will offer encouragement for further exploration. The following gives a few suggestions of beginning activities for the novice teacher to try in the classroom. However, there are many choices other than these that the teacher may prefer as starting points to suit present needs. Keep in mind that complex activities can be broken down into more manageable segments.

- *Pre-School and Early Grades* – "Insects" in the Science/Life section and "The Golden Egg Book" in Language Arts are excellent beginning activities for this age level. The story line in each case is simple and involves only one or two characters. The first two or three exercises listed in all the Primary Tools categories (except "Create and Copy" and "Action/Reaction") are also wonderful beginning activities for this age group as is a session exploring scarves.

All the Language Arts/Story Enactments (except "Stone in the Road'") are suitable material for a pre-school through grade school group.

- *Grade School* – "How the Rhinoceros Got His Skin" and "The Lion and the Mouse" from the Language Arts section are favorites with grade schoolers and make enjoyable introductions to drama/dance activities. The first half of the Grammar section in Language Arts is rich with movement exploration and also includes good beginning material. In addition, the Story Enactment and Poetry portions of Language Arts are excellent for beginning class plans. The first half of the Life and Earth Science sections also have great appeal for grade school age children while offering new challenges.

- *Middle School* – The International Stories listed in the Social Studies section are, in general, more complex and appropriate for the 5th - 7th grade age group. Because the stories are complex, however, the time must be taken to prepare the participants for the best introductory lesson. The "Body Sculpting", "Action/Reaction", "Dancing Words", "Locomotion", and "Characterization Locomotion" exercises generate enthusiasm and are good introductions to basic drama/dance concepts for this age group. "Shadow Sleuthing", "Environmental Education", and "The Three Major Classifications of Rocks", all in the Science/Earth section, are complex but very appropriate beginning activities for older grade school and middle school participants.

With these basic teaching tips at the teacher's disposal, confidences can be assured and a successful beginning to the drama/dance program launched.

HOW TO USE BASIC DANCE ELEMENTS

The teacher's conscious integration of the fundamental dance elements – Space, Time, Force and Body – is vital to the success of a drama/dance program. Creative dance, as defined in the Main Introduction, is highly effective in producing dynamic curriculum enactments. The dance elements in the following chart will enable the teacher to direct participants toward movement variety and expression. The teacher should familiarize the participants with these elements and the dance vocabulary involved through introducing appropriate Primary Tools exercises, such as "Dancing Words", "Action/Reaction", "Locomotion", and "Body Sculpting". These exercises may be tailored to focus on one dance element, or a combination of elements. The example that follows illustrates how some of the dance elements as presented in the following "Elements of Dance" chart, can be used in conjunction with the "Push/Pull", exercise found in the Primary Tools.

Space: Push your partner from one side of the room to the other.
Time: Push your partner slowly.
Force: Push with all your might.
Body parts: Push with your shoulder.

Or, using all the four of elements combined, one might give the directive: "Push your partner slowly and gently on a low level using your head."

Imagery vs. Movement Exploration

The drama/dance teaching method set forth in *Leap Into Learning!* requires that participants demonstrate academic concepts through movement and sound. The result of any activity will be far more innovative and dynamic if the students are guided toward variety in movement through the use of the dance elements. It is ineffective to give directives such as "Move like a tree" or "Be a tree", which rely primarily on mental imagery, whereas, a quick guided exploration of appropriate body movements incorporating dance elements can better promote exciting tree-like characterization.

To illustrate this point, the poem "Silver" in the Language Arts section involves enactments of trees. The teacher might have participants begin by exploring an aspect of *space* through the directives and questions: "Show me the *shape* of your tree. Is it crooked or straight? What *level* has your tree grown to? Is it a high, middle-sized, or low tree?"

Next, add exploration of *body moves:* Ask: "When the wind blows, show me how your tree bends, twists, shakes, collapses." Allow time for each move before making the next suggestion.

Try the element of *force:* "Now the wind is blowing sharply, making sudden fierce blasts. Now it is blowing gently. Is your tree's response rigid and *tight* like a big hard oak or supple and *loose* like a young sapling?"

"Which *body parts* represent the branches? Try

making the branches with your legs in the air. Now make branches with arms swaying overhead. Let your back and rib cage move with the wind. Move your fingers only. Let your tree move to the music as you *focus* your eyes upwards."

One can just imagine the unique and lively trees that will emerge from such an in-depth study of these dance elements.

Any aspect of curriculum that the teacher wishes to try through drama/dance techniques can be explored in this manner. Experience in using the dance elements as a means of encouraging expression and variety will quickly develop with practice. This approach will protect the teacher from the pitfall of relying exclusively on mental and verbal imagery.

In applying dance techniques to curriculum, study the curriculum material closely and consult the following chart to gain insight into which elements would best serve to depict specific curriculum material. One or two of the elements can be introduced very briefly, or an in-depth approach can be taken as demonstrated in the "tree" example.

The chart lists the basic elements of dance, categories within each element, and examples, as found in an excellent and highly recommended resource book, *First Steps in Teaching Creative Dance to Children* by Mary Joyce. (See Bibliography.)

The participants will begin to automatically incorporate variety in their movement as they become familiar with the dance terms used by the teacher.

Elements of Dance

Body	*Body parts*	Outer: head, shoulders, arms, hands, back, rib cage, hips, legs, feet Inner: muscles, bones, joints, heart, lungs (breath)
	Body moves	Stretch, bend, twist, circle, rise, collapse, swing, sway, shake
	Steps	Walk, run, leap, hop, jump, gallop, skip, slide
Space	*Shape*	Body design in space
	Level	High, middle, low
	Direction	Forward, backward, sideward, turning
	Size	Big, little
	Place	On the spot, through space
	Focus	Direction of gaze
	Pathway	Curved, straight
Force	*Attack*	Sharp, smooth
	Weight	Heavy, light
	Strength	Tight, loose
	Flow	Free-flowing, bound, or balanced
Time	*Beat*	Underlying pulse
	Tempo	Fast, slow
	Accent	Force
	Duration	Long, short
	Pattern	Combinations

Dance Element Game

The children in this photograph are studying the dance elements through the use of a rocket ship prop. Each star has the term "Body", "Space", "Force", or "Time" hidden on its back. The planets around each star bear the aspects of that element. The planets surrounding the "Force" star, for instance, are "attack", "weight", "strength", and "flow".

In the activity pictured here the child shown is flying the rocket ship to the star or planet of his choice. He will then lift the star or planet from the board and turn it over to reveal the dance element, or aspect of the element, written on the back. This game can be played simply to reinforce awareness of dance vocabulary or the group can explore, through movement, whatever dance word is revealed.

Sharing the Activity Through Discussion

A guided discussion following the physical activity of an enactment helps settle down the group and provides an opportunity for participants to verbalize and to share ideas. Most important is that the leader approach each class session with a positive tone. Let the participants know what makes a good enactment by pointing out those things done well, such as:

- *Good use of dialogue*
- *Appropriate volume when speaking*
- *Following storyline or curriculum scenarios accurately*
- *Explicit use of facial expression*
- *Interesting and convincing characterization through body movement and voice modification*
- *Creative and conscious involvement of the basic dance elements*
- *Effective portrayal of emotion*
- *Awareness of levels and spacing*
- *Good interaction and cooperation between players*

The group may come up with other important aspects to add to this list. Begin discussions with a statement such as, "Raise your hand if you wish to share something you saw in the enactment that was especially well done." With younger children it works well to ask, "What did you like best in our drama/dance activities today?" The responses can be useful for re-enactments but the main aim of discussion is for the children to verbalize what they saw, heard, or experienced during enactments. Try to keep discussions brief and to the point. Depending on the group and the enactment the leader may wish to add questions such as, "What do you think could have been done better and *how* would you improve it?" For some members, this may invite attacks of a personal nature and it must be clear that the comments be specific and at the same time constructive. Those who give critiques must also be required to share a constructive idea for improving the action or dialogue. It can be valuable to encourage older students to offer suggestions on what can be improved. This feedback enables the participants to develop a critical eye and ear, note inappropriate behavior, as well as improve the enactment with positive suggestions and solutions.

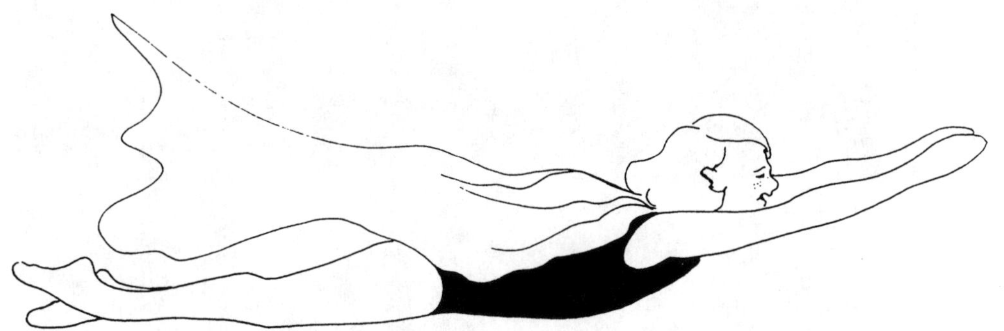

PRIMARY TOOLS
The Warm Ups

INTRODUCTION TO PRIMARY TOOLS

The Primary Tools Section that follows abounds with a rich selection of exercises to choose from for drama/dance purposes. Each curriculum class plan found in Section Two of this book has been carefully paired with the selections from the Primary Tools. Within the class plan format the Primary Tools are called the "Warm-ups." The importance of introducing these warm-up exercises prior to each drama/dance activity cannot be overstated. As one would not hand a young child a book and expect him or her to read it without first teaching the fundamental reading skills required, likewise a certain foundation precedes drama/dance curriculum enactment. The Primary Tools are the foundation upon which this teaching method is based and are presented in the form of movement games, stretches, pantomime, physical contact studies, and other playful skill-developing activities. The Primary Tools prepare the group with specific physical, verbal, and interactional skills while establishing a relaxed atmosphere conducive to learning.

Within the class, the warm-ups help to break down inhibitions and provide an outlet for the child's need to move and interact with peers. Through the warm-ups individual abilities are witnessed by the group, and explicit skills are developed.

Some Primary Tools are simple and need no introduction whereas others build upon prior exercises. For instance, before approaching the more complex exercise, "Group Sculpting", it is advisable to conduct "Shapes," Partner Sculpting", and "Positive/Negative Sculpting" to better prepare students for group sculpting techniques.

The Primary Tools were designed with three fundamental goals in mind: To *build group and self-esteem, establish discipline* and *build basic drama/dance skills,* all of which are valuable in establishing a solid foundation in order to carry out further drama/dance activities.

Building Group and Self-Esteem

Of primary importance in conducting warm-ups or any drama/dance activity is the focus on building group and individual self-confidence. Although this book centers upon the teaching of dance and drama, and its integration into the curriculum appears to be the primary aim, the authors of this book feel that the *first* goal of this work is to develop group and self-esteem. For without esteem, participants vie for position and retreat from exploration out of fear of being considered foolish. As a result, learning is held at a standstill. Such a situation cannot set the tone for a productive learning environment.

Encouragement, by emphasizing those tasks done well, lays the groundwork for a truly positive environment in the classroom. The recognition and approval of each individual participant is of tremendous importance in forming a successful learning atmosphere. It is valuable to acknowledge that individuals will contribute to the group in different ways. Whereas one child may show leadership qualities, another may shine as an inventor of unique dance movements. If the child showing leadership is also bossy, emphasize the positive aspects of his or her leadership abilities first and let the negative aspects of bossiness be brought out in group discussion. Then insist on concrete suggestions from group members of how to lead without bossiness. If criticism comes out in the discussion, make sure that it is not personally derisive. Require that each criticism be coupled with a suggestion on how to better the enactment. The teacher should make it a primary goal to scout out each participant's strong points and integrate these qualities as much as possible into daily activities.

Also, make it clear that participants are not to be laughed at or put down for their efforts. Emphasize and reinforce those tasks that are done well by individuals and by the group during active portions of the class. Within reason, ignore less desired behavior and call attention to desired behavior by showing enthusiasm. For example, when conducting the "Jump/Freeze" exercise, ignore the few wobblers and exclaim, "Excellent! I can hardly see a muscle moving! You're as frozen as icicles."

This positive reinforcement, combined with a familiarity with rules and procedures, will be the key to inaugurate a successful program, paving the way toward tolerant, eager, imaginative participation by both teacher and participants alike.

Establishing Discipline

The second goal after esteem is discipline. It is necessary to start a program with one or more warm-ups that establish rules and procedures. Rules are designed to help participants to work harmoniously together by learning cooperation and safe behavior. The category on "Control Mechanisms" found in the Primary Tools will give the class greater freedom to conduct activities, yet maintain order. When success rather than misbehavior is emphasized, these rules may be approached with an air of delight and challenge to guide the class in succeeding at the required task.

Away from the restraints of desks and chairs, yet

within the regular classroom, new discipline challenges undoubtedly will arise. For example, socializing is the most common disruption to the progress of drama/dance classes. In such cases, "The Wise Old Owl" exercise helps curb talking and redirects attention to the activity itself. Reciting this poem with hand gestures reminds the participants that cues and information are missed when socializing. The teacher may also re-establish order in the classroom by simply singing out the participants' names, a song, or playing a musical instrument.

The "Jump/Freeze" exercise makes a superb introduction to discipline in beginning drama/dance classes. To restore order at any time during an activity or enactment, the teacher can call out "Freeze" or beat the drum as a cue for participants to freeze both action and talk. In this manner, the classroom can become lively and yet be controlled in an instant.

It may be advisable at times to separate participants who are friends or enemies if their interaction is disruptive to the progress of the class. A teachers' aide or parent volunteer can also be very useful in handling disruptive participants. If need be, have a particularly unruly participant sit out an activity and watch. In some cases an undisciplined class may need to be stopped to address the problem and discuss or resolve a solution.

Challenging the group members to demonstrate a rule empowers them and encourages desired behavior. When some participants are being forgetful, reinforce the rules again by giving the participants opportunities to actually demonstrate the rules. For example, at the outset or during a locomotion exercise, the leader might say: "Let's see who knows what to do once you get to the other side of the room. Ready, get set, go!" Then follow this up with, "That's right! So many of you remembered to turn around when you arrived at the wall and to stand quietly. You are ready for the next locomotion activity." Once basic rules are fully understood, the class will have better opportunity to enjoy the challenges of the more creative or academic activities.

Building Drama/Dance Skills

The third goal of the Primary Tools is to develop the basic movement and dramatic skills that enrich the enactments. Through these skills those students involved develop the means to express themselves and the explicit tasks given them. As any craft or skill, such as learning to play the piano, certain fundamental skills need to be learned and practice is essential to success. The teacher should not be reluctant to repeat Primary Tools exercises, stories, or curriculum activities, remembering that skills and refinement only develop through repetition and renewed interpretation. As in other crafts, the more proficient one becomes the more enjoyment one derives from the activity.

The ultimate goal in all of drama/dance application is the demonstration of esteem, discipline, and the learned drama/dance skills combined in an effective enactment, be it a display of lightning electrons leaping within a cloud or the silver moon dancing from tree to tree to accompany a poem.

It should be noted that each Primary Tools category has a specific skill building purpose. For instance, the category "Stretches" offers exercises that awaken consciousness of the body and slowly increase the parameters of each body's capabilities. Because stretches are not often a necessity to an activity enactment, they are infrequently mentioned as warm-ups in the class plans. They are, nevertheless, of great value and stretches should definitely be included at the teacher's discretion to prepare and focus the body for the upcoming movement tasks.

The "Body Sculpting" skills are basic to all the drama/dance teaching methods. Through these exercises, the participants shape themselves to represent the curriculum material, be it a group sculpture of a swamp, numeral, rocket ship, or a dinosaur, with each person shaping him or herself to represent a part of the whole.

"OK Bumping", "No Bumping", and the "Action/Reaction" exercises that enable the participants to dynamically interact with each other add an exciting dimension to enactments.

The "Movement Games", "Locomotion", and "Create and Copy" categories awaken both teacher and participant to the infinite possibilities in body movement and use of space. A child tends to move all of his or her body at once with little consciousness of the movement variety available. These categories teach the use of body parts, body moves, levels, space, movement dynamics, timing, and all the basic dance elements that truly bring enactments to life!

Other Primary Tools categories focus on the conscious development of characterization, pantomime, and voice that transforms the participants. Guiding and nurturing the participants in these areas bring depth and sparkle to enactments.

As introduced in the category on "Props", the use of scarves in drama/dance activities adds a magical effect. The inclusion of scarves is well worth the effort they take to make or the price of purchase. They add a flair of excitement and a new visual dimension. In addition, self-consciousness diminishes as participants focus on this colorful, flowing prop and its movements.

Thus, the Primary Tools section overflows with a rich variety of ideas to build and strengthen skills based on exercises geared toward providing an enjoyable experience for all involved.

Selecting Warm-ups

The exercises and games in the Primary Tools section may be used simply because they become class favorites or they may be selected with a specific aim in mind. That purpose may be as diverse as to introduce a new pantomime task, to develop characterization for a story enactment, or to practice physical interaction with a partner.

When preparing to teach a given topic through a drama/dance approach look carefully at the chosen material for the movement, interaction, and pantomime content. If the material is complex, involving numerous drama/dance elements, concentrate on one aspect at a time. It is important to have a clear goal for each session and determine specific skill developing exercises within this Primary Tools section that will assist in achieving that goal. For instance, to enact atomic fission certain dance techniques are brought into play – sculpting and physical contact. For this activity it is required to recreate the basic structure of an atom through sculpting exercises, then practice collision and breaking the atom apart through Action/ Reaction exercises such as "No Bumping" and "OK Bumping".

If necessary, divide an activity over several class sessions, concentrating on one aspect of the activity at a time during each session's warm-up and enactment. In this way an understanding of a complex curriculum activity builds over several sessions. The material is reviewed, and yet new aspects are explored and developed with each re-enactment.

Each curriculum class plan activity found in Section Two of this book is written up in a format that includes warm-up suggestions from the Primary Tools in Section One. These are merely suggestions and it is envisioned that the teacher, with experience, will soon develop a keen eye for pairing warm-ups with new activities.

For example, while a sculpting exercise is recommended for the "Discovering Dinosaurs" activity outlined in the Science section, the teacher may prefer to use an adaptation of "Animal Walk". This exercise focuses on locomotion allowing the participants to imagine how these ancient beasts moved about their terrain.

Reviewing warm-up exercises is recommended even with an experienced group. Remember that one of the most important benefits of the warm-ups is to physically prepare the participants for the main activity. Students who have come from extended periods of sitting require a locomotor or aerobic type exercise such as "Run, Skip, Jump", or stretches, to prepare the body and expend pent-up energy before concentrating on the curriculum task. On the other hand, participants coming from physical activity may require a calming exercise such as "Spaghetti" to help them relax and refocus energy.

In other words the warm-ups serve as important transitional tools . They help the leader and participants move from intellectual acquisition of information to creative, physical, and verbal expression. The Primary Tools' purpose is to develop drama/ dance skills and limber both mind and body, encouraging imaginative thought and action.

Prefacing each of the different categories within the Primary Tools section that follows is a brief description of that category's objectives which may assist the teacher in the selection and use of these tools.

Stretches

INTRODUCTION

Stretches are an important component of any physical activity. They release tension and increase mobility, readying the body for further activity. The following section includes some basic yoga stretches, such as the "Cobra", as well as stretches combined with imagery ("Juice"), and poetry ("Who Has Seen the Wind?"). Using imagery makes stretches interesting but may mask the physical goal of the exercise, especially for younger age groups. Without hampering the fun, occasionally point out the physical goal of the exercise and suggest how the participants can best achieve that goal. Remind participants, if necessary, to straighten legs, reach far, and make an effort to stretch the muscles. The quieter stretches may also be used to re-center and calm down the class at the close of a drama/dance session readying them for the next class.

JUICE

Objective: To stretch the back and the legs, especially the inner thighs and hip joints.

Activity: Sit in a circle formation with participants. Demonstrate how to sit with the soles of the feet together.

Explain that in the center of the circle is some delicious fruit and that each person is to be a machine for making fruit juice. Call on someone to name a specific fruit. At this point, everyone stretches forward, picks some fruit and places it under his or her knees.

As fruit squeezing machines, everyone proceeds with the following actions:

- Turn the juice squeezer on by pressing toes. (You may invent push button noises as this is done.)
- Place your hands on knees and press

Fruit squeezing machines making juice

knees repeatedly to the floor as you "squeeze the fruit into juice".

- Turn off your machine (press toes again).
- Place your hands on either side of one knee, twist towards that side, lean down and "slurp up the juice".
- Lean over and slurp to the other side keeping the soles of your feet together at all times to get maximum twist and stretch.

Repeat the juice squeezing sequence with other fruit suggestions.

Extended Activity: Continue to stretch legs and back by altering the shape of the juice as follows:

- Stretch your legs directly out in front, with legs together.
- Pick some more fruit.
- Pile the fruit on top of your knees.
- Turn on your machine.
- Smash the fruit into "juice" with your nose by leaning forward from the waist touching nose to knees.
- Turn off your machine.
- Spread your legs wide apart, scooting backwards if more legroom is needed in the circle and bend forward again, this time nose to the floor, slurping up "juice".

TWINKLE, TWINKLE LITTLE STAR

Objective: To stretch inner thighs, hips and back of leg areas and to practice "turnout" at the hip joint as used in dance techniques.

Getting Started: Have participants sit in a circle formation with legs spread wide apart so that neighboring toes touch. An aerial view of all the legs together in this position forms a star-like geometric shape. Point this out to the class. Emphasize that knees should be straight and legs rotated at the hip joint to turn out. In the correct position the knee caps will not point in toward each other but will point up to the ceiling or out to the sides.

Activity: Recite the following nursery rhyme or sing as everyone performs the accompanying actions.

TWINKLE, TWINKLE LITTLE STAR

. "Twinkle, twinkle little star . *Lean forward, stretch arms in front of body and wiggle fingers.*

. How I wonder what you are, . *Stretch and lift arms up overhead, opening them out in a wide gesture while looking up, then bring arms back down to the sides.*

. Up above the world so high.   *Lean to right side,*
stretch and lift the
left arm up over the
head and then down
over right leg. Re-
peat to the other
side.

. Like a diamond in the sky..   *Roll backward on-*
to your back. Lift
both legs in the air
and make a diamond-
shaped opening with
them by placing soles
of feet together and
knees apart.

. Twinkle, twinkle little star .   *Lean to right side,*
how I wonder what you are." *stretch and lift the*
left arm up over the
head and then down
over right leg. Re-
peat to the other side.

BEND AND STRETCH

Objective: To stretch the back of the leg and sides of the waist.

Getting Started: Stand in a circle or spread out in the room. During the exercise, when bending forward emphasize straight legs. For maximum benefit in the side stretches, caution the participants not to lean forward but directly to the side. As simple as this is it is often a big favorite.

Activity: Recite the poem as you do the movements.

1. *"Bend and stretch*

1. Bend down with arms and back in front then reach over head with two hands.

2. *Reach for the stars.*

2. Reach over head with one arm and then the other.

3. *Here goes Jupiter*

3. With arms over head, bend at the waist and reach to one side.

4. *There goes Mars."*

4 Bend and reach to the other side as in 3.

Repeat 1-4

Repeat 1-4

WHO HAS SEEN THE WIND?

Objective: To stretch the waist, sides, back, and shoulder muscles.

Activity: Stand with the participants in a circle formation or spread out in the room allowing plenty of space to the sides of each participant. Initially, participants should stand with legs slightly bent and spread apart to match shoulder width. Demonstrate while informing the participants that the torso must be directly to the side, not leaning forward during side stretches. Recite the poem and demonstrate the actions as everyone follows along. Recite the poem again as everyone repeats the actions.

"WHO HAS SEEN THE WIND?"
By Christina G. Rossetti

Narration	Actions
"Who has seen the wind?	*Raise shoulders up and down in a gesture of questioning.*
Neither you nor I;	*Arms raised, bend at waist toward one side and then to the other.*
But when the leaves hang trembling,	*Make a trembling gesture with hands over head.*
The wind is passing by.	*Swing arms and upper body around in a circle from the side, down front, to the side and over head, twice.*
Who has seen the wind?	*Repeat shoulder gesture.*
Neither I nor you;	*Repeat waist and arm bends to each side.*
But when the trees bow down their heads	*With arms still raised, make one slow circle with arms and upper body to side, down front, to other side, then over head.*
The wind is passing through."	*Repeat two circles as above, but quicker.*

CAT AND DOG BACKS

Objective: To strengthen and stretch the back muscles.

Activity: Demonstrate the following back stretches as the participants copy the actions and sounds:

CAT BACK
- Kneel on hands and knees.
- Arch the middle of the back up.
- Look down and back at legs while tucking the chin in and the bottom under.
- "Hiss like a frightened cat.

Reverse the stretch with the *dog back*.

DOG BACK
- Sag the middle of the back down leaving the bottom up.
- Lift your chin up towards the ceiling.
- Keep the knees on the floor.
- "Howl" like a dog.

Repeat the cat and dog back stretches several times, alternating one with the other.

Cat back

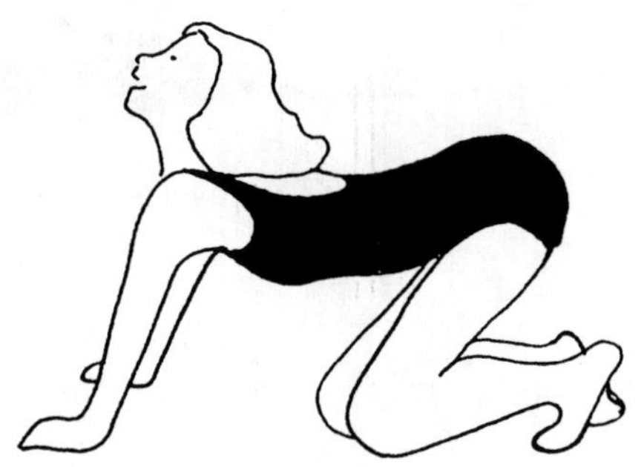

Dog back

COBRA

Objective: To stretch the back, stomach and neck muscles.

Activity: It is suggested to go right from the exercise "Do Your Ears Hang Low", page 45 , to this stretch. After the last word in this song "low", slide right down onto the floor and begin the Cobra pose as follows:

- Kneel down
- Slide hands out front until you are lying on the floor, stomach down
- Relax and take a breath
- Place your hands on the floor by your shoulders and push away from the floor with the arms lifting shoulders, chest, and stomach but not hips
- Look up at the ceiling, arching your back
- Lie down again; relax
- Put your arms down along your sides and lift shoulders and head without using arms
- You may stick your tongue in and out like a snake and "hiss"

- Lie back down again and completely relax your back muscles
- Breathe deeply
- Repeat the Cobra as often as you wish.

Extended Activity: Try a "Superman! Superwoman!" version of the Cobra pose, this time demonstrate as follows:

- Lie on the floor on your stomach
- Place your arms up beside your ears
- Say, "Superman! Superwoman! Up, up and away!"
- Do actions similar to the Cobra pose, lifting your arms, head, shoulders, legs, and feet off the floor using your back muscles
- Hold that position for a few seconds and lie back down
- Relax

Note: Make sure to couple this stretch with the "Cat Back", page 19 , to stretch the back in the opposite direction as well.

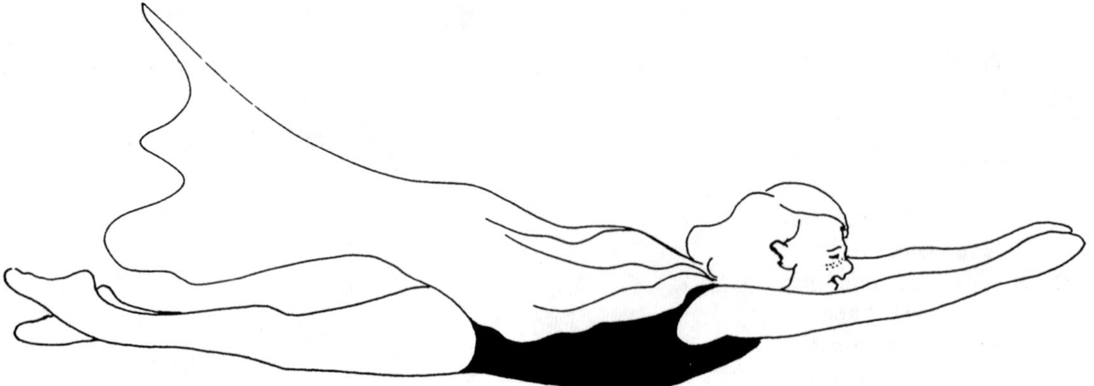

Superwoman Cobra

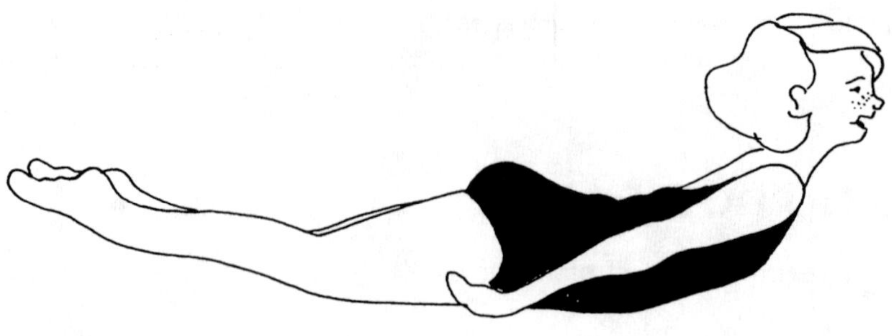

Basic Cobra

THE CLOTHES WASHER

Objective: To twist-stretch the waist and back muscles.

Activity: Have participants sit in a circle formation. Instruct them to:

- Bend the knees up and place the soles of the feet on the floor in front of the body.
- Grab the right ankle with the right hand and place it beside the body with the knee bent and the inner part of the leg touching the floor.
- Allow the left knee to fall forward so that the outer part of this leg touches the floor.

Because the legs look somewhat like the letter "Z", this is called the "Z-position" in modern dance.

Inform the group that they will be making the motions of the agitator in a washing machine, twisting while remaining in the "Z" position and following the narration. The leader narrates and demonstrates the following actions as the participants copy the actions.

Narration	*Actions*
"Open the lid."	Reach an arm above your head as if lifting the lid.
"Throw in the clothes."	Pick up pretend clothes in front of you and throw them into the washer and on top of your head.
"Add some soap."	Scoop up pretend powdered soap and sprinkle overhead, adding a big sneeze.
"Close the lid."	Pretend to close lid over your head.
"Turn on the machine."	Turn knob and add knob noise.
"Wash the clothes."	Put hands on your hips and twist from one side to another to imitate an agitator, while making a "swish-swash" noise.
"Slow down."	Gradually, slow down twisting, then stop.
"Let the water flow out."	Move hands out on the floor in front of you and lean forward.
"Take out the clothes."	Motion to open lid, reach in and take out the clothes. Reverse legs and repeat exercise.

Clothes washer actions

Control Mechanisms

INTRODUCTION

The key to a successful control mechanism is to elicit willing cooperation through challenges and a playful approach. It is equally important to clearly articulate the rules and what is expected of the participants before and during each exercise. Challenging the group members to demonstrate the rules through a warm-up (rather than by simply dictating what is expected) empowers them and encourages desired behavior.

Through the early introduction and well-timed use of the control mechanisms the teacher can manage lively lessons and remain in control at all times. The "Jump/Freeze" exercise is an excellent beginning for a drama/dance class. It is beneficial to use an adaptation of this "Jump/Freeze" exercise at any point during activities to restore order. Once this is learned the teacher can call out "Freeze" (or beat the drum as a cue) to quickly freeze both action and talk during an activity or enactment. In this way events can become lively and yet be controlled in an instant.

Socializing is often the most common disruption to the progress of a drama/dance class. If group members have a strong need to socialize, let them know there will be time alloted for sharing during the discussion period. If socializing persists during an activity, "The Wise Old Owl", in this section, is an excellent control mechanism to curb talking and redirect attention to the activity.

One can also regain order by regrouping the participants into a circle formation. This helps focus the participants' attention so that the teacher can regain control. For example, a teacher could say, "Let's see if everyone can be standing in a circle by the count of ten." This countdown can become a game by using a rhyme such as "One, Two, Buckle My Shoe", or a foreign language, *"uno, dos, tres, ..."*

With experience teachers will find additional solutions to suit the group's discipline needs. With the aid of control mechanisms, the teacher will meet with success and reap the rewards of an effective drama/dance program.

Freezing in the midst of the action

JUMP / FREEZE

Objective: To establish a control mechanism for stopping the action.

Getting Started: It is important to share this activity as both fun and challenging. *Stillness* (freezing) is a very effective dynamic for movement activities. The ability to freeze the action and sound is an invaluable control device for the leader of the group. Explain that you will provide sound by beating the drum, playing a record, tape or instrument, or singing. Participants are to jump while the music is happening and *freeze* as soon as it stops. The goal is to freeze as quickly and totally as possible. Enhance results by saying, "Do not blink an eyelash, do not make a sound!"

Activity: Have participants spread out in the space so that they are not close to anyone or anything.

The leader plays music or a rhythm while participants jump, then freeze when the sound stops. Repeat the process several times with varying music, rhythm or time lapse.

Extended Activities: Call out some variations in movement or stillness such as:

- Explore different types of jumps: little/big, silly/serious, rounded/jagged, to the beat of the music.
- Freeze in different shapes: small/large, symmetrical/asymmetrical; rounded/pointed; balanced on one foot; low, middle, or high-level shapes.
- Try a variation called "Run/Freeze", in which any locomotion is stopped in mid-movement using the above rules.

NO BUMPING

Objective: To eliminate the hazard of bumping into walls and other participants during locomotion and other movement activities.

Getting Started: This crucial warm-up should be approached as an exciting challenge in teaching participants complete body control. In addition, it serves to establish guidelines in locomotion and other movement activities while minimizing potential injuries.

Activity: Ask participants to spread themselves out at one end of the room and run across the space from one end to the other *without* bumping into one another. Tell them to stop short just before they arrive at walls, desks, or other obstacles at the opposite end of the space. Once that is achieved

they are to turn around and stand quietly, ready for instructions.

Praise participants who are successful and have these members demonstrate, one at a time, to the group how they were able to stop quickly and safely. Repeat the activity until everyone is successful.

Repeat the activity to incorporate other locomotion movements such as a *skip, run, hop,* and *glide.* When confronting a hard-core bumper who delights in disobeying the rules, ask him or her to sit and observe as others demonstrate. Then ask for the observer's insights on what makes a successful stop (slowing down, using a jump to stop quickly, etc.), then let the observer demonsrate what he or she has learned.

OK BUMPING

Objective: To learn to bump or come into contact with another participant in a way that is OK for both parties involved, eliminating unnecessary aggression or embarrassment.

Getting Started: Explain to the group the objective of this activity without mentioning embarrassment. Bring up the topic of unnecessary roughness if you feel it will be an issue.

Activity: Have participants choose partners and work in pairs, spreading out in the space. Instruct partners to gently bump shoulders to a drum beat or hand clap, and to stop bumping when the sound stops.

Call out other body parts to bump gently in the same manner - hips, backs, stomachs, bottoms, knees and elbows, avoiding sensitive areas such as the head.

Whenever appropriate, stop action and conduct a short discussion with the group on what worked well and what did not. For instance, if some participants are being hurtful, stop and discuss the objective - to bump without hurting.

Extended Activity: Have participants spread out in the space and work individually. Begin action by walking in all directions. Guide the activity by calling out different movement directives such as: skip, run, change direction, use different levels, etc.

Direct the group towards the center of the space, having participants move quickly and closely around each other *without bumping.*

Now, direct the group to slow down, move closer to each other, and *bump without hurting.*

Keep the group moving at all times. After several

THE WISE OLD OWL

explorations, direct participants to re-use the entire alloted space by moving *away from* instead of towards each other. Inspire the use of a wider movement vocabulary with more movement suggestions such as found in the "Dancing Words" exercise in this section.

Objective: To quiet a group, control unwanted behavior and refocus attention on the leader through acting out a poem.

Getting Started: Use this poem unannounced and when necessary in the middle of any class or discussion. Teach it to the participants and explain that whenever this poem is heard, they are to stop whatever they are doing or saying and recite the words and perform its actions together. After the poem is completed, participants are to remain quiet and pay careful attention to any new instructions.

Activity: "The Wise Old Owl"

Words	Actions
There was an old owl,	*Fingers around eyes*
Who lives in an oak.	*Arms up as tree branches*
The more he saw,	*Fingers around eyes*
The less he spoke.	*Finger to lips*
The less he spoke,	*Finger to lips*
The more he heard.	*Hands cupped behind ears*
Why can't we be	*Hands out to sides,*
	Shoulders up in
	questioning gesture
Like that wise old bird?	*Fold hands in front*

The Wise Old Owl

INTRODUCTION

Locomotion is defined as "the act or power of moving from place to place". Anyone who has observed a child learning to walk or crawl knows that locomotion is of major importance to the child. It is the source of much joy and the focus of hours of determined action. It has been scientifically documented that locomotion, such as a baby's crawling, develops the intellectual capacities of humans in a crucial way. Thus, locomotion activities and warm-ups are invaluable inclusions in any well-rounded educational program.

Before conducting locomotion warm-ups, clear the space of any obstructions (See "Move that Museum Piece" found in "Teaching Tips", Section One.) and indicate the boundaries of the area to be used. Simple locomotor activities can be organized by lining up the participants across one end of the space. If there is not ample space for all participants to comfortably stand side by side, several lines, one behind the other, may be formed.

Clearly announce what cues you will use for informing the first line of participants to move (locomote) in unison across the space to the opposite side of the room. Such cues as, "Ready, get set, skip!" or, "One, two, three, gallop!" are some ideas that work well. Participants often jump the gun, so to speak, and move before these cues are given. Keep them attentive by occasionally calling out: "Ready, get set, stop!" This catches those who have advanced prematurely, and alerts them to listen more carefully next time. Explain that this is not a race and emphasize that the fastest is not necessarily the best.

Give precise instructions as to what is expected from participants while in locomotion and upon reaching the other side of the space: Participants must stop *before* reaching any barrier, turn around and wait quietly while watching the next group travel across the space. These rules can be practiced with the locomotion exercises that follow in this section. "No Bumping" is recommended as the first locomotion exercise for beginning groups and offers a built-in control mechanism. An adaptation of the exercise "Jump/Freeze" such as "Run/Freeze" is also very helpful as an initial lesson for learning control.

Make it clear that participants are to stop once on the other side of the space. In the event that any participants run right back across the space after the initial crossing, discuss why this is not a safe idea. Participants may easily crash into someone else who is still traveling in the initial direction.

In some cases the locomotion exercise can serve as an end in itself, while in other cases locomotion can be chosen with a specific objective in mind such as to prepare participants for improvising dance steps or to portray character roles. For instance, in portraying character roles, the contrasting characters found in Aesop's Fables "The Tortoise and the Hare" (fast and slow), and "The Lion and the Mouse" (big and little) are classic examples of characters that can be developed favorably through locomotion explorations. Participants who have experienced practice time locomoting such specific characters have better opportunity to present superior enactments later, having already internalized the characterization through body movement.

The following section on locomotion aims to increase both the mental and physical agility of participants through locomotor exercises based on the basic components of dance – use of the body, space, force, and time – along with characterization building skills. It serves the classroom as an invaluable primary tool for conducting the innumerous activities found throughout this book.

ROUND THE CIRCLE
By Kristen Bissinger

Objective: To warm bodies up, practice locomotion in a circle, traveling either right or left, and staying in group formation.

Getting Started: This dance game introduces some important basics in cooperation and group consciousness:

- Forming a hand-holding circle without excessive arm-yanking and crack-the-whip type activity is the first hurdle.
- Establishing the rule that everyone must remain in his or her place in the circle (no passing allowed).
- Maintaining an *even* circle formation as the group travels.

Maintain a firm but joyful attitude with these rules. Help the participants to discover what is needed to keep the circle traveling evenly. Those who feel crowded may slow down their movement to fit the circle or move outward, thus enlarging the circle. Practice making the circle larger and smaller as the group locomotes.

Challenge the group to form the circle quickly by counting to ten or reciting a rhyme by the end of which all members must be standing in a circle.

Have the group members repeatedly spread out in the room and on cue re-form into a circle without bumping. Make a game of it and comment on what makes this cooperative effort work.

Activity: Have participants: hold hands, face center, and create a large circle; drop hands and step back to enlarge the circle; turn to the right. (The teacher may call out instructions when necessary, for example, "Kathy, turn towards Joey," and so forth.)

Sing the song and lead the participants in the actions either to the right or left. Keep the group alert by occasionally calling out "Turn around," and repeating the song and activity in the opposite direction immediately upon completing it in one direction.

Call out locomotor activities and directions or ask participants for locomotor suggestions such as, gallop, spin, hop, etc., to be incorporated into the song and actions.

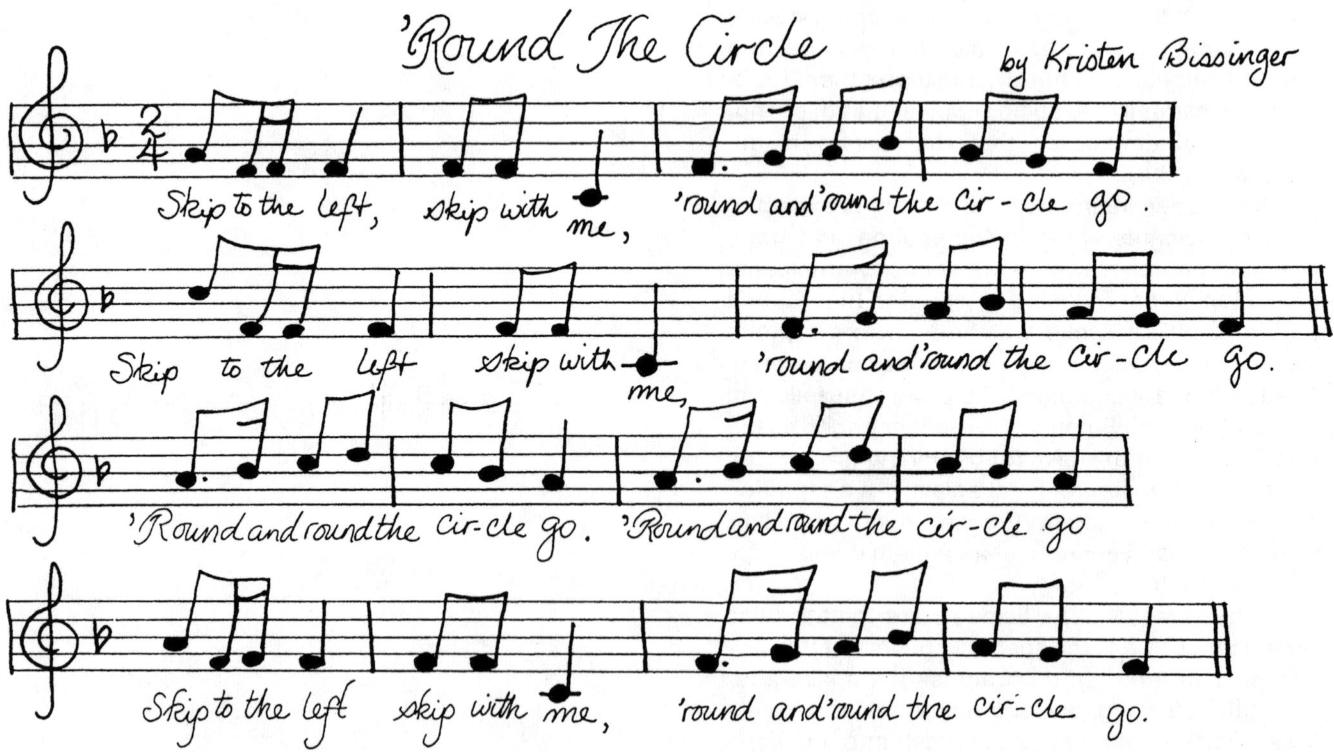

RUN, JUMP, SKIP

Objective: To introduce the basic locomotor movements.

Getting Started: Ask the group to brainstorm a list of all the possible ways a person can move across a given space.

walk	run	jump	skip	hop
stomp	leap	slide	slither	tiptoe
roll	prance	gallop	spin	cartwheel
skate	fly	swim	crawl	hobble

Warm-up: Prepare the group for this locomotion exercise by explaining what locomotion involves and practicing the rules found in the "Introduction to Locomotion" text, such as the "No Bumping" exercise, page 23 .

Activity: Line up participants and call out any one of the movements on your list for the participants to perform from one side of the space to the other. Review the rules if necessary.

When necessary, demonstrate or have a participant demonstrate the locomotor movement correctly.

Explore a variety of locomotion in this manner.

Extended Activity: Continue exploration of the following dance elements through locomotion:

* *Pathways*, such as: zigzag, curved, spiral, wandering, or diagonal.
* *Directions*, such as: forward, backward, and sideways.
* *Levels*, utilizing vertical space, such as: low-level (scooting, slithering, rolling, and crawling), middle-level (crouching position), and high-level (leaps, jumps, and movements with arms above the head).

A group in locomotion

EMOTION LOCOMOTION

Objective: To dramatize emotions as expressed through the body in motion.

Warm-up: Expand verbal and movement vocabulary through exercises based on emotions, such as "If You're Happy and You Know It" on page 35 , or "Guess How I Feel" on page 36 .

Activity: Line the class up for locomotion. Explain to the class that they will be expressing the physical feelings and emotions that are called out while they travel from one side of the space to the other. Call out one of the following per crossing.

hot	angry	surprised
cold	joyful	sad
sneaky	tired	scared
bold	energetic	shy

Add or subtract emotions as suits your aim or concentrate on just a few that are needed for your specific enactment goals.

If the participants simply run, tell them to slow down and give a short preparatory statement before each feeling, such as: "It's blistering hot, your clothes are sticking to you with sweat and you desperately need a drink of water."

CHARACTERIZATION LOCOMOTION

Objective: To strengthen characterization skills through locomotion while developing an awareness of how the use of different body parts help define a character.

Getting Started: The following exercise can be done with older participants (fourth grade and older) as a general study of characterization, or confined to the study of characters involved in a story the class is planning to enact. Invent a list of character traits and body parts through which they can be portrayed, or use the following list with the participants.

* *Timid or bold* - chest
* *Picky or sloppy* - neck or mouth
* *Energetic or lazy* - legs
* *Cheerful or melancholy* - arms and shoulders
* *Fat or thin* - stomach
* *Focused or dreamy* - eyes
* *Young or old* - back
* *Kind or wicked* - eyes

Note the accompanying body parts beside each pair of opposite character traits. These, and /or

Exploring activities in locomotion

other appropriate body parts, may be suggested to the participants to build a physical characterization.

Warm-up: Conduct "If You're Happy and You Know It", page 35 , with older participants. Stand with the participants in a circle formation and call out a trait *plus* an accompanying body part through which the trait can be expressed. The leader can demonstrate an example or call on a volunteer to demonstrate, then have everyone try it. For example:

- *Timid* - contract chest
- *Bold* - expand chest.

Activity: Line the participants up in preparation for locomotion (as instructed in "Introduction to Locomotion"). Call out a specific character trait and accompanying body part and ask participants to travel across the space expressing that trait through action. Other body parts may contribute to the characterization in addition to the part specified.

If participants have difficulty expressing certain character traits, ask for specific examples of a character trait and this may help them to visualize the trait. For example: *Superman is bold.* The partpcipants can concentrate on moving like Superman in order to achieve the look of boldness through locomotion.

ANIMAL WALK

Objective: To explore expression through animal characteristics in locomotion.

Getting Started: Excellent preparation for this activity is to have participants observe animals in motion, either live or on film. Discuss with the group how the animals observed move. Use of space, dynamics, body parts, tempo, and weight are all contributing factors to the characteristic movement.

Activity: Focus on useful aspects of the previous discussion and specify the actions that characterize a variety of animals. Conduct this exercise as described in the "Introduction to Locomotion" text and have participants perform the following locomotor movements. For example:

Fox – Quick zigzag pathway, nose to the ground

Chicken – Squat and walk low to the ground, moving head in and out

Elephant – Slow heavy steps, use an arm as a trunk

Pony – Prance or gallop, chest out and head held high

Giraffe – Stand tall, stretch arms, legs and neck as long as possible and walk slowly, nibbling with lips

Bear – Lumber from side to side with bent knees,, limp wrists held out in front

Penguin – waddle from foot to foot, heels together, toes apart, arms at sides, hands flexed

Extended Activity: Concentrate on animals to be enacted in a particular story, aiming to develop an appropriate movement vocabulary for each animal character. For example, in the story of "The Lion and the Mouse" from *Aesop's Fables:*

Lion – Move on all fours, chest out, head held high; walk slowly with strong shoulders; roar, shake mane, show claws and teeth, pounce; stretch like a cat, yawn, flop down and curl up.

Mouse – bend or curl over with arms pulled in and paws in front; tiptoe quickly, looking nervously this way and that; stop with eyes wide and attentive; scratch with front paws, pick up a grain, nibble on it with teeth bared; clean face with paws, look back quickly and scamper away.

STACCATO/LEGATO LOCOMOTION

Objective: To inspire contrasting dynamics in locomotion through imagery.

Getting Started: Often a movement or character quality can be more fully expressed once it has been explored with a contrasting quality such as the quick, sharp *staccato;* and smooth, even *legato* dynamics utilized in musical pieces. This exercise in contrasting movement dynamics can enrich characterizations for story and history enactments as well as reinforce exaggerated, decisive action useful in Science and Math activities.

The leader's tone of voice helps serve to guide the movement qualities of this exercise. For instance, a slow speaking manner, either delicate or weighty, encourages slow movements, while lively speech helps activate fast movements. Drumming or clapping, recorded or live music can also be incorporated to help define the tempo.

Because quick movements expend more energy, and slow movements require more concentration, it is best to offer exercises that alternate between the two dynamics for a balanced program.

Activity: Prepare the participants for locomotion as suggested in "Introduction to Locomotion" and ask them to imagine the following scenarios as you guide them through alternate sharp and smooth movements. Remember to utilize appropriate voice tone in narrating imagery.

Scenarios

- *Hot Sand (quick)* – "Imagine that the floor is covered with hot sand and you have to pick your feet up quickly as you run from where you are to the cool ocean on the other side of the room." (High prancing and lively arm movements.)
- *Mud (slow and heavy)* – "The floor is covered with thick mud, up to your knees. Slowly sink in and pull out each leg as the mud tries to suck you down." (Add sucking sounds.)
- *Firecrackers (fast)* – "Imagine that each one of you is a string of tiny firecrackers. I will come and light each one of you and you will explode over and over again from this side of the room to the other." (Jump up and shoot arms and legs in all directions, "bang" or "pop" sounds can be included.)
- *Bubbles (slow and light)* – "Now you are all bubble soap. I will come by and blow each of you into a big bubble. You will fill up with air and very slowly float to the other side of the room where you will burst." (Blow on the back of each participant's neck as they expand.)
- *Mouse (fast)* – "You are a tiny mouse darting all about a field with quick sharp movements."
- *Dinosaur (slow)* – "You are a two-ton dinosaur slowly grazing and walking on giant feet."
- *Runner (fast)* – "You are a champion track star running a race."
- *Astronaut (slow)* – "You are an astronaut walking on the moon where there is little gravity so that you float and move about very slowly."

LOCOMOTOR LIFT

Objective: To experience the feeling of weight by actually lifting and carrying another person or heavy object as might be needed in a story enactment or group sculpture. Or to experience the sensation of excessive weightiness, useful in depicting such characters as a dinosaur or giant.

Activity: Have participants choose partners equal to, or nearly equal to their own size or weight.

One partner in each pair stands behind the other. The partner in front crouches slightly (bending forward while bending knees). The partner behind droops his or her body weight forward over the bent partner's back. The bent partner then straightens the legs to lift the partner slightly off the ground and tries to walk a short distance bearing the partner's weight.

Switch roles and repeat, so that each participant receives a chance to carry and be carried.

Though a story or activity may not actually call for one person carrying another, this experience will result in a superior portrayal of the carrying of a heavy object or enactment of a large and heavy character.

INTRODUCTION

Copying is a basic mode of learning and a wonderful way to share the ideas and movements of others. While the process of creating keeps a learning activity interesting and relevant for those involved, it is also empowering. All children of any age level, whether accelerated learners or those with learning disabilities, benefit from "Create and Copy" activities. The "Mirror Game" develops special thinking skills, while "Opposite Actions" challenges participants to translate a verbal cue into its opposite. The "Copy Hop" is extremely useful to the classroom as it can be adapted to explore a movement vocabulary centered on any chosen theme. Copying games can remain on an elementary level in which one movement is shared and then copied by the group. Or, the concept can be developed into a more complex lesson with a sequence of movements strung together, for participants to remember and copy.

Sound and movement is explored throughout this book in various combinations. However, the exercises in this section present some games involving abstract sound and movement to help strengthen participants' awareness in each of these categories. Advanced age level participants will enjoy challenging each other with more complex and faster paced variations of these simple warm-ups.

COPY HOP

Objective: To develop self-esteem, encourage observation skills, copying and movement creation, and to explore movement themes.

Activity: Stand with participants in a circle formation. Explain that each person who wishes will have a chance to make up a simple motion such as a jump, arm swing or spin. When called upon, a participant will go to the center of the circle and repeat his or her motion over and over again. Those in the outer circle will copy the motion repeatedly while chanting or singing the performing person's name in the following song:

> Here's to *Mary* and the way she does the Copy Hop.
>
> Here's to *Mary* and the way she does the Copy Hop.
>
> Here's to *Mary* and the way she does the Copy Hop.
>
> Copy Hop!

Have everyone clap their hands on "hop". "Mary" then returns to her place in the circle and another participant is chosen. Let everyone who wishes a turn perform an action, including the leader.

SHARE-A-MOVEMENT

Objective: To encourage confidence and observation through movement creation and copying the movement of others.

Getting Started: Have participants sit in a circle formation. Demonstrate to the group a simple movement to imitate, such as a raise of the arm, tilting of the head or fluttering of eyelids. Ask participants to copy the movement in unison several times.

Activity: Have each participant initiate a movement for the group to copy.

Repeat the procedure, but this time in an accumulative manner. First, one action is demonstrated by a participant and repeated by the group. Then, the next person in the circle initiates an action and the two actions are repeated in sequence by the entire group, and so on, until everyone has contributed a movement and the series of actions has been demonstrated.

This is an excellent activity for memory recall. Ask the group to repeat the procedure in a standing position using any part of the body.

If a participant does not know what to do or the movement ideas are repetitious make suggestions such as: "Make a movement with your foot," "Let's see a twisting movement," "Can you share a slow movement on a low level?" Use any combination of the elements of dance, page 8 , as suggestions.

SHARE-A-SOUND

Objective: To explore vocal expression in preparation for enhancing characterization, sound effects, radio plays, dance accompaniment, etc.

Getting Started: Have participants sit in a circle formation. Explain that the group will be exploring sounds: both vocal sounds (sounds that are made with the mouth, throat and vocal chords), as well as percussive sounds (such as clapping, slapping, and stamping).

Warm-up: As a sample make a sound (such as clucking, kissing, clicking fingers, slapping) for

Sharing sounds with the group

everyone to repeat in unison to the best of his or her ability.

Now, ask everyone to try all the different sounds that they can think up. Indicate that copying is permitted and have everyone start making noises, simultaneously, and at random.

If participants seem shy in coming up with sounds, the leader can continue to provide sounds while encouraging copying, clapping, and other actions. On the other hand, if the group is excessively noisy, or gets heavily into gross sounds and this proves disturbing or inappropriate, simply stop the activity and ask for quieter versions of the same sounds. The leader may ban the gross sounds or if these are not too disturbing these sounds can be allowed to run their course and as the novelty wears off, those involved will move onto other sounds.

Activity: The above warm-up explores sounds at random for practice. Now, ask for a volunteer to demonstrate only *one* sound and have the other participants copy that sound in unison. Repeat each sound several times. The creation of more difficult sounds (such as the popping noise made with finger and cheek) can be explained by their initiators. In this manner, attempt one by one, all of the sounds the group dreams up.

This activity is to be used as preparation for "Share the Sound and Movement" found below, and can be used as accompaniment for dancing to sound poetry such as the poem "Row" in the Language Arts section of this book.

SHARE THE SOUND-AND-MOVEMENT

Objective: To explore how different sounds suggest companion movements.

Warm-up: Conduct the previous exercises in this Session, both "Share-a-Sound" and "Share-a-Movement", with the group.

Demonstrate to the group a simple sound/movement sample, such as a:

- Quick explosive sound while shooting hands up like a rocket ship
- Vibrating "motorboat" sound (made with lips) while wiggling shoulders back and forth
- Long "ohhhh" sound while swaying the body in a slow, graceful motion

Activity: Ask participants to explore some sound and movement combinations on their own for a short time period. Afterwards, have each person share a sound and an accompanying movement with the group. After each sound/movement idea is shared, have the group first try mimicking it together in unison, then pass the sound/movement around the circle so that one participant after another copies it. Also point out and encourage the *exact* copying of the energy level, inflection, timing and all aspects involved in the original interpretation. Emphasize *simple* sound/movement combinations so everyone can be successful and accurate.

Extended Activity: Have the group explore sound and movement while in locomotion, in unison. For example, the quick explosive sound while shooting hands up like rocket ship may be matched with energetic leaps. Use a drumbeat, cymbal crash, or loud sound as a freeze control mechanism.

Give participants ample time for exploration. Mention that copying is permissible and encourage variety by calling out suggested variations in level, tempo, and types of sound (such as percussive or vocal, sounds made with feet and other body parts).

Divide the class in half or into smaller groups, and have the individuals in each group share some of their sound/movement ideas while group members watch and listen.

MIRROR GAME

Objective: To develop observation and concentration skills as well as teach unified movement.

Getting Started: Have participants choose partners and spread out in the space.

Warm-up: Use a variety of stretches to limber and stimulate body awareness such as those found in this section: "Bend and Stretch", "My Hands Say Hello", "Who Has Seen the Wind?", and "Cat and Dog Backs".

Activity: In each pair, one partner is the leader and the other represents the mirror image. In conducting movements, the leading partner moves very slowly while the mirror partner follows the movement and copies it as exactly as possible, and at the same time. (Performed well, one should not be able to differentiate who is leading and who is following.) Encourage the leading partner to experiment with a variety of interesting movements utilizing various parts of the body by calling out body parts and moves.

After a few minutes of practice, change roles and repeat the process with new movements.

Discuss what worked well, what did not, and why. Stimulate conversation by asking: "Was your partner slow enough?" "Did he or she do movements you could/could not do?" "Were the movements simple enough to follow?" "Could you see your partner clearly at all times or did some movements put you into a position where seeing was difficult?"

Extended Activity: Add new interest to the activity with the following variations:

- Let the leadership pass back and forth between the two partners without preplanning or consultation. This exchange of leadership may happen in quick succession or with long periods of leadership by one leader. In any case, neither partner should hang onto or avoid leadership.
- The leader partner may experiment with tempo by adding some quick movements or movements with a rhythmical quality for the mirror partner to repeat as promptly as possible. In this case slight delay in mimicking movements is acceptable.
- The leading partner creates movements and the mirror partner copies the movements but varies them somewhat. For example, adding or subtracting movements, changing the timing, levels or dynamics, or repeating some movements. The leading partner may stay still periodically to allow time for the mirror partner's variations.
- Have participants arrange themselves in groups of three. Each group stands in a triangle formation so that all three face one direction. One person stands out front and two stand beside each other and behind. The person in front leads the movement, be it stationary or locomotor and the two behind the leader copy the movements as accurately and quickly as possible, similar to the mirror game.

These threesomes can travel forward in the direction of the leader, move sideways or move backwards as the leader dictates.

When the person leading *turns* to the right, the follower to his or her right immediately takes over as leader of the group. The former leader becomes a follower. Thus as a leader turns one way or the other a new leader takes over from where the former leader left off.

INTRODUCTION

Exploring and developing a character can be highly rewarding and provide in-depth material for story enactments and dramatic interpretations. A character has many components – a voice, personality, movement characteristics, gestures, feelings, relationships and motivations. Participants will find fascination in creating and expressing the qualities that differentiate a pompous king from a bumbling court magician, a slow turtle from a fast and boasting rabbit, and a brave explorer from an evil pirate. The following section includes exercises for giving a character dimension. Refer to the Locomotion section for additional assistance in expressing how specific characters move ("Animal Walk", "Emotion Locomotion" and "Characterization Locomotion").

IF YOU'RE HAPPY AND YOU KNOW IT

Objective: To develop physical and facial expressions demonstrating various emotions.

Getting Started: Have participants stand in a circle formation. Open up discussion about how we show feelings through gestures and expressions (facial and body). Physical feelings such as being "cold" or "itchy", as well as emotional feelings, like being "scared", "happy" or "surprised", all make suitable examples for exploration.

Activity: Sing the song, "If You're Happy and You Know It Clap Your Hands". Ask participants to raise their hands if they can suggest other feelings and accompanying actions to add to the basic song.
Examples:
"If you're *angry* and you know it *stamp* your feet."

"If you're happy and you know it"

"If you're *surprised* and you know it *jump* and say 'Oh' " (throw hands up, open eyes and mouth wide in surprise).
"If you're *cold* and you know it *shiver* and *shake.*"

The leader may wish to demonstrate a few examples initially to get things rolling and spark ideas. The leader may also need to help out occasionally when a participant has provided an example of a feeling but no appropriate movement to go with it, or vice versa.

Another exercise with a similar objective in this section is called "Guess-How-I-Feel" and may also be utilized to explore feelings. However, the exercise "If You're Happy and You Know It" moves along much more quickly and requires less waiting and guessing time making it appropriate for younger age groups and groups abiding by a limited time schedule.

GUESS-HOW-I-FEEL

Objective: To practice expressing feelings and emotions through posture and body movements.

Getting Started: Have the group sit in a circle. Ask for suggestions of words that describe feelings and physical sensations as well as emotions. Demonstrate how not just the face, but many parts of the body can be called into play to express feelings – back, chest, head, hands and legs. For example, to express shyness, the head might hang, arms pull in, chest collapse and knees turn in.

Activity: Ask participants to suggest some feelings to be expressed through physical actions and gestures.

Have a volunteer stand up, and turn his or her back to the group for a few moments of preparation. Then the volunteer must turn to face the group and briefly express a feeling through posture and gesture.

"We're so sleepy"

The volunteer then sits down and calls on someone in the group to guess what feeling was enacted. Words that have the same general meaning such as "angry" and "mad" should be accepted as correct, though the actor may indicate he or she had another word with a similar meaning in mind, if that is the case.

The next actor is then chosen and the game continues as before. After four incorrect guesses, the actor may state the feeling that was intended.

GUESS-WHO-I-AM

Objective: To develop characterization through body movement and posture.

Getting Started: Have participants sit in a circle formation. Choose a theme that fits the classroom's current needs – a decision that may be based on the enactment for which the group is preparing or the age and interests of the group.

For example:
- Reptiles
- Animals of a particular habitat such as ocean or forest
- Types of people based on age, personality, occupation
- Fantasy or fictitious characters such as Superman, the Joker, science fiction idols, or a witch.
- Characters from stories the participants have read or enacted during the year.

Activity: Ask participants to raise their hands when ready to demonstrate a specific character that fits the study theme. When called upon, a participant should attempt to express the character of choice through a combined display of physical actions, facial expression and pantomime only (no dialogue!). This can be performed inside the circle formation or outside the circle in another designated location. The presentation should be short, lasting anywhere from two seconds to one-half minute.

Upon completion of the character expression, the actor sits down and calls upon someone in the circle who has raised a hand to guess what character was being stated. When the character is guessed correctly, a new actor is chosen to enact another character. Or, after five incorrect guesses the actor is permitted to reveal the character attempted and another actor is chosen to take a turn.

COSTUME BALL

Objective: To convey feelings and emotions through body expression.

Getting Started: Discuss with the participants how the body is capable of expressing a wide assortment of feelings. Ask for some clues the body might give to illustrate "sadness" (drooping shoulders, limp arms, slouched back, legs turned in), "happiness" (raised or swinging arms, chest open and shoulders back, fingers spread out), or "anger" (tense muscles, clenched fist, stomping or kicking feet).

Cut out eye holes in large paper bags and write a word describing an emotion or feeling on each bag.

Warm-up: Conduct the "If You're Happy and You Know It" exercise, page 35 .

Activity: Have the participants put the bag-masks over their heads and emphasizing exaggerated movement, line up as if entering a ball. One person can serve as the grand marshal and announce the arrival of each guest by the word written on the mask. For example: "May I present Mr. Angry, Ms. Ecstatic, etc."

As each guest is announced, the guest enters the room using the *entire* body to express the word on the mask. Ask participants to remain in character until all guests have arrived at the ball. Thye may mingle, march, or dance to music. Stop the music and exchange masks so the event can be repeated and new versions of emotional expressions explored.

Extended Activity: Assign each participant an emotion or feeling to be conveyed through the body. If the group is large these may be duplicates.

Give each person a new paper bag with eye holes on which to draw a bold, exaggerated facial expression of an assigned emotion.

Place the masks face down and mix the bags up. Give each person a bag-mask without letting him or her see which emotion it expresses.

Have the participants keep the bags face down until their turn. Without seeing the image drawn on the bag, each participant places his bag over his head and performs his assigned emotion for the group. The primary challenge of this activity is that one emotion will be expressed through the body and, quite possibly, another emotion or feeling will be expressed by the mystery mask.

Afterwards, ask: Which was stronger, masks or movements? Were the body movements decisive enough to overcome the mask? What was the effect of this mixed message? What was the effect when the mask and movements expressed the same emotion?

MASKED BALL

Objective: To investigate the face as a tool for conveying emotions.

Getting Started: Brainstorm with the group and develop on the chalkboard an extensive word list that describes the many expressions the face can conjure:

happy	*angry*	*sick*
surprised	*suffering*	*tired*
nervous	*ecstatic*	*bored*
sorrowful	*seething*	*sneaky*
sad	*arrogant*	*terrified*

Warm-up: Demonstrate some of the expressions listed above. After each portrayal discuss and compare with the group how facial movements define a particular expression. For example:

- *Joy* - Upturned mouth and eyes
- *Anger* - Flared out nostrils, lowered eyebrows
- *Surprise* - Raised eyebrows, rounded, open mouth

Encourage participants to exaggerate facial movement using the following exercises:

- Open mouths as large as possible; make mouths as small as possible.
- Puff cheeks out; suck them in.
- Open eyes as wide as possible; narrow eyes so that they can barely be seen through.
- Wiggle the nose.

Activity: Ask two or three participants at a time to come to the front of the acting space and demonstrate for the group expressions that illustrate a range of emotions in a single category, such as:

sad	*sorrowful*	*tragic*
satisfied	*happy*	*ecstatic*
annoyed	*angry*	*enraged*

Have participants pretend that they have masks on, using the traditional mime technique of putting on and taking off an imaginary mask. This may be done by having the leader recite a word to be expressed such as "happy" while the actor moves the hand across the face as if putting on a (happy) mask, then moving the hand in the opposite direction as if taking the mask off, or "erasing" it. Lead the activity by reciting the word to be expressed. Each time an imaginary mask is removed, the face should remain in "neutral".

Masks may take on specific character as well as expression, such as a:

- Clown who is happy
- Monster who frightens people
- Person who ate too many green apples.

Now invite all the participants to a masked ball, and ask them one by one to show their masked emotions as they enter the ballroom.

CHARACTER SKETCHES

Objective: To practice physical, gestural and vocal characterization along with skit development.

Getting Started: Ask participants to bring in newspaper or magazine pictures and articles on some interesting personalities to share with the group. Discuss what makes them unique, such as looks, intelligence, lifestyle, talents, personality, etc. These could encompass politicians, humanitarians, artists, writers, rock, sports and motion picture stars.

Warm-up: Conduct "Character Locomotion" as found in this section. Some examples are:.

- *Regal king* walking with chin in air and chest puffed out.
- *Mouse* skittering in a zig-zag pathway of short, quick runs.
- *Old man* hobbling with small, shaky steps.
- *Witch* swooping about as if flying on a broom.
- *Robot* walking with mechanical jerks.

Now try a voice exercise by reciting this rhyme in a normal voice.

> Roses are red,
> Violets are blue,
> If I were a (*mouse, king*)
> I'd flip somersaults for you!

Repeat the same rhyme as if you were a:

- Pompous king, (bombastic)
- Tiny little mouse, (squeeky)
- Very sleepy hippopotamus, (yawny)
- Feeble old man, (quavering)
- Cackly, wicked witch, (cackly)
- Mechanical, jerky robot (monotone)..

Activity: Make up a number of flash cards with a

specific character written on each one. The class may assist in compiling these cards. Place the cards in a hat and ask each participant to draw one card, then develop a short personality sketch around this card title. No story content is required for these initial sketches. Instead, focus on the expression of a strong personality type through movement in the space and an idiosyncratic behavior such as a gesture or habit. Challenge participants to think up an idiosyncrasy for their character. The king could tug at his beard, the mouse constantly bump into things, and the robot occasionally make sputtering sounds when exasperated.

After five minutes, ask participants to further develop their characterization by adding simple dialogue in a characteristic voice. For example, the witch might be leaping and stirring her brew while singing cackly incantations. The feeble old man might shuffle, scratch his head and mutter the grocery list over and over.

Extended Activity: Ask two participants to pair up and create a short skit utilizing their character's traits in a situation with conflict.

For example, a story built around an eccentric hairdresser and electronic robot may involve the hairdresser trying different solutions to grow hair on a bald headed robot. Challenge the participants to retain their characterizations throughout the skit.

Objective: To further develop characterization through visual transformation or simply experience makeup exploration.

Getting Started: Bring in theatrical makeup color sticks and eyebrow pencils, powder (optional), hairpins and clips, cold cream, Kleenex, washcloths, mild soap, several towels and a large mirror. Give each child a *small* dab of cold cream to smear all over his or her face. This aids in makeup removal later. Pin hair away from faces.

Activity: Let younger children improvise the decoration of their faces in small groups in front of the mirror.

An older group can be shown some basic character makeup designs from which to choose.

• *Old Person* – Wrinkle up the face and follow the natural lines with an eyebrow pencil around eyes, mouth and forehead.

• *Young Woman* – Extended eyeliner, eye shadow, lipstick, and rouge.

• *Native American* – Geometrical designs, lines, spots, and bold colors.

• *Cat* – Whiskers, divided and extended lip, dark nose, and whiskery eyebrows.

• *Clown* – Red nose and cheeks, big lips, peeky eyebrows.

Several makeup personas can be explored in a single session by starting with the makeup sugges-

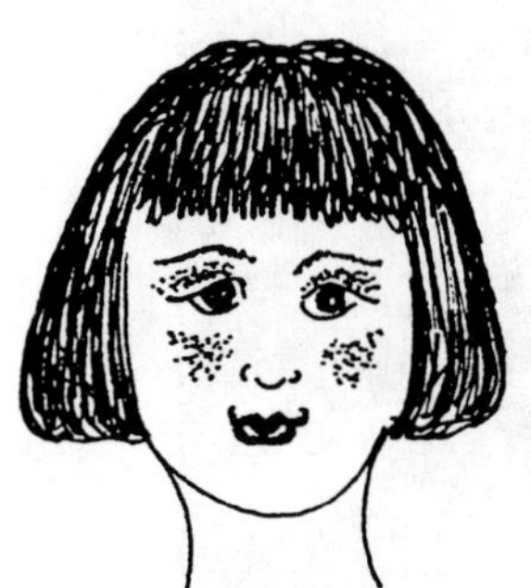

Young women

old person

clowns

Basic make-up designs

A child becomes a lion through make-up artistry

tions for the old person or young woman and then superimposing a bolder character makeup such as the clown, cat, or Native American.

Participants may be encouraged to create an imaginary character through makeup, mimic the makeup of a famous character, such as Batman, or apply makeup appropriate for a character to be enacted.

To remove makeup have participants smear their faces with cold cream removing as much makeup as they can with tissues. Faces can then be washed with warm water and mild soap on washcloths.

Cat

Native American

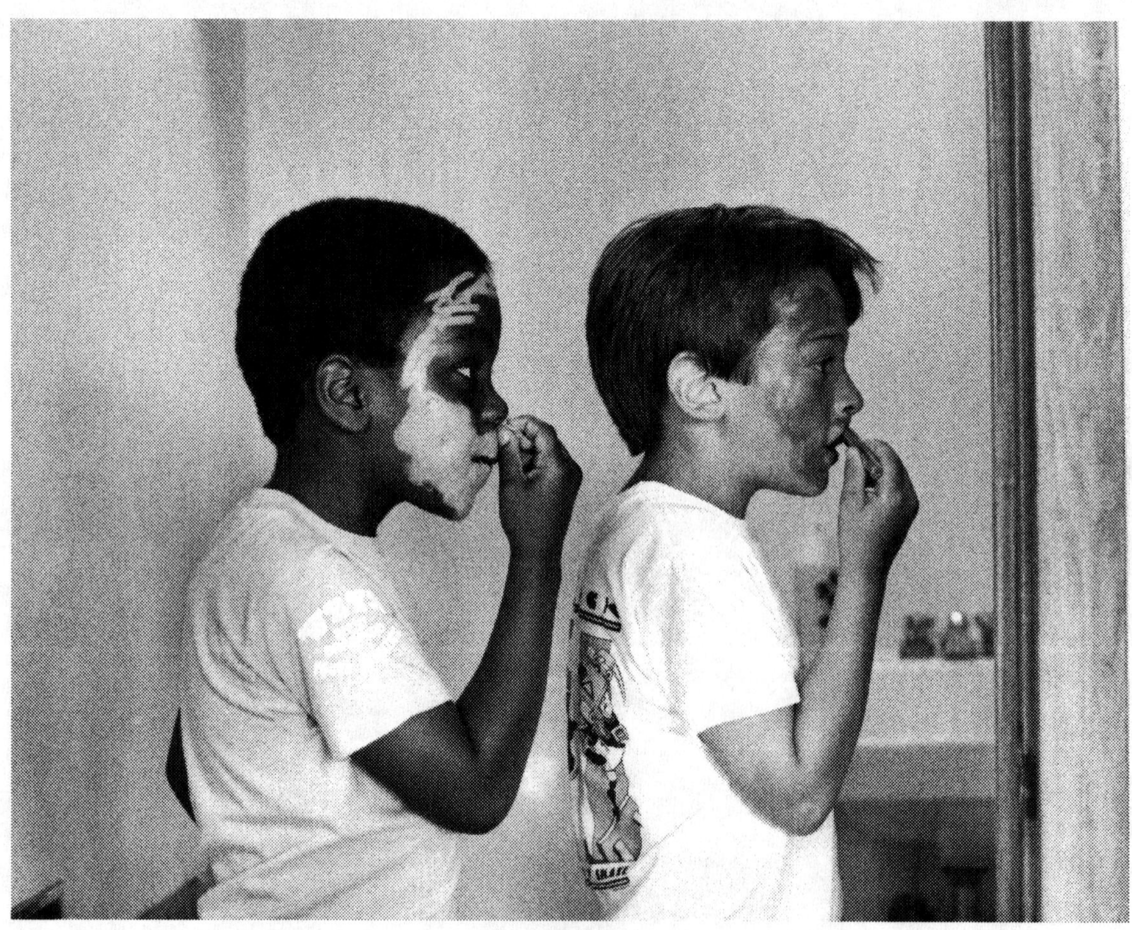

The Tin Man and the Witch of the West
apply their silver and green faces   (Wizard of Oz)

This section includes an assortment of games that involve movement patterns designed to fit the words or ideas in the songs. In the case of "Do Your Ears Hang Low?", for instance, the whole body represents floppy ears and expresses the actions and gestures in response to the words of the song, providing an enjoyable means of practicing stiff and loose movement control. The teacher should feel free to design movements for other songs or adapt existing songs to teach specific concepts in movement exploration. For example, "Here We Go Round the Mulberry Bush" is an excellent song to practice pantomime. Consider adapting popular folk, rock, or rap music in the same manner for older groups. Brainstorm with the group members to come up with possible movement solutions of their own invention.

MY HANDS SAY "HELLO"

Objective: To increase awareness of separate body parts and movement capabilities apart from the rest of the body.

Activity: The song in this activity is geared towards the younger child, but the activity is a valuable one to conduct with older participants as well. If confronted with embarrassment or resistance by the older age group, persevere and simply have fun with the actions. Challenge the older group to use imagination in striving for real variety in movements or achieving true "isolation" (moving only the specified body part while the rest of the body remains still). Model willingness to play and they are sure to come around!

Begin the activity standing with participants in a circle formation and singing the following words to the tune of "The Farmer in the Dell":

> My hands say "Hello"
> My hands say "Hello"
> Every time I see my friends
> My hands say "Hello".

Ask participants to move only the body part specified in the song. Start with the hands and have participants wave hands in a normal fashion the first time around. Then ask the group to further explore hand movements of other sizes, speeds, shapes and dynamics as the song is repeated. The leader can encourage creativity by demonstrating a "hand dance" with as much variety as possible while repeating the song.

Ask participants to raise their hands to suggest different body parts to move during the song. The activity flows more continuously if the leader sings "my", *pauses* and points to someone for a body part suggestion, such as feet, knee or elbow, etc.; then immediately proceeds with the new body part and its' movements to the song.

NAME GAME

Objective: To learn each other's names while becoming aware of the syllable divisions and rhythms of each name.

Getting Started: Talk about syllables and how names may vary in the number of syllables or beats that they contain. Mention some examples. Ask participants to raise their hands if their first names have only one syllable, then two, three, etc.

Warm-up: Have participants sit in a circle with their legs crossed. Explain to them that they are going to play a rhythm game with their names. They will beat out the rhythm of everyone's name with their hands on their thighs.

Make up a simple rhythm pattern using a series of long or short beats to go with a name. For example:

My	*name*	*is*	*Nan*	–	*cy.*
(long)	(short)	(short)	(long)		(long)

Repeat this idea three times with all the participants following while slapping their legs.

Go around the circle as each participant repeats the procedure using his or her own name and the rest of the group joins in with the beat.

In playing this game, the rhythm of the sentence tends to make one emphasize the first syllable of the name, so in a name like "Michelle", where the emphasis is on the second syllable, instead of the first, allow for a pause,

My	*name*	*is*	*(pause)*	*Mi*	–	*chelle.*
(long)	(short)	(short)	(short)	(short)		(short)

Stand in a circle and perform the isolation exercise, "My Hands Say Hello", page 43 , to get participants up and moving while exploring the various body parts we use in dance.

Activity: Still standing, spread out the participants in the space. Ask them to create movements that emphasize the rhythms in their names. For example:

Nan	*cy*
(spin around)	(stretch both arms up quickly)

DANCING WORDS

If the participants are new to each other and seem to hang back, mention some possible movements, such as: jump and various stretches, head nod, shoulder lift, arm swing, kick and spin. As an example have particpants try a few movement combinations that you, as the leader, design to go with your own name such as: jump — jump — nod; or swing — swing — twist.

After an exploration time, in which the leader, circulates helping those that appear to need it, gather everyone into a circle formation and have each person share his or her name dance as others copy it. Sing or say, "Her/His/My name is ___________," adding the appropriate name and movement.

Objective: To involve participants in moving and exploring a wide variety of body movements and movement qualities.

Getting Started: Share with the group the objectives of this activity and discuss the variety of non-locomotor body movements (achieved in a stationary position) that they are familiar with, such as swinging or twisting.

Prepare for the exercise by finding some interesting music or plan to use a drum.

Activity: Have participants spread out in the space and ask them to try the movements that follow while in a stationary position. As the group shows readiness (no bumping or talking, and ability to control

Children slapping rhythms to "Name Game"

level of excitement), you may expand the exercise to include moving about the space while performing the dancing words.

Call out the dancing words on the list below, one at a time, giving time for exploration of each type of movement. Encourage variety by parts, giving specific examples of the basic elements of dance:

- Space
- Time
- Dynamics or force
- Use of body parts

Combined with the following movement words:

bend/straighten	*stretch*
swing/sway	*shake*
twist	*rise/fall*
float	*wobble*
bounce	*jab*

You may add specific locomotion directive (such as walk, skip, slide, etc.) in combination with these dancing words and basic dance elements for more complex action.

DO YOUR EARS HANG LOW?

Objective: To stretch the back, neck and leg areas while exploring loose and stiff movements, as well as tempo changes.

Activity: Have participants stand in a circle formation and ask them to copy your actions. Explain beforehand that this exercise will begin slowly and gradually, then speed up. Conduct the following actions to the song with participants:

DO YOUR EARS HANG LOW?

Song	*Actions*
Do your ears hang low?	*Bend forward at waist; arms and head dangle forward, hanging down (entire body can represent ears)*
Do they wobble to and fro?	*Wobble or rock your feet from side to side while swaying your knees, back, arms, and wrists loosely*
Can you tie them in a knot?	*Make a quick hand gesture to represent tying a knot*
Can you tie them in a bow?	*Make a similar, but altered, gesture to represent tying a bow*

Song	*Actions*
Can you throw them over your shoulder,	*Throw both hands over one shoulder*
Like a continental soldier?	*Stand stiffly with heels together and salute sharply*
Do your ears hang low? (a little faster)	*Repeat the first forward bend from the waist*

Repeat the entire sequence three or four times building up a slightly faster pace each time.

I'M A PUPPET ON A STRING

Objective: To practice correct alignment in body posture, releve' in ballet first position, as well as stiff and loose movement qualities.

Getting Started: Arrange participants in a standing position in a large circle formation. Sing the song while demonstrating its accompanying movements, then have participants copy them. This is a very popular exercise and can be repeated with success.

Activity: Have participants pretend to be puppets and stand at arms' length from each other while standing very straight and rigid, as though held up by imaginary strings attached to their heads. Have them proceed with the following actions:

I'M A PUPPET ON A STRING

Song	*Actions*
"I'm a puppet on a string."	*Stand in first position, (heels together and toes apart) and releve'(go up on toes then place heels back on floor again). Repeat four times.*

Exploring puppet actions

"I can leap."	*Do a little leap from one leg to the other leg, while remaining in place.*
"I can spring."	*Place feet back to first position. Jump up and down three times.*
"I can move my arms like this."	*Bend arms at elbows and move stiffly up and down, holding hand flat, like a doll's hands.*
"I can even, blow a kiss!"	*Bend over stiffly at waist. Place hand to mouth, then release as though blowing a kiss.*
"I can reach my arms up tall."	*Lift arms up, bit by bit, as though climbing a ladder until arms are fully up and dancer is up on toes as in releve!*
"But loose my strings and I will fall."	*Completely relax all body tension and slowly collapse to the floor.*

SPAGHETTI

Objective: To practice conscious muscle tension and relaxation.

Warm-up: Conduct the exercise "Do Your Ears Hang Low", page 45 , and "I'm a Puppet on a String", page 45 . If your group has not performed these before, practice movements involving both stiffening the body and making it loose and floppy. Also focus on tightening and wobbling specific body parts such as the hands, arms, legs, back, and head.

Activity: Ask participants to stand in a circle formation. Tell them that they will represent uncooked spaghetti and that they are to make their bodies as tall and stiff as possible.

The leader should take on the character of a little old lady or man and pretend to look for something to eat and discover the spaghetti. Improvise your own version or use this story:

"Once upon a time there was a little old lady who was very hungry. She went to her cupboard and found some spaghetti. But it was too hard to eat as it was (leader walks from person to person testing spaghetti for hardness), so she put it into a pot (push everyone toward the center of the space), poured in some hot water (make the sound and gesture of pouring a big pitcher of water over the spaghetti), and turned on the stove (make the sound and gesture of turning on a giant knob). Soon the water started to bubble and steam and the spaghetti got limper until it was all soft and wobbly in the pot (everyone gradually grows limper and limper, until wobbly). Then she turned off the stove and tested the spaghetti to see if it was done."

In the end, the leader rolls everyone onto his/her back, encouraging each to be loose and limp. To best achieve this, the leader can go to one person at a time, grab hold of the feet and shake and pull the legs gently, but firmly, to achieve a floppy movement. Shake and pull arms in the same manner and try gently rolling the head from side to side as the "spaghetti" lies limp and unresisting. Encourage each spaghetti to be quiet and relax encouraging looseness of limbs with comments like "Oh, yes, this piece of spaghetti is loose as a goose" or "This piece of spaghetti is just soft enough for my old teeth".

Some participants may be stiff on purpose. If this happens, one may wish to go on to the next, letting that participant know that the you will return when he or she is "fully cooked". Other participants will carry some tightness unintentionally and in this case work with them gently until the limb or neck relaxes.

The remaining "spaghetti", not being "tested", should use the time to simply relax. Discourage talking by saying, "Spaghetti doesn't talk!"

FOCUS

Objective: To raise awareness and the ability to focus both visually and physically on a direction, object or other point of focus. (Adapted from a lesson on focus found in *First Steps in Teaching Dance to Children* by Mary Joyce.)

Getting Ready: Discuss the meaning of focus with the group. When we place focus on something, we place all our concentration and interest on it. To practice this concept, have the group concentrate on various objects in the room noting that the eyes play an important role in focusing. Follow this up by having participants show focus by directing arms and pointing fingers at various objects. Next, encourage whole body focus by leaning, pointing and moving toward the object of focus.

Warm-up: Ask participants to spread out in the space. One at a time, call out objects of focus: wall, floor, ceiling, clock, light fixture, door knob, or other object as participants use eyes, arms, or other body parts or gestures to indicate the object of focus.

Repeat the exercise and ask participants to respond with quick sharp changes of focus from one object to another. Then try the exercise again with slow gradual changes of focus.

Expand this warm-up to include some locomotor activities with the following exercise:

• Have participants line up along one side of the space. Explain that their assignment is to travel (run, walk, etc.) to the other side of the space while changing their point of focus. Cue participants by calling out focal points such as, look behind you, down at the floor, at your hands, up at a light fixture, etc., as they locomote to the other side of the space.

Conduct a simple scenario that demonstrates changing focus with the addition of changing levels and tempo. Before the participants move across the floor again, explain the change of focus actions you will ask them to do: First, they are to crawl

The use of focus in this scene makes dramatic content strong

halfway across the space pretending to look for something. Ask them to imagine what they might be searching for (lost money, a toy, pet gerbil, etc.). Halfway across the space, they find the object, jump up and run the rest of the way. As they run, they are to show with their focus that someone is chasing after them. Try this several times gradually accumulating the series of actions if this is too complicated for the group to grasp all at once.

Activity: Have participants imagine that they are entering a haunted house. Challenge them to use change of focus and levels as they travel through the house and imagine what they might see or do there. Each participant must concentrate fully on his or her own ideas without interfering with the actions of others. For fun, they might add facial expressions showing horror, surprise or delight as they come across strange things in the house.

Play some haunted house sounds or improvise some spooky sudden noises for the group to react to.

Enact this idea in two groups, one half acts, while the other half watches. Share comments on what worked well and was convincing or interesting to watch. Then reverse roles and repeat with a new set of actors.

Extended Activity: Ask participants for suggestions of situations in which focus would be an important factor. Examples: A car race, a wrestling match, building an art project, catching a butterfly, putting on make-up.

Divide participants into pairs or small groups with the assignment to decide on a skit involving all members of the small group. Each scene must involve focus, locomotion, and change of level. (The leader may create other criterias in addition to focus for advanced age groups to suit a particular purpose, such as physical interaction between participants.) Give participants five to fifteen minutes to practice their scenes before performing them for the class. Follow up with a short discussion; what worked and what did not for each scene?

INTRODUCTION

Pantomime is a challenging and useful addition to drama/dance activities. It eliminates the need to have the actual objects involved in an enactment and the pre-occupation with those physical objects that often detracts from the enactment itself.

The three activities included here provide pantomime experience in defining an object through gesture and usage, as well as full-body expression of activities, such as dressing oneself and eating. The magical quality of pantomime is enhanced here through music and guessing games.

WHEN I WAKE UP IN THE MORNING

Objective: To practice pantomime appropriate for an enactment and also to transform pantomime into dance.

Getting Started: Open up discussion with the participants on some of the things they do when they wake up in the morning.

Make up a tune that can be sung repeatedly two or four times to the words "When I Wake Up In The Morning, I Jump Right Out Of Bed."

Activity: Stand with the participants in a circle formation. Sing the song "When I Wake Up In The Morning" and ask everyone to sing along and *jump* on the words "I jump right out of bed".

Ask the participants to suggest other activities to replace the words "jump right out of bed". These may be pantomime suggestions such as "brush and brush my hair" or "go right back to sleep", or movement suggestions such as, "run and fall right down", or "spin and spin around". The teacher may limit the suggestions to a particular theme such as work, play or early morning activities to prepare for an enactment.

One may guide the participants to transform pantomime action into dance, by:

- *Enlarging or diminishing the movements.*
- *Letting the initial pantomime movement carry them into locomotion.*
- *Repeating the movement with variations.*

- *Changing the tempo.*
- *Doing the movement with different body parts such as: stirring a witch's pot with the elbow, toe, head, finger, etc.*
- *Combining pantomime with body moves such as stir and skip in a circle.*
- *Varying the force involved in the movements.*
- *Combining any of the above variations with the pantomime.*

These dance and pantomime explorations can then be utilized in a drama/dance enactment, creating a fuller expression of story, poem, history, or wherever appropriate.

EATING

Objective: To introduce and explore basic pantomime skills.

Getting Started: Explain, or elicit from your group the definition of pantomime; it is expressing or acting out an idea using body and facial movements only. True pantomime does not include sound or dialogue.

Warm-up: Conduct the "Juice" exercise, page 16 . Concentrate on the pantomime involved in this exercise, with added comments which encourage clearer pantomime gestures, such as: "Focus on the way your hand grasps that apple. Can we see the size of the apple in your hand or does it seem to disappear once you've grabbed it? Take a bite out of that apple. Show me how crunchy or how juicy it really is.

Activity: Sit with the participants in a circle formation. Ask each person to think of a favorite food and practice individually how that food is eaten. Is it a:

- *Chocolate bon-bon, picked out of a box with two fingers and delicately savored*
- *A slice of pizza with greasy, stringy cheese*
- *Crumbly cake eaten with a fork*
- *Grapes picked off a vine and popped into the mouth one by one*
- *Slippery noodles being eaten with chop sticks?*

Ask participants to think about the food that they have chosen and how it must be eaten differently from other foods.

After a few minutes of practice time, have volunteers take turns to pantomime eating while others guess what food is being focused upon.

THE MAGIC BALL

Objective: To develop skill in outlining and using pantomimed objects.

Getting Started: Have participants sit in a circle formation.

Explain the game by saying:

"I have a Magic Ball. (Pantomime the tossing and catching of a ball.)

It's magic because it's invisible but I can make all sorts of things out of this ball. First let's see you catch it!" (Toss the ball to someone you feel will play along. Ask that person to toss it to another person until everyone has handled the imaginary ball.)

Activity: Continue the dialogue by saying:

"Now I'm going to make this Magic Ball into something I can use. Raise your hand when you think you know what it is." As though the ball is clay, mold it with a few simple gestures into a tool or object which can be easily identified through pantomime. Clearly outline the object's shape with your hands and show how it is used. Some excellent beginning examples are a fishing rod, baseball bat, pen, hammer or prop needed in a story to be enacted.

Have participants guess by raising hands. The person who guesses correctly, or someone else who is ready, can be the next mime and mold a new object from the Magic Ball. Squish your object back into a ball and toss it to the next mime. Stress that the object should be a simple one and actions must be performed up off the floor for all to see clearly.

I have a magic ball

INTRODUCTION

Everyday objects can serve as inspiration for pantomime, challenge imagination, or merely give visual focus. How to use a single prop, such as an egg beater, may elicit as many ideas as there are members of the group. Is it magic? Does it refuse to beat eggs? Does it talk? The exercise "'Prop Bop" will help bring these imaginative suggestions into action.

The section on "Scarves" offers the teacher a most versatile tool for curriculum enactment. Scarves can be used both as props and costumes, through dance they help express music and depict wind, waves, erupting volcanos, and innumerable other concepts.

USING SCARVES

As props, large, colorful, lightweight scarves made from a translucent and flowing material offer endless possibilities for adventure in movement with drama/dance activities. Scarves can easily represent concepts such as waves, fiery flames, air currents, tornadoes or billowy clouds. With just a little imagination, scarves can be converted into instant costumes by wrapping and tucking them around the body for a cape, veil, skirt, diaper, gown or turban. Since large ready-made scarves are relatively expensive to purchase and hard to find, consider investing in some translucent fabrics of various colors, particularly the primary colors – red, yellow, blue, as well as green, black, and white. When making your own scarves, simply leave the selvaged sides of the material, and turn under and hem the cut ends. For best results make the scarves large enough so that participants can envelop themselves in them, but not so large that when tied around the waist or tucked in the collar, they drag on the floor and tend to cause falls.

A scarf size can be determined by the size of the participants and the intended use of the scarf. Most material comes in 47"or 52" widths. Large scarves, 39" wide x 47" or 52" long, work well with adults and larger children. With this size, one person can manipulate each end to produce good wave effects, or it can accommodate a number of participants under the scarf for special group uses, as in depicting a volcano, underwater scene. or cloud. For children, pre-school through third grade, a 36" wide x 47" or 52" long scarf makes a more manageable scarf size for individual use.

BASIC SCARVES

Objective: To introduce scarves through exploration and establish the rules involved in the use of scarves.

Getting Started: Read "Introduction to Scarves" and prepare a scarf for each participant.

Establish the rules; scarves are not to be:

- Tied around the neck (tucked in the collar is okay).
- Sucked or put in the mouth.
- Used as whips or to entrap others.
- Stepped on (they can be dangerously slippery on hard smooth floors such as wood or linoleum).
- Work individually; no talking or interacting.

Some participants will have a hard time with this last rule. If necessary, stop the action with a "freeze" and make it clear that this is a solo exploration. There will be time later for group efforts and discussion.

Activity: Have each participant select a scarf and find a space away from others or objects. Instruct participants to stay in their spots and explore what movements they can do with their scarves.

A variety of musical selections can elicit variety in movement. Allow time for individual exploration. Then call out movement possibilities: circles, figure eights, angular movements, snake-like movements on the floor, throwing the scarf in the air, twisting it, flattening it out on the floor, draping it over one's head or other ideas.

Next, direct the group to move around the room while exploring a variety of scarf movements. Have participants move with the music and freeze when it stops.

Ask each participant to share a favorite scarf movement with the group, then have the group copy it.

Magic under the big scarf

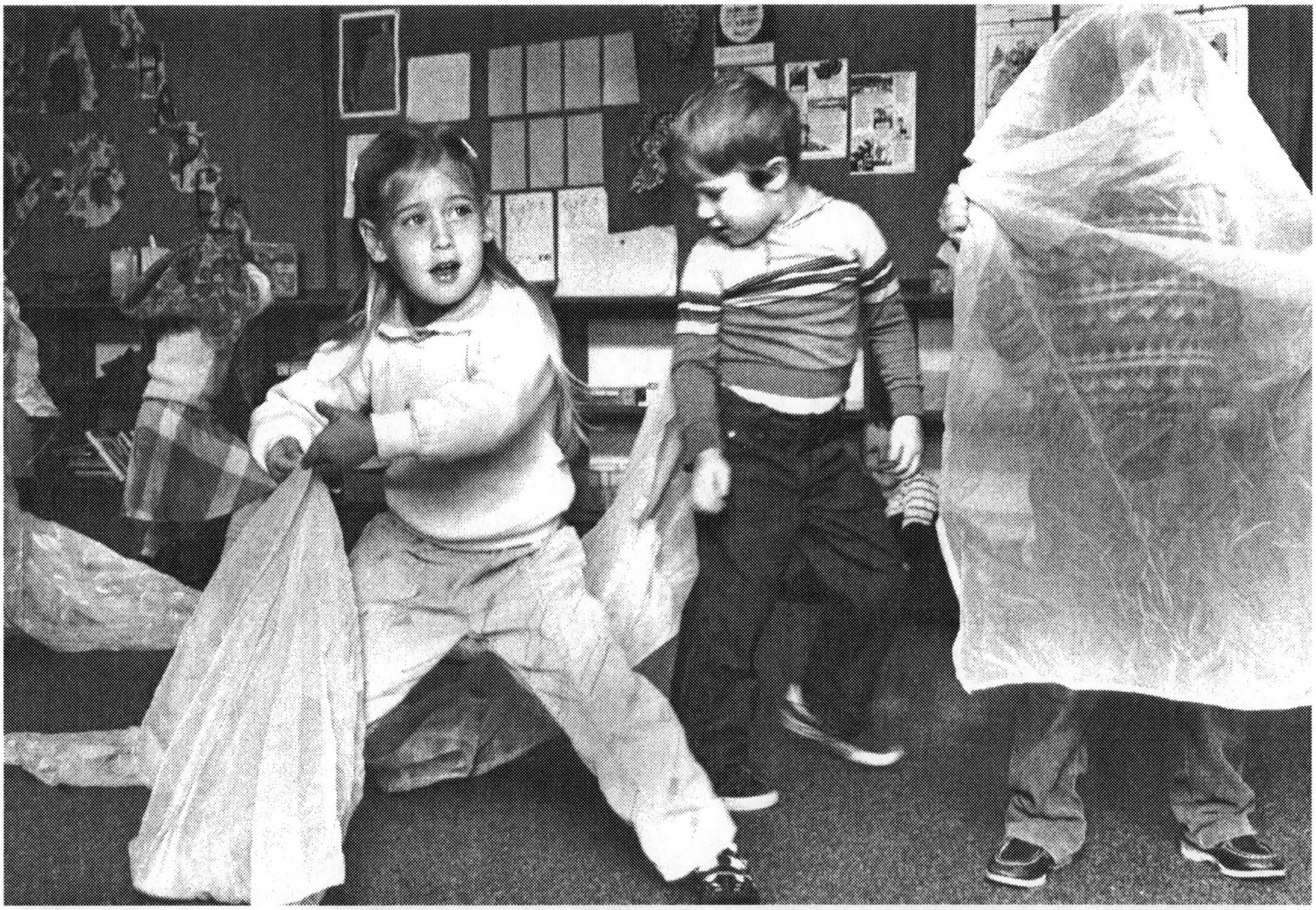

Children exploring characters with scarves

Creating an ocean with scarves

MULTIPURPOSE SCARVES

Objective: To explore a variety of ways scarves can be used in drama/dance.

Warm-up: Conduct the exercise "Basic Scarves" page 51 .

Activity: Several activities on the use of scarves follow:

Color Images – Have participants sit down with the scarves draped over them. Tell them to relax and view the world through their scarves. Ask them to think about the questions you will ask, without answering out loud. Ask: "How does it make you feel to be surrounded by the color of your scarf? How does it make the world around you appear different? What does the color of your scarf bring to mind?"

Ask participants to create one or two movements to express each of the images that the scarf's color evokes. For example:

Red - Firecrackers (explosive jumps)
Blue - Clear skies (steady walking with open, floating scarf); Blueberries (curl up and roll)

Environments – Include scarves when enacting *Instant Scenery* on page   . For example:

Ocean – Several participants simulate water by waving large blue or green scarves between them. Others use scarves and bodies to sculpt and recreate ocean habitat (seaweed, fish, crabs, and sand) while under the large scarves.

Mountaintop – Dark scarves cover still bodies to simulate mountains. White scarves produce billowy cloud movements around the mountains, as colorful scarves enact birds soaring about the mountains.

Rainstorm in a Garden – Divide participants into four groups: butterflies, flowers, rainstorm (wind and rain) and sun.

Spread out the flowering plants, each with a scarf, to create a garden in the room. Gather in one spot those participants representing the sun, to shine on the garden and have them practice flashing or floating out their scarves as rays.

Send out the butterflies, with scarves over their shoulders as wings, into the garden to fly and flutter from flower to flower, stopping to drink nectar and walk with very long, spindly legs.

As the rain and wind of the terrible rainstorm sweep in, the sun is hidden and the butterflies flutter away frantically to hide under the flowering plants.

Finally the rainstorm blows away, the sun comes out and the garden is calm and sunny again. The butterflies come out to fly and feed again.

Energy – Concepts such as air currents, moving molecules, combustion, and sound waves can be illustrated with flowing or flashing scarves.

Props and Scenery – Props and scenery can be improvised through the use of scarves. A twisted scarf makes a rope, a flat scarf when held up high makes a canopy or roof. Caution must be used when a scarf is used as a rug, for scarves are often slippery underfoot.

London Bridge – Play "London Bridge" with two participants holding up a long scarf representing the bridge while others file through one at a time. Make sure everyone is going in the same direction. The scarf is brought down on the phrase "my fair lady" and catches the person under it. This person must take the place of one of the bridge-holders and the game continues.

Costumes – Pass out scarves and have participants work individually or in pairs to create as many costume designs as they can within ten minutes. For example:

* *Draped over shoulders* - Bird, bat, super-hero, Dracula,
* *Draped over head* - Bride, old woman, ghost,
* *Tied* - Arm sling, leg bandage, corset, eye patch, sash, diaper, skirt, dress or hat.

Have each team or individual show a favorite costume to the group. Then have pairs develop and present short skit, centered around characters created with scarf costumes.

Magic Scarves – Have participants imagine that the scarves possess magical powers. By sitting under the scarves they are transformed into other creatures. Remove the scarf to reveal a plant, mammal, reptile, dinosaur, monster, human character, or machine to be guessed by the other participants. Categories may be chosen beforehand or left to individual whim.

BALL TOSS
BRAINSTORMING

Objective: To promote quick thinking and sharing of ideas around a central theme while focusing on any aspect of the curriculum.

Getting Started: Have ready a specific topic and a ball that is easy to catch. Stand participants in a circle formation.

Activity: Introduce the topic. For example:

* *Modes of transportation*
* *What does the sun do?*
* *Names of towns and cities in a state*
* *Characters previously dramatized*
* *Themes that might make a good poem, dance or drama*

The ball is tossed and whomever catches it must call out an example which fits the topic, plus repeat the previous example called out.. For instance, in the theme *transportation,* you may say "trains" and throw the ball to a participant who repeats "trains" and adds a new example, such as "canoes" or "bicycles". This participant then tosses the ball to another participant. The next person repeats "canoes" and adds another idea, and so on.

This activity can be approached in a factual or subjective manner, depending on your theme and aim. It also serves well as a quick quiz and memory recall exercise, or simply as a brainstorming session to elicit a list of ideas to motivate "group thinking" about a particular topic.

PROP BOP

Objective: To inspire skit creations through the use of ordinary household objects.

Getting Started: Make a search for some interesting items or ask each participant to bring in a special item from home to share with the group such as a: wire whisk, hammer, ball, bag of nuts, sponge, perfume bottle, etc.

Activity: Arrange the objects on a table and have each participant choose one object. Provide practice time for each participant to explore his or her object in a brief enactment. Let participants take turns presenting short demonstrations using the objects, such as hammering nails (hammer), spilling a drink and sponging it up (sponge), applying scent (perfume bottle), etc. Then divide the group into pairs to develop more complete skits around the objects.

Extended Activity: Objects may be used imaginatively rather than literally. For example, the sponge may become a wallet; the hammer, a baby; the cardboard tube, a telescope. (Refer to the "Bag of Props" activity in Language Arts.)

Using a sponge prop

Body Sculpting

INTRODUCTION

The teacher will soon discover these contact dance games called "sculpting" to be some of the most useful tools and central to a drama/dance method of teaching. Once the concept of sculpting, using the body as malleable sculpting material, is understood, the technique has endless uses. Participants can work together to create with their bodies, the internal parts of Alexander Graham Bell's first telephone, the nucleus of an atom, an insect for science, an historic building for social studies, and numbers and geometric designs for math. Possibilities are as varied as the imagination allows, from simple shapes conducted by one or two persons, to complex environments formed by a large group.

SHAPES

Objective: To build awareness of the body's ability to achieve a variety of shapes.

Getting Started: Have the group members sit in a circle formation. Once all are seated ask everyone to freeze and take a look at his or her body shape. Are there some holes in the shape? Crossed parts? Angles or straight parts?

Explain to the class members that they will be exploring a variety of shapes that the body can make.

Warm-up: Call out specific body shapes for your class to try while remaining in the circle formation. For example:

- *Rounded/straight*
- *Twisted/crossed*
- *Angular/smooth*
- *Low level/high level*
- *Big/small*
- *With holes, without holes*

If desired, include shape concepts that the class can use later when enacting a particular story or aspect of curriculum study. For example:

- Large and small shapes for such story characters
- Angular for machinery
- Rounded for planets
- Crossed to represent positively charged electrons

Activity: Ask the participants to move around the room to the tempo of a drum or other music. When the music stops they must instantly form a motionless shape. Right before stopping the music the leader may call out a specific type of shape to be created by the participants.

After exploring the idea in unison, one half of the group may sit to one side and observe while the other half demonstrates the shape activity.

The awareness developed in this activity is a basic tool for dance, and preparation for "Partner Sculpting" and "Positive/Negative Sculptures" and "Group Sculpture" that follow.

PARTNER SCULPTING

Objective: To explore body shapes, physical contact and trust.

Activity: Have participants select partners and work in pairs. Spread the pairs out in the space. Ask partners to decide whom will be called "A" and whom "B".

Partner Sculpting

Partner "B" is to stand still (but not rigid), as partner "A" "sculpts" him or her into different shapes and positions. There is to be no talking or verbal instructions between "A" and "B". Partner "B" is to be relaxed and move in any way partner "A" places him or her, holding that position until moved again by partner "A". Partner "A" is, of course, to be considerate of "B" by not forcing a movement that is either painful or anatomically impossible. The shape imagery may be totally abstract or take on a specific form useful for story enactment or the curriculum such as a flower, tool, animal, or vehicle.

The majority of participants will use their hands to move their partners. To encourage diversity, the leader may wish to call out different body parts that partner "A" is to use when moving "B" such as: "Partner "A", sculpt "B" with your elbow (head, hip, shoulder, knee, etc.)." When calling out a succession of body parts, give time for exploration for each new part before going on to another.

When the group has come up with an interesting array of sculptures call 'freeze' so that the shapes and positions can be assimulated and viewed for a moment by everyone.

Then call out "relax" and switch roles. Partner "B" will now sculpt "A".

Extended Activity: Group sculptures can also be achieved by having one or more participants sculpt a larger group of participants in the same manner.

For shape imagery:

• theme can be selected such as: cats, machine, dinosaur, insect, wind, or mountain. Or, the sculpture may simply be an abstract shape.

• The concept of symmetrical and asymmetrical shapes can be sculpted.

• An aspect of scenery such as a: temple, boat, magical forest, or rocket ship all make fascinating subjects for group sculpture.

• A group sculpture may be used as the start-

ing point for a dance. The shape is formed, the music starts and participants dance or move from that beginning shape until the music (or dancers) stops. As an innovative approach, a series of different improvisational dances may even be started from the same beginning shape. Afterwards, discuss each dance and how it differed or was similar to previous dances.

POSITIVE/NEGATIVE SCULPTURES

Objective: To discover the concept of positive and negative space and use it to create interesting body shapes and interrelationships.

Getting Started: Explain to participants that in this activity the body mass is called "positive" space and the empty spaces that the body encloses are called "negative" spaces or "holes". As a point of comparison, the negative space in a doughnut is also the hole.

Ask participants to strike a pose that will produce as many negative spaces or holes as possible, then freeze. While they hold their positions, point out the holes that can be found in each person's body shape.

Explore this same activity on high, middle, and low levels.

Have participants pick partners and work in pairs to form additional holes between the partners' bodies.

Activity: Improvise a Sensational Sculpture involving everyone in the class. This can be done in three sculptured stages:

Completed partner sculptures

58

Sculpture #1

Sculpture One – One participant begins by forming a pose that includes as many holes as possible. It should be a pose that can be held comfortably for a long period of time. Ask four or more additional participants to come up, one at at time, to connect to the original participant's pose and add on more holes by using their bodies and the space between their bodies, then freeze.

Sculpture Two – Ask a second group of four or more participants to fit into the holes that the first group formed and fill up the negative spaces while creating interesting shapes with their bodies, then freeze.

Sculpture Three – Ask the first group, Sculpture One (positive space) to gently move away, leaving behind only those that fit into the holes, Sculpture Two This is the third and final sculpture.

You might wish to introduce the concept of symmetry and asymmetry to this exercise. First have each participant form a symmetrical shape with his or her body. Next, try asymmetrical shapes individually. Teams of participants can work together to form symmetrical group shapes by arranging themselves identically on either side of the sculpture so both sides are balanced.

Sculpture #2

Sculpture #3

A group sculpture of Mr. McGregor's gooseberry net

"Oh no! Peter Rabbit is caught in a gooseberry net!"

GROUP SCULPTURE

Objective: To work as a group to create an image through body sculpting techniques.

Warm-up: Conduct the exercises "Shapes" page 56, "Positive/Negative Sculpting", page 58 and "Partner Sculpting", page 56 (optional).

Activity: Divide the participants into groups involving five or more members each.

Whisper to each group the name of something the group must illustrate through body sculpture. Examples: flower, sun, specific insect, amoeba, lobster, chariot, tepee, dinosaur, etc. The objects may be centered around a theme or chosen at random.

Give the groups five to ten minutes to form the sculptures. Then have each group show its shape in sculpted still form, and with movement added, if appropriate, for the rest to guess.

Extended Activity: Tell a story or an event in history and discuss with the participants which aspects of the scenery, props and characters could be done through group sculpting. Give each group one of these aspects to depict through group body sculpting.

Retell the story, calling on each group to enact its group sculpture when appropriate.

INSTANT SCENERY

Objective: To create still and moving sculpture, in which everyone sculpts themselves to represent an aspect of an environment or scenery.

Getting Started: Fabricate with the group a list of environments, such as: *desert, ocean, jungle, forest, arctic,* and *swamp, discuss what composes them, and how these environments differ from one another.*

Warm-up: Make sure the group has experienced the exercise "Shapes", "Partner Sculpting" and "Positive/Negative Sculpting" on the preceding pages, at some time before this exercise.

Activity: Focus on a specific environment such as a swamp. Involve all the participants in sculpting, using their bodies to form shapes representing plants, animals, earth, water, or any idea that will help define the environment. Participants may work singly or in groups to form appropriate images with their bodies. For example, to form the swamp: five participants may link together to form a snake, one form a drooping tree, six become stagnant swamp water, two an alligator, two shape into twisting vines, and another a swamp boat. To promote spontaneous thought and action, call out a slow count of ten as participants rush into positions to

Group sculpture of a volcano

sculpt the swamp environment. Call out "Freeze",
then "Move", so that participants can express the
still shape as well as elements in the environment
where action is appropriate, such as: a moving
automobile, swaying trees, undulating snake,
machine parts, swimming fish, etc.

Strengthen the exercise by calling out a contrasting environment and repeat the procedure.
Afterwards compare how environments differed or
were similar to one another.

Extended Activity: This excellent technique can
also be used to model instant scenery or objects for
acting out stories. The possibilities are endless.
Participants can combine forces to sculpt descriptive and interesting environments, or aspects of an
environment, such as:

graveyard	*traffic jam*
zoo	*rocket ship*

circus	*sofa*
botanical garden	*water fall*
fast food joint	*tombstone*
kitchen	*science laboratory*

For example: a kitchen challenges participants
to represent such objects as faucets, stove, ref-
rigerator, clock, mixer, toaster, sponge, and dish
rag. Action such as the whirling of a beater and
popping of toast can be added to the still forms
when cue "Move" is given, to bring them alive.

• Guessing sculpted environments can also be
made into a game. Divide the class in half. Have
members of each half take turns sculpting themselves into a still scene that can be taken into
action on the cue of "Move". Members in the other
half must then guess what the scene is and describe its action.

Instant Scenery

INTRODUCTION

The contact dance structures included in this section lend power and excitement to this method of teaching. There are many enactments in which participants must be in direct contact with one another, as in a fight scene, or in the study of friction, magnetism, or rock metamorphosis. For maximum safety, it is important to stress to the participants that these exercises be practiced with *care, control,* and in *slow motion.* The partners must actively work together to produce the illusion of a fight and that takes real cooperation. Actual impact with any force can be avoided altogether by having partners stay at a safe distance from one another, using slow motion, "pulling punches" and utilizing isometrics (tensing muscles), which gives the appearance of effort. In most cases, blows toward the head and face must be avoided. Thicker areas of the body, such as buttocks, thighs, and upper arms offer safe grounds for action/reaction contact. As a general rule, be observant and make sure there is ample space and supervision of these warm-ups at all times.

Push and Pull actions

PUSH AND PULL

Objective: To introduce action/reaction response and direct physical contact with one another that can be integrated into controlled fight scenes in stories and drama.

Getting Started: Explain to the group that you are going to do a pushing exercise using three levels of intensity – low, medium, and high. Have the group pair into partners named "A" and "B". (Partners of equal weight and size are recommended.) Make sure there is plenty of space for action to occur. If space is limited, have a smaller number of pairs perform the exercises while the remaining pairs observe action, allowing all pairs a turn. Explain clearly to the group that the pushing exercise is to be achieved with *constant* and *even* pressure, not shoving or punching.

Caution: Have all exercises here be performed in *slow motion* for safety reasons and avoid such areas as the face and stomach. Especially caution during the high intensity activity.

Activity: Begin with having "A" push "B" with *medium* intensity. "B" should resist or at the same time push back with medium strength. Partner "B" should allow partner "A" to dominate pushing around the room. Most participants will start by using their hands to push. Encourage use of other body parts. Call out, "Now partner "A", push with your hips (shoulders, heads, knees, etc.)." Give time between each new body part for exploration. Mention other levels such as crouching or crawling on the floor to give variety. Now switch roles. Partner "B" will push "A".

Have "A" push "B" again and try the exercise pushing with "all their might" (high intensity: strong but steady pushing; no crashing or bumping) and resisting with "all their might". Tell the "B" partners to firmly root themselves into the ground so they cannot be moved. Again call out different body parts for pushing and give both partners "A" and "B" a chance to push.

For the last exercise have partner "B" be light as a feather or soap bubble (low intensity) while "A" pushes "B" very lightly. Partner "B" should respond by floating with a gentle, light movement in the direction being pushed offering no resistance. As "B" floats about, partner "A" should gently control "B", making sure that person does not bump into objects or other people. Some light, airy music can help to set the mood for this version. Try different body parts again and coach the "B" partners to be aware of where how they are being pushed so that they can respond appropriately.

Switch roles and repeat.

Further develop this exercise by having the partner being pushed, close the eyes to learn to "trust" the pusher.

As a variation, try conducting the entire activity using the opposite concept - pulling.

Expanded Activity: This pushing and pulling activity is a very useful warm-up that can be used with stories for the class to dramatize. Some excellent examples of stories that include either pushing or pulling sequences are:

PULLING

"The Lion and the Mouse", *Aesop's Fables*
(the lion is tied by the hunters and tries to pull himself free.)

Hugin and the Turnip by Isabel Wyatt
(all characters pull the turnip)

The Golden Goose a traditional English Tale
(a group of characters get stuck to the goose and each other and try to pull away)

PUSHING

The Gingerbread Man a traditional English Tale
(the old woman pushes as she forms the cookie dough)

"The Kitten and Falling Leaves" by William Wordsworth
(Refer to poetry in Language Arts Section)
(the kitten pushes as she plays with the leaf)

MOCK BATTLE

Objective: To learn to choreograph a varied and safe action-reaction "dance" that can be used in fight scenes for story enactments.

Getting Started: Discuss "Mock Battle" as it is performed in movies and on television. Do the actors really knock each other down? Or, do they make a punch look real without actually hitting or hurting one another?

Demonstrate a stomach punch on a participant using *slow motion* and working *with, not against,* your opponent. Show how the hand stops short of contact with the body.

Activity: Have the group divide into pairs ("A's" and "B's") and practice mock punches and counter

Partners in mock battle

punches on one another in slow motion. Partner "A" makes a move, "B" reacts; partner "B" makes a move, "A" reacts. Remind them that *it is crucial that all action is conducted in slow motion for safety.* Emphasize that no one is to actually hit or kick another person. Encourage the use of different levels and body parts: use feet, elbows, shoulders, etc. Have each pair spend some time practicing in slow motion various actions and reactions, including falls. Strongly caution against face "hits".

After some practice, sit the group down and have each pair share some of their best moves. Again, remind them to use slow motion and not be carried away as they show what they've worked on. Encourage the group to comment on what worked, what did not, and why.

Caution: If participants in the group are violent, unpredictable, or uncooperative, attempt this activity with extra care. In this case, it may be advised to explore this activity in small groups of one, two or three pairs at a time, so that the teacher can observe how well participants are following the rules of no actual body contact and total cooperation between partners.

On the other hand, this is an especially popular activity and can be therapeutic for participants needing an outlet for explosive type energy and closer involvement with peers.

In conducting the activity, be sure to provide each pair with plenty of space. If therapy is the chief aim, come prepared with a pillow or punching bag for participants who are not yet able to "pull their punches".

MACHINE MADNESS

Objective: To create action/reaction movement to depict a machine useful in curriculum enactments.

Getting Started: Brainstorm with your group a list of machines, real or imaginary.

Warm-up: Conduct "Shapes", page 56 , then divide into pairs for "Partner Sculpting", page 56 .

Activity: Proceed with an adaptation of "Mock Battle", page 64 , in which the goal is machine-like action. "A" does an action aimed at "B". "B" reacts with an appropriate reaction then responds with an action of his or her own which "A" must react to. These series of two actions and two reactions are then repeated.

Have an exploration period and then ask each couple to settle on an action/reaction series that the couple can repeat for the group to watch.

Emphasize clear, precise movement to capture the machine-like quality.

INTRODUCTION

This section includes exercises to care for the vocal chords and throat, enhance awareness of the use of breath, and increase volume through practice in voice projection. The "Who's Speaking?" exercise helps the participants develop character voices and emotional expression through the voice. These can be equally valuable to both student and teacher as they strengthen vocal expression.

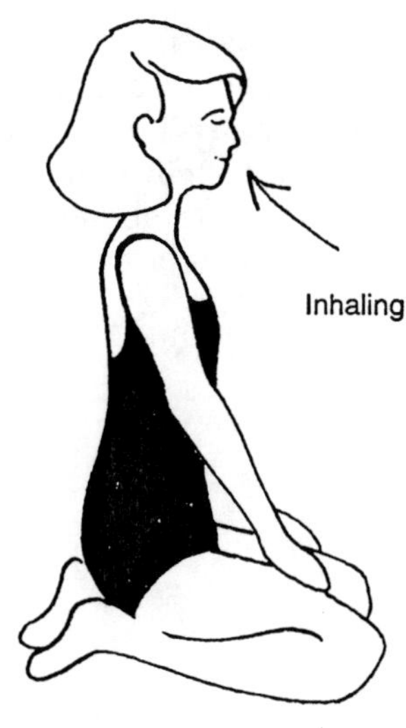

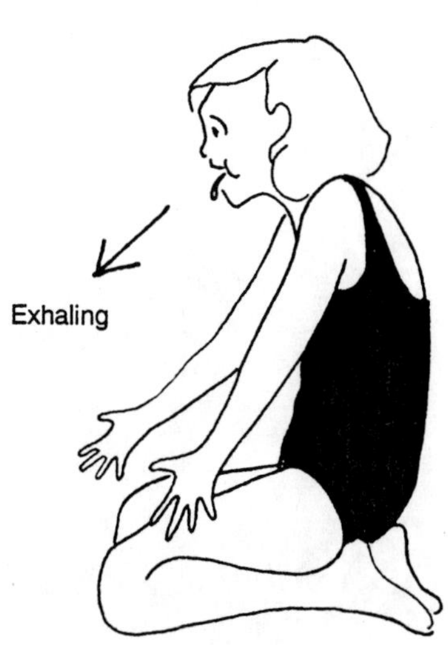

Lion Pose

WHO'S SPEAKING

Objective: To complete a characterization by adding the element of voice to facial and body expression.

Getting Started: Discuss with the group how a voice might sound if portraying "sadness" (slow, soft), "excitement" (high, fast), "anger" (gruff, staccato).

Activity: Ask participants to recite a nursery rhyme or well known song lyric using a descriptive emotional tone. For example: recite "Humpty Dumpty" as if sad, angry or happy. The same poem or other well known poems may be explored vocally expressing feelings such as:

> *hot* or *cold*
> *sleepy* or *wide-awake*
> *aggressive* or *timid.*

Integrate body and facial expressions along with the voice exercise above to develop total characterization.

Utilize increased vocal skills from this exercise in group enactments of literature or historical events under study.

LION POSE

Objective: To loosen throat muscles in order to project the voice properly, or to help alleviate a sore or tired throat, and to practice sudden, fierce dynamics.

Warm-up: Instruct participants to:
- Yawn big and wide, consciously opening and stretching the back of the throat.
- Experiment with widening the opening at the back of the throat. If possible, press the back of the tongue down and say "ahhh" (as in a doctor's throat examination).
- Repeat the same wide mouthed stretch, only this time stretch the tongue way out and down toward the chin.

Activity: Instruct participants to:
- Sit up on the knees with toes curled under so that the bottom side of the toes and balls of the feet are on the floor and the heels are not.
- Place the palms on the knees, close the eyes and breathe in through the nose.
- Strongly and suddenly exhale through the mouth, forcing the back of the throat to open as if yawning.
- Stick the tongue out and open the mouth as wide as possible.

- As this is done, shoot the arms and hands forward with the fingers spread apart, suck the tummy and bottom in and round the back.
- Open the eyes as wide as possible.

BREATHING

Objective: To learn how to project the voice and use the breath to its full capacity.

Getting Started: Explain to the group the importance of proper breathing for maximum brain and body functioning, voice projection and relaxation. This exercise may be conducted before or after a drama/dance activity. Before an activity, the aim is to increase breathing and center participants. After an activity, its aim is to relax and calm down participants.

Activity: Initially this exercise may cause giggling, but if the leader perseveres through this stage, the exercise can be very effective. Have participants lie on their backs with knees up and soles of feet flat on the floor while resting hands gently on the abdomen and relaxing completely.

Instruct them to:

- Take in a deep breath through the nose while pushing (expanding) the abdomen *out.*

- Hold the breath a moment, then blow the air *slowly* out the mouth.

- Repeat the breath exercise, adding a "haaa" sound while slowly exhaling.

- Repeat the breath exercise, making sure tummies are pushed out (fully expanded) at the same time increasing the volume of the "haaa" sound. (When the abdomen is pushed out, this allows the diaphragm to push down, towards the abdominal area, allowing extra room for the expansion of the lungs.)

- To demonstrate the lesser lung capacity when the abdomen is tight, have participants suck in and tighten the abdomen, then inhale air through the nose into the upper chest area only. While still pulling in the abdomen exhale slowly, making a "haaa" sound. (Ask participants if they feel the difference in the amount of air taken in with these two breathing techniques.)

Repeat the first exercise several times aiming to relax the throat, abdomen, and chest while making a large full sound on the exhale.

Extended Activity: As a variation to this activity:

- Try exhaling with a series of short, loud "ha" sounds, using the abdominal muscles to push out the air. Challenge participants to try this, one at a time, so that you can determine what each participant's ability is with this assignment.
- Conduct this same exercise in both sitting and standing positions.
- Use a short sentence, instead of the "ha" sound, in which each participant must project from the abdomen.

Warn the participants against screaming in which the throat becomes constricted and no regard for the abdomen is taken. The throat can be loosened with yawns then gradually increase in volume, making sure the abdominal muscles are expanded and relaxed, not contracted.

CURRICULUM CLASS PLANS

THE CLASS PLAN FORMAT

The structure of this book provides an easy format and a large resource of ideas for the teacher to tap into. Section One, called Primary Tools, consists of a selection of warm-ups which may be used purely for drama/dance exploration and enjoyment. However, the main purpose of the Primary Tools in this book, is to prepare the participants for the curriculum activities as outlined in Section Two.

Section Two presents a selection of curriculum class plans designed specifically for grades K - 7, focusing on the areas of Language Arts, Science, Social Studies and Math.

Each class plan includes a section describing the objective of the activity, hints for getting started, suggested warm-ups from the Primary Tools section and the curriculum activity itself. In this way the teacher and participants are better prepared, both mentally and physically, for the curriculum enactment at hand. Each class plan is set up in the following manner:

• The *Objective* clearly states the overall goal of the activity, whether it be learning a factual concept such as why the sky appears blue, gaining understanding of a culture through a story enactment, or practicing the multiplication tables.

Usually the objective has a single focus but at times, several objectives may be involved.

• *Getting Started* helps to guide the teacher on how he or she and the participants must prepare for the curriculum lesson. This may encompass sharing information, brainstorming, explaining concepts, conducting research or gathering materials.

• The *Warm-up* is a crucial aspect to an activity's success. The warm-up is designed to prepare the participants to be physically equipped to enact the movement, dialogue, interactional, and dramatic content of the curriculum activity.

• The *Activity* section includes the main curriculum material and an explanation of how it is to be enacted.

• The *Extended Activity* is included for some topics. This section guides the teacher to further study and enactments appropriate to the topic covered in the main Activity.

Building New Class Plans on a Drama/Dance Foundation

Leap Into Learning! contains numerous class plans built on drama/dance exercises. In each case these exercises are tailored to teach specific curriculum. When forming a class plan around curriculum material that is not covered in the course of this book search the Primary Tool section for warm-ups that will be helpful in enacting the lesson. In the main introduction, "The Basic Elements of Dance" will help the leader to break down the movement and interactional content involved in an enactment. As an example, when enacting "Earth, Sun and Moon Orbits" the earth and moon must travel at different *speeds,* in circular *pathways,* without physical *contact.* The dance elements of speed and pathways can be explored through warm-ups such as the "Locomotion" exercises, and the absence of physical contact can be practiced through the Primary Tools exercise, "No Bumping".

Curriculum requirements may also be approached through the enactment of stories. The Social Studies activity "Carry Your Own Weight", for instance, incorporates a story about taking on responsibility within a group. History and literature are naturals for drama/dance enactments but in the following chapters you will also find examples of science, math, and grammar lessons taught through stories as well.

There are also stories that cover more than one topic. *The Fire Stealer**, an Ojibwa Native American tale, is an excellent example of such a story. In this story, the hero, Nanabozo, can transform himself into animals and trees. He travels to the North to steal a torch of fire guarded by an old warrior and his daughter. When Nanabozo returns triumphant, the flames reflect off the river onto the trees' green leaves, changing them into fiery oranges, yellows, and reds. Each fall Nanabozo works this same magic on the trees reminding his people that he stole fire for their benefit and taught them how to use it without fear.

This story, then, has dramatic themes of fire and transformation, and emotional themes of fear, bravery, and compassion.

The class plan for this story would be built around a study of emotional expression through the Primary Tools, "Guess How I Feel", and "Emotion Locomotion". "Body Sculpting" and "Characterization Locomotion" aid in exploring the transformation and characterization requirements. To add color and dynamics fire and leaf color change might be explored through the "Multipurpose Scarves" exercise and "The Elements" activity found in the Science section. Finally, the complexity of a story such as *The Fire Stealer* inspires further interdisciplinary study. It suggests thematic exploration of: fire prevention, combustion, Native American cultures, fear and how to overcome it, and the scientific explanation for why the leaves change color. (Refer to the Science section for "Photosynthesis" and "Leaf Color Change".)

This method of building on a drama/dance story enactment is thus a most effective and excellent means of presenting material while motivating children in the process of learning.

**The Fire Stealer*
an Ojibwa Native American tale
retold by William Toye,
Oxford University Press, 1979.

LANGUAGE ARTS

A full enactment of "The Wizard of Oz"

INTRODUCTION TO LANGUAGE ARTS

Undeniably, Language Arts is rich territory for applying drama/dance techniques. The world of poetry and story can be interpreted freshly so that even the most ordinary things can come alive and be exciting. Through imaginative drama/dance interpretations the participants can become rhinos full of irritation because of cake crumbs under their skins in Rudyard Kipling's "How the Rhinoceros Got His Skin". They can dance to silvery-toned music inspired by the poem "Silver", by Walter de la Mare or, be an egg that will not be easily patched together again in Mother Goose's "Humpty Dumpty". The material from which to select is boundless and drama/dance serves as an excellent base upon which to bring the elements of poetry and story development to life: rhythm, intonation, alliteration and form, as well as plot, sequencing, character, conflict and resolution are all essential aspects of study in the Language Arts curriculum and can be assimilated with great enthusiasm through drama/dance activities. Ample material is also included here to help encourage participants to invent their own stories. Activities included in this section, such as "Dining Out" and "Bag of Props" focus on developing story writing skills through team work and improvisation. Refer to the Social Studies International Stories section for additional material excellent for enactment.

As a teaching technique which kinesthetically reinforces the participants' understanding of curriculum concepts, drama/dance is invaluable in introducing new vocabulary and parts of speech. In the activity "Jump, Spin and Wobble", for instance, students are challenged to express verbs through movement. The classroom comes alive as the verbs are enacted and energized, or put into skit form for added meaning. Drama/dance teaching techniques in this section also help motivate students to absorb some basic language components such as letters, nouns, verbs, adjectives, prepositions, synonyms, antonyms and homonyms.

The sharing of literature and language in such a creative and entertaining mode can provide the classroom with a most rewarding and educationally effective experience.

INTRODUCTION TO POETRY

Poetry can be explored through drama/dance in a variety of ways. In selecting a poem it is very important that the poem appeals to you, as the teacher, so that it may be read (or, better yet recited) with wholehearted enthusiasm. It must, of course, appeal to the participants themselves, by being age or development appropriate, containing material and style that the group can relate to or fully understand. The subject of the poem, the mood created through the reader's voice quality and inflection, and the use of dramatic timing are all essential to the success of a poem's reading.

In presenting a poem you may wish to emphasize one or several of its aspects:

- *Rhythm*
- *Rhyme*
- *Dramatic content*
- *Alliteration or the sounds of the words*
- *Mood or movement quality*

One or more of these aspects, or any movement theme that is appropriate to the poem (such as rounded versus quick and sharp movements) can be explored through warm-ups. After this preparation, participants can improvise their own drama/dances based on the warm-ups and their own inspirations. For example, in the class plan in this section for the poem "Silver" by Walter de La Mare, the warm-up "Share the Sound and Movement" helps participants to get in touch with sounds and the movements that they inspire. In this case, alliteration is emphasized by concentrating on the "s" sound and the word "silver" with the many images it brings to mind. The combination of familiar topics (the dark, moon, dog, mouse) and the magical mood of the poem make it rich material for drama/dance enactments.

"Chip-Chop" by I. Tupaj emphasizes the rhythm of chopping wood and comes alive when participants are asked to produce their own chopping movements to the poem's rhythm.

Drama/dance inspired by a poem can be left at an improvised stage with exquisite results. Still, if a structured or more polished piece is desired, start with ample improvisation using ideas drawn from the warm-up selection in Section One, such as "Shapes" and "Dancing Words" to imbue the participants with a variety of movement vocabulary possibilities. The participants can demonstrate favorite movement ideas for different sections of a poem and the group or leader can select which movements will accompany each part of the poem. Then have the group repeat the chosen movements in unison with the poem until all are familiar with the sequence and movements.

Another valuable approach to presenting poetry through drama/dance requires the participants to learn pre-planned body movements for illustrating the poem's content. Prior to the class, the teacher studies (or memorizes) the poem and designs expressive actions to accompany it. The group is taught, through demonstration and repetition, to recite the poem while enacting the accompanying pre-planned motions while in unison. Such an example is found in the poem "Hunter and Hare" found in this section which serves as an excellent prototype for pre-planned actions. It also provides an ideal example showing of an action-oriented poem in which the participants use full body movements while remaining in a stationary position. Starting the school day or the drama/dance session with a number of poems conducted in this manner, either from a standing position behind desks or in a circle formation, can produce striking results and serve as a physical and verbal outlet while strengthening group unity. This simple method also is beneficial for developing memorization skills as well as providing successful presentational material with minimal class time.

Poetry offers a vast and rich world from which to select material. The following poems and accompanying movement suggestions demonstrate only a fraction of the possibilities for combining poetry with drama/dance activities. Last, but not least, are those poems written by the students themselves which they will greatly enjoy bringing to life.

NURSERY RHYMES

Objective: To explore locomotion and rhythm patterns through nursery rhymes.

Getting Started: Have participants share some of their favorite nursery rhymes with one another. Teach the participants some of your favorite rhymes or familiarize them with lesser known rhymes.

Warm-up: Practice some rhythm exercises with the group - stamping feet and clapping hands to the underlying pulse of various nursery rhymes being recited. Emphasize quick beats for some verses, as in the "Hippity-Hop" sample below, or slower beats for others, as in "Baa, Baa Black Sheep, Have You Any Wool?". Point out and demonstrate to participants the use of accent on certain syllables. For example, in "Humpty-Dumpty" the first syllable is accented, the second syllable is less emphasized. Conduct "No Bumping", "Run, Jump, Skip", and "Jump/Freeze", pages 23 , 27 , and 23 , to prepare for locomotion with the rhymes.

Activity: When acting out a nursery rhyme, begin with simple locomotion from one side of the space to the other. Add some informal pantomime actions with the second or third repetition. Some examples follow:

HIPPITY-HOP
(Hop and Jump)
"Hippity-Hop to the barber shop
To buy a piece of candy.
One for you and one for me
And one for sister Mandy."

First, have the group hop and jump from one side of the space to the other side as the rhyme is recited. This can be done very informally. Upon reaching the other side of the space, instruct the group to line up side-by-side again and pretend to give and receive candy with the participants on either side of them.

Now, challenge the group to repeat their hops and jumps back across the space, as the rhyme is recited, but stop when they hear the word "candy". They are then to give and receive the pretend candy from those on either side of them and continue across the floor to the other side.

SKIP TO M' LOU
(Skip)
"Skip, skip, skip to m' Lou,
Skip, skip, skip to m' Lou,
Skip, skip, skip to m' Lou,
Skip to m' Lou m' darlin'."

This rhyme may be conducted with all members first skipping by themselves, then pair off and have partners skip together, across the floor. Participants may gallop if they have not mastered a skip.

RIDE A COCK HORSE
(Gallop or Prance)
"Ride a cock horse to Banbury Cross,
To see a fine lady on a white horse,
With rings on her fingers,
And bells on her toes.
She will make music wherever she goes."

Have participants begin this rhyme with a regular gallop or prance gait across the floor. On the second or third repetition, add a dance in a free-form style as the "lady" jiggles her toe bells and shows off her rings.

HUMPTY-DUMPTY
(Side-Slide)
"Humpty-Dumpty sat on a wall,
Humpty-Dumpty had a great fall,
All the King's horses and all the King's men,
Couldn't put Humpty together again."

Have participants do a side-slide movement with an emphasis on the first beat. This movement is perfect for the rhythm of Humpty-Dumpty.

Develop "Humpty-Dumpty" into a dramatization by having participants pick partners. One partner represents an egg. The other represents the King's horses and men. As the poem is recited all partners enact their parts.

Encourage the eggs to make themselves round like big eggs, and then to roll or waddle across the room, sit down in mid-air on an imaginary wall, then fall, making themselves into broken and jagged shapes on the floor. The other partners gallop across the room on pretend horses and try to fix up Humpty-Dumpty. Each time they are set back on the wall, the Humpty-Dumpties fall down and break again. Afterwards, the King's horses and men gallop back across the room to their starting place. Recite the poem slowly as each part is enacted.

You may wish to add:

"Then along came his mother and 'clickety-clack'
She put him together and set him right back."

With this the leader can go to each egg and right Humpty-Dumpty into a standing position, having everyone reverse roles with his or her partner and re-enact the rhyme.

PUSSY-CAT, PUSSY-CAT
WHERE HAVE YOU BEEN?
(Tip-toe)
"Pussy-cat, Pussy-cat,
Where have you been?'
'I've been to London,
To visit the Queen.'
'Pussy-cat, Pussy-cat,
What did you there?'
'I frightened a little mouse,
Under her chair. "

Ask participants to locomote in a straight course across the space with a sneaky, tip-toe movement, then, on a second round, follow a winding course. Speed up the voice on the line , "I frightened a little mouse under her chair", and ask the participants to enact these lines with a quick dash and pounce.

In the second interpretation, participants all play the part of the cat, the leader is the "inquirer" and the Queen, and the mice are imagined.

LITTLE MISS MUFFET
(Skip, Creep and Run)
"Little Miss Muffet,
Sat on a tuffet,
Eating her curds and whey.
There came a big spider,
Who sat down beside her,
And frightened Miss Muffet away."

Read the rhyme as all participants locomote across the space, first skipping, then repeat the rhyme as they creep, then run.

Have participants act out this rhyme as a duet, choosing partners and enacting it at least twice (reversing roles). Establish ahead of time where Little Miss Muffet will sit and in which direction she will run when frightened. One partner plays Little Miss Muffet who skips along and sits down, and pantomimes eating with a bowl and spoon. The other partner plays the spider who creeps up to Little Miss Muffet in a spider-like position. Direct participants to build suspense by having Little Miss Muffet not notice the spider until it is quite close, at which time she responds by turning, seeing the spider, and jumping up in surprise and fear as she runs to a pre-determined spot on the other side of the space.

It might be of value beforehand to discuss with participants the term "tuffet". (Two plausible suggestions have been a tuft of grass or a pillow with tufts sewn on it. Webster's defines it as a low seat.) Also, if the group does not know what curds and whey are, they can be described as foods similar to cottage cheese or yogurt containing thick clumps and runny liquid.

Extended Activity: As a follow-up to "Little Miss Muffet" you may wish to counteract this archetypal frightened reaction to spiders by gathering or observing harmless spiders, studying how they are helpful to humans. *Charlotte's Web* is one of many positive stories about spiders and insects. Because insects are an important aspect of the whole ecostructure, it is necessary to expose children to their merits as well as their sinister connotations. Many youngsters have a natural fascination with insects and this curiosity should be encouraged, not turned into repulsion or fear. (See the "Insects" activity in the Science Section.)

Little Miss Muffet

"CHIP-CHOP"

Objective: To explore the poem's theme, its strongly-accented rhythm, and the use of strong rhythmical movement.

Warm-up: Ask the group for some examples of movement used when chopping wood.

Spread the group members out in the space and encourage everyone to pantomime log splitting actions with hearty enthusiasm: legs spread apart, arms swinging up overhead and down on the log in big broad chopping strokes.

Establish a steady rhythm of one quick beat and one slow beat with a rhythm instrument or clapping.

Next, expand the movement from simple pantomime into dance by encouraging repetitive sharp movements to the rhythm using different body parts, levels and directions.

Activity: Read the poem, "Chip-Chop", with a clear strong rhythm, placing emphasis on the word *chop*. (The word *chip* comes on the quick up-beat of the rhythm and is used to indicate raising the axe while the word *chop* accompanies the axe coming down.)

The group should retain a steady chopping action, two chops per line, throughout the poem. (In the second line, the chop will be on *wood* of the word *woodman* and on *chopper,* and so on throughout the poem.)

Once the rhythm and action is established, ask the group to recite the poem with you, as they chop.

CHIP-CHOP

Chip-Chop, chip-chop
The woodman with his chopper chops.
Chip-chop, chip-chop
Stout and strong and proper chops.

On beeches, oaks and larches too
His hatchet brightly rings,
And while he chops so cheerily
As cheerily he sings.

by I. Tupaj

THE KITTEN AND THE FALLING LEAVES

Objective: To dance with enjoyment to the actions of a poem which involves rolling, spinning, leaping, falling, contact with a partner, and kitten characterization.

Warm-up: Conduct "I'm a Puppet on a String", page 45 . Ask participants "How else can you fall?" Have the participants watch and copy each falling suggestion. Encourage variety and verbalize the characteristics of each fall. Examples: melting fall, jump-fall, forward, side, and backward falls, slide-fall, spin-fall, and floating fall.

Practice kitten moves through locomotion: run, run-leap, run-leap-roll, run-slide, prance, chase tail in circles. Emphasize the use of levels.

Have the participants choose partners. The partners take turns spinning, rolling, and leaping around each other as a kitten might play with a wind-tossed leaf.

Activity: Have the participants stay in pairs and read or recite these excerpts from the poem "The Kitten and the Falling Leaves."

Have the pairs decide which partner will dance the kitten and which the leaf. Spread the pairs out in the space and recite the poem again with pauses, giving time for the participants to dance and interact. Then ask the participants to switch roles and repeat the poem and action.

Sit down and share with the group what the participants most enjoyed in dancing the poem. Add comments on what was done well and what might improve the enactment: use of levels, space and pathways, more movement by the leaves, more interaction between kittens and leaves, etc.

Divide the pairs into two groups and have one group of pairs watch as the other group dance, and vice versa.

THE KITTEN AND THE FALLING LEAVES

See the kitten on the wall
Sporting with the leaves that fall!
Withered leaves, - one, two, three,
From the lofty elder-tree.

With a tiger-leap half-way
Now she meets the coming prey.
Lets it go at last, and then
Has it in her power again.

by William Wordsworth

The Kitten and the Falling Leaf

THE HUNTER AND HARE

Objective: To introduce the participants to a lively poem enacted through pre-set dramatic action while standing in a stationary position.

Warm-up: Begin with the "Round the Circle" exercise, page 26 . Incorporate into this exercise some of the basic actions that occur in the "Hare and Hunter" poem such as leaping, hopping, and stomping.

Encourage the group members to mimic your own actions for some of the animal activities found in the poem: down like a little rabbit and wiggle the nose, nibble some hay, dig, sit up quickly, then fall asleep.

Activity: Recite the poem while performing hand and arm motions, appropriate to the poem's actions for the children to follow. You may wish to design your own motions, or follow those described below.

Afterwards, consider enacting the poem more completely, allowing participants to create their own actions.

To begin, arrange the class members in two parallel lines, one behind another, to represent collectively the hunter in back and hare in front. Each of these characters should conduct actions when appropriate.

SNOWFLAKES WHIRL THROUGH WINTER NIGHT

POEM	ACTIONS
Snowflakes whirl through winter night,	Make swirling motions with hands above heads (all).
Clothe the earth in glowing white, Down beneath the snow so deep	Sweep hands from one side to the other, down toward the earth (all).
Master Hare lies fast asleep.	Place hands beneath cheek in sleeping gesture (all).
Hark! What's that? A noise I hear.	Suddenly stand up straight, eyes wide, hands up like two ears on top of head (hares).
Hide, now hide your head and ear.	Cover head with arms and crouch low (hares).
Up above the snow white ground Huntsman walks with heavy sound.	Make four stamping steps for each line (huntsmen).
Green his cap with flying feather	Two hands come together above head to indicate peaked cap on head; then one hand sweeps back on side to indicate feather (hunters).
Brown his coat for wintry weather.	Cross arms in front, hands on biceps for "coat" and "cold" (hunters).
Both his boots are big and black.	Make four stamping steps (hunters).
Bow and arrow on his back.	Draw bow (hunters).
Slowly, softly place your boot	Crouch and take two steps in place; one looking right, one looking left (huntsmen).
Quietly if you wish to shoot.	Take two more slow steps in place for "quietly" and "wish," looking to one side and then the other (hunters).
"But alack!"	Throw hands up (hunters).
The ice goes crack.	Clap hands (all).
Down a hole Hunter roll!	Make hand-over-hand rolling motion: bend forward (hunters).
And my hare???	Bend forward, hands on thighs (hares).
With a leap de-lop-lop-lop	Take three jumps forward on "lops" (hares).
Off he capers, hop, hop, hop.	Take three jumps backward on "hops" (hares).
Laughing loud, "Ha-ha-hee-hee Huntersman you can't catch me."	Hold tummy and shake in laughter (hares).

Then he nibbles at some hay,	Fold hands in front like paws (hares).
Wipes and sweeps the snow away,	Make wiping gesture towards sides (hares).
And once more falls fast asleep 'Neath the snow so white and deep.	Place hands under cheek in a sleeping gesture with head to one side (hares).

Hunter and Hare by M. Meyerbort

This sort of group recitation with actions requires extra practice for some participants will catch onto the words quickly and tend to lead the presentation, while others will grasp the ideas more slowly.

by M. Meyerkort taken from *Winter*
published by Wynstones Press,
Brookthorpe, Gloucester, U.K.

"SEAL"

Objective: To explore a poem through dance motivated by the sounds and images of the poem.

Warm-up: "My Hands Say Hello", page 43 , helps to encourage movement of individual body parts.
"Bend and Stretch", page 18 . (Optional)
"Do Your Ears Hang Low?", page 45 , is an excellent practice of sharp and floppy movement qualities.

Explore through locomotion some actions taken from the poem such as "swim". First ask the group to "swim" from one side of the room to the other. Further elaborate and explore the movement with directions such as: "Swim on a low level like a seal", "swim varying your level", "dive and swim, darting this way and that", and "now, add some twists".

Read the poem, and let the group see how the poet has chosen to write the poem on the page.

Activity: Have everyone spread out in the space. Re-read the poem as the participants dance to it. If necessary remind them to use the whole floor space and as many levels as possible. Also repeat lines such as "A flip of the flipper, A flick of the wrist" to give the dancers a chance to explore the movement suggested.

Break the group in half or in smaller groups and have half act as audience while the other half dances.

Extended Activity: Have half the group become underwater creatures: seaweed, crabs, sharks, etc. These creatures may arrange themselves in small groups using characteristic movements in a limited space, while the other half dance as seals and use the whole space, darting in and out, over and among the sea creatures.

SEAL

See how he dives
From the rocks with a zoom!
See how he darts
From his watery room
Past crabs and eel
And green seaweed,
Past puffs of sandy
Minnows feed!
See how he swims
With a swerve and a twist,
A flip of the flipper,
A flick of the wrist!
Quicksilver-quick,
Softer than spray,
Down he plunges
And sweeps away;
Before you can think,
Before you can utter
Words like "Dill Pickle"
Or "Apple Butter",
Back up he swims
Past stingray and shark
Out with a zoom,
A whoop, a bark;
Before you can say
Whatever you wish,
He plops at your side
With a mouthful of fish!

by William Jay Smith

Exploring seal actions

ROW

Objective: To explore both sounds and images which lend themselves easily to expression through movement in this appealing poem.

Warm-up: Use the "Staccato/Legato" locomotion exercise, page 29 , to explore these movement qualities.

Use an adaptation of "Jump/Freeze", page 23 , during some of the above locomotion exercises.

Through "Dancing Words", page 44 , explore a variety of movements to help expand the participants movement "vocabulary".

Activity: Read the poem "Row" by Ralph Pomeroy. Point out the seven different descriptive segments, almost like seven small poems within the poem.

Read each of these separately and discuss with the group the actions and movement qualities evoked by each segment.

Following are examples of movement for the first three segments:
- Slapping, clapping, percussive, and wave movements
- Hopping, stretching, and contracting
- Floating

Spread the group members out in the space. Recite each segment several times and allow the participants to improvise dance movements to it.

Encourage repetition of movements and the choosing of favorite movements for each poem segment.

Recite the entire poem several times as the participants move to it.

In conclusion, share the dances with just two to five dancers performing at one time, as others watch.

ROW

Slap. Clap.
The lake's back
laps the flat
boat. Croak,
goes a frog,
croak. Flo-
tillas of vanilla
water lilies
float. Moats
of air flare, filled
with day-diamonds,
flame. Tame
turtles lurch
like dreadnoughts
across murky
floors. Oars

dig dingles
in the sun-shingled
roof of the water.
Pines shine,
singing their green creeds.

by Ralph Pomeroy

SILVER

Objective: To improvise dance inspired by the alliteration, mood and characters introduced in the poem "Silver", by Walter de La Mare.

Getting Started: Read the poem 'Silver' and discuss with participants the alliteration and the definition of words that they might not understand such as "shoon", "casements", "thatch", and "cote".

Warm-up: Prepare the participants to dance with a variety of stretches such as: "Who Has Seen The Wind?", page 19 , "Juice", page 16 , "Cat and Dog Backs", page 19 and/or with the exercise "Dancing Words", page 44 .

Tailor the Locomotion exercises in Section One by concentrating on the action described in the poem, such as:
- Slow floating walk
- Zig-zag pathway (rather than straight across)
- Tip-toe
- Scamper
- Creep and "catch"
- Use of levels (high, middle and low movements while crossing space

Incorporate the "Focus" exercise, page 47 into this locomotion activity.

Explore "Pass the Sound and Movement", page 33 , with emphasis on "s" sounds.

Compile a list of image words that the participants associate with the word "silver" such as "sparkling, strong, shining, rich," etc. Have participants spread out in the space and individually compose a movement for the word "silver". Have those that are willing share their composition as others watch. Of all those shared choose one "silver" movement for everyone to copy and learn. If competition is an issue or time is limited, the leader may compose a simple "silver" movement and teach it to the group.

Activity: Still spread out in the space, have the participants explore movement in unison as each improvises his or her own dance to the sounds, words and images evoked by the poem as it is read aloud.   Enrich the reading with mood and voice quality, the use of bells, a triangle, or appropriate music. Vary the tempo of the reading and allow pauses for movement. Incorporating pathways, levels, tempos and freezes, each participant moves as he or she feels inspired. These improvisations may then be shared by small groups or with half the class members watching and half dancing.

Extended Activity: Divide the class into two groups. Group A dances the moon, the doves and the fish with scarves if scarves are desired and available.   Group B dances the trees (with still shapes), the casements, the dog, the mouse, and, using the scarves from Group A – the stream. Each time the word "silver" occurs in the poem, everyone dances the composed "silver" movement.

Before the group dance interpretation arrange the trees in the space, then establish the locations where the dog, doves and the stream with fish will be danced. The poem, may be danced just as it is written emphasizing the use of still shapes to compliment and contrast with the movement or altered a bit to allow for more movement on the part of the dog (stretching, howling, prowling), and the doves (flying out of their coop and back again).

Reverse parts and have the original A group dance the B part and vice versa. Discuss what is working well and what is not. Then dance it two more times with half of the class dancing while the other half watches. Follow with a short disucssion at the end of each showing emphasizing positive feedback.

SILVER

Slowly, silently, now the moon
Walks the night in her silver shoon;
This way, and that, she peers, and sees
Silver fruit upon silver trees;
One by one the casements catch
Her beams beneath the silvery thatch;
Couched in his kennel, like a log,
With paws of silver sleeps the dog;
From their shadowy cote the white breasts peep
Of doves in a silver-feathered sleep;
A harvest mouse goes scampering by,
With silver claws and a silver eye;
And moveless fish in the water gleam,
By silver reeds in a silver stream.

by Walter de La Mare

JABBERWOCKY

Objective: To enjoy the imaginative use of sounds and images in the poem and to translate these into expressive humorous movement.

Getting Started: The leader may gain some insight into this poem by reading *The Annotated Alice* by Lewis Carroll with notes by Martin Gardner. This can be helpful but not necessary, for the participants will receive their own impressions from the nonsense words in the poem.

Warm-up: Limber bodies with a variety of stretches from Primary Tools

Use "Staccato/Legato Locomotion", page 29 and "Characterization Locomotion", page 27 , to explore a monster, knight in shining armor, unusual animal movements and dynamics across the floor.

Conduct "Share the Sound-and-Movement", page 33 . If the participants have not explored "Share-A-Sound" and "Share-A-Movement" previously, make sure they start with these exercises before attempting "Share the Sound-and-Movement.".

Activity: Read or recite "Jabberwocky" using expressive intonation and emphasizing the sounds of the words. Discuss with the participants what images come to mind with such words and phrases as "slithy toves", "gyre", "gimble", "mome raths outgrabe".

Ask volunteers to share movements that they feel express such words.

Have participants spread out in the space and individually move in unison to the poem as it is read. Slowly repeat the poem several times allowing the participants time to explore movements and physical characterization. Make sure to include intonation inspired by the discussion.

As a solo, each participant takes on all the characterizations within the poem.

Share the solos in small groups (two to five performing at once) until everyone has had a chance to perform for the others. Each group's performance can be followed by discussion.

JABBERWOCKY

'Twas brillig, and the slithy toves
    Did gyre and gimble in the wabe:
All mimsy were the *Borogroves*,
    And the mome raths outgrabe.

"Beware The *Jabberwock*, my son!
    The jaws that bite, the claws that catch!
Beeware the *Jubjub bird*, and shun
    The frumious Bandersnatch!"

"He took his vorpal sword in hand:
    Long time the manxome foe he sought –
So rested he by the *Tumtum tree,*
    And stood awhile in thought.

And as in uffish thought he stood
    The *Jabberwock,* with eyes of flame,
Came whiffling through the tulgey wood,
    And burbled as it came!

One, two! One, two! And through and through
    The vorpal blade went snicker-snack!
He left it dead, and with its head
    He came galumphing back.

And has thou slain the *Jabberwock?*
    Come to my arms my beamish boy!
O frabjous day! Callooh! Collay!
    He chortled in his joy.

'Twas brillig, and the slithy toves
    Did gyre and gimble in the wabe:
All mimsy were the *Borogroves,*
    And the mome raths outgrabe.

by Lewis Carroll
From *Through the Looking Glass*

All Mimsy were the Borogroves

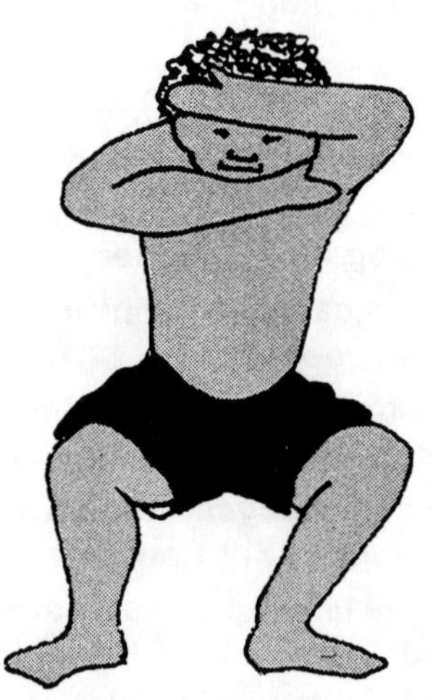

"An hast thou slain the Jabberwocky?"

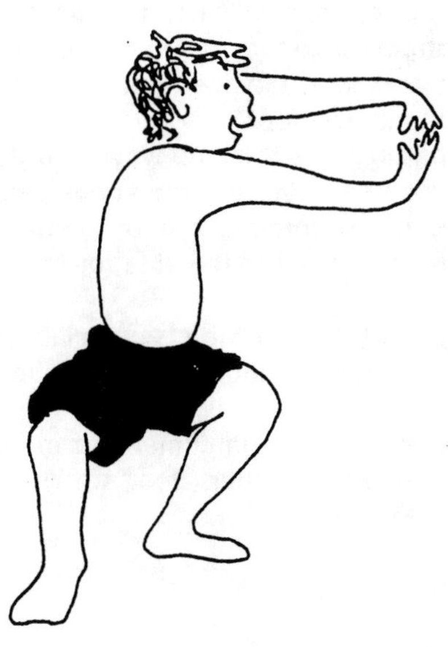

"The Jabberwock, with eyes of flame..."

BODY LETTERS

Objective: To reinforce letter and number recognition through body shapes.

Getting Started: Have participants practice writing different-sized letters or numbers in the air with their fingers, hands, and arms.

Ask participants, one at a time, to write a letter or number in the air. Have the rest of the class guess which letter or number it is.

Warm-up: Explore the "Shapes" exercise, page 56 .

Activity: First, demonstrate to the group the formation of a letter with body-shape by making a capital "T" (stand tall, feet together, arms straight out at shoulder level and head bent to one side). Follow this up with a series of activities in letter and number shapes:

• Spread participants out in the space and challenge participants to individually body sculpt the letters in their own names, and any other letters they wish to explore.

Choose participants to demonstrate each one of the letters in the alphabet, from A to Z. Point out the importance of facing the letter in the right direction for the audience to view clearly.

• Discuss what letters may best be achieved by several participants and try those in small groups. For example, three participants may form a "W". One member bends over with hands and feet on the floor and bottom up, to form the middle of the "W". The second and third members stand at the first member's hands and feet.

• Have participants think up ways and demonstrate how to de-emphasize certain body parts that are not involved in forming a letter shape. (For example, lean the head to the side for the capital letter "T".)

• Conclude by having the class collaborate to form the name of your school or a story title being read or enacted.

• Geometric shapes and numerals can also be explored in the same manner. (See "Are You Two?" in the Math Section.)

NOUNS AROUND TOWN

Objective: To reinforce what constitutes a noun.

Getting Started: Explain to the group that a noun can be a person, place or thing. To illustrate these ideas, write some sentences on the board and ask the class to name the nouns in each sentence.

Warm-up: To build awareness of nouns, ask participants to walk randomly in the room while calling out the names of nouns that they see inside the room and through the windows. Direct attention to areas of the room, or categories of nouns that are overlooked.

Have participants sit in a circle and share favorite nouns discovered through the exercise. Next, lead your group in a brainstorming session on the most unusual or interesting nouns that they can think up.

Explore "Character Locomotion", page 27 . Follow this up with an adaptation of "Instant Scenery", page 61 , aimed at creating imagery of a specific place or thing through body sculpture.

Activity: Divide the group into teams of three or more members each. Give each team a sentence or have each group create a sentence which incorporates at least two nouns. Each group must first act out the nouns in the sentence, separately, then act out the entire sentence, with nouns integrated, for the rest of the class to guess. Allow five or ten minutes for teams to spread out and practice the noun and sentence enactments. Ask each team, one at a time, to present its enactment in front of the class. When the nouns are properly guessed, the group presenting enacts and discloses its sentence.

For example:

• The *monster* slunk evilly around the old *tree*.

• Our *dog*, *Spot*, fetches the *ball*.

• Parrots can talk and pick up *crackers* with their *toes*.

• Superman flew through the *air* and landed on the *Empire State Building*.

• The mad *elephant* tore down the *tree* and headed toward our *car*.

• The *hammer* and *nails* are all over the *floor*.

• Silently, the *butterfly* circled the *flower*.

• The two *babies*, lost in the *woods*, cried until the *wolves* found and cared for them.

BERRIES AND BEARS
Prepositions

Objective: To understand prepositions and prepositional phrases and how they are used in a sentence.

Getting Started: Fabricate and define a list of prepositions and prepositional phrases with the class. Explain that a preposition is a word that indicates the relation of something (a verb, noun, adjective, etc.) to something else.

Warm-up: Start with the simple locomotion exercise "Run, Skip, Jump", page 27. Adapt this exercise by placing obstacles in the room and asking participants to perform a number of prepositions and prepositional phrases such as:

- Skip *around* the post
- Jump *over* the ruler
- Sit *on* the chair
- Scoot *under* the table
- Walk *with* your hands *above* your head
- Tiptoe *through* the chairs
- Walk *up* to the chair hand-*in*-hand *with* the person *next* to you

After each sentence has been performed ask a volunteer to name the prepositions or phrase involved.

Activity: Divide the class into small groups of two to four participants each. Ask each group to design a short scene involving five or more prepositions or prepositional phrases and enacted by everyone in the group. A story example follows:

BERRIES AND BEARS·
by Kristen Bissinger

Zak and Lia decided to go berry picking. They got their pails and walked *across* a field, *around* a pond, *over* a fallen log, *through* the woods, and *under* a fence. There they found their favorite berry patch ready and ripe *for* eating. They began to pick and put the berries *in* their pails and *in* their mouths.

On the mountain lived a family *of* bears. They knew the berries were ripe, too, so they headed out *in* search *of* the berry patch. They lumbered *down* the mountain, *around* a pond, *over* a fallen log, *through* the woods, *under* a fence and they began to eat berries.

Both the bears and the children began to eat *at* the edge *of* the patch. They backed their way *into* the center *of* the patch eating as they went. When they got *to* the center *of* the patch, they bumped *into* one another. Both children and bears jumped *with* surprise and ran *out* the way they had come: *under* the fence, *through* the woods, *over* the log, *around* the pond. The bears climped *up* their mountain and *into* their cave *with* a huge sigh *of* relief. Zak and Lia ran *across* the field *into* the house, panting, laughing and glad to be safe *at* home.

Exploring prepositions

JUMP, SPIN AND WOBBLE
Verbs and Adverbs

Objective: To teach about words that express actions (verbs) and words that can alter these actions (adverbs).

Getting Started: Introduce action verbs to the class and build a word list on the chalkboard:

run	glide	slip
wave	spin	fly
jump	wobble	dance
leap	rotate	scoot

Warm-up: Have participants arrange themselves at random in the space. Call out action words, one at a time, for them to interpret individually, while in unison.

Activity: Ask participants to work in teams of two or three members each to develop short skits that center around action verbs. For example:

Jump – People hold a jumping competition; or, a magic jumping bean when eaten, causes people to jump.

Spin – Two people spin a third person who represents a top

Fly – A mother bird teaches a baby bird to fly for the first time.

Extended Activity: Add the element of adverbs to the verb activity. Discuss the three forms of comparative adverbs: *positive, comparative and superlative.* Compile a list of interesting adverbs on the chalkboard by first listing a verb and then follow it with a listing of comparative adverbs to describe it. For example:

Jump – High, higher, highest; or, wildly, gracefully

Cartwheel – Fast, faster, fastest

Wobble – Roughly, more roughly, most roughly

Have participants spread out in the space. Call out some of the verb and adverb combinations in the list for participants to perform individually, while in unison.

Ask each participant to enact one of their favorite verb and adverb combinations while others watch.

BLOBBING AROUND
(Adjectives)

Objective: To explore adjectives through group movement exercises.

Getting Started: Discuss adjectives with the class and build an adjective word list on the chalkboard:

wobbly	tired	energetic	tall	bouncy
big	tough	ragged	circular	bashful
little	senile	sharp	angular	reluctant
funny	lazy	smooth	bold	silly
rickety	undulating	lumpy	collapsible	agitated

Discuss definitions of a blob (a shapeless mass, an amorphous something that can change shape).

Explain to participants that they will explore "adjective blobs" – blobs with characteristics that are defined by one adjective. The leader will discover that some adjectives are well suited for use in this activity while others are not.

Warm-up: Create a locomotion exercise, adapted from "Emotion Locomotion", page 27 , centered around adjectives. Call out adjectives, one by one, that lend themselves to movements, and have participants locomote, as inspired by the adjectives, across the space. Have participants move in unison or in small groups. If the adjective is not clearly expressed in the movements, repeat the exercise after some clarification or call on an individual who has expressed it successfully to demonstrate the movement to the group.

In addition, "Share the Sound-and-Movement", page 33 , helps encourage playful sound and movement possibilities.

Activity: Hold up some sheets, blankets or bedspreads and explain that these will become the "skins" that will be used to transform participants into life-sized blobs for interpreting adjectives. (This activity can also be performed without a covering with the group acting together in a cluster or blob-like formation.)

Collaborate in teams of three to six members each. Have each team arrange itself under a single "skin" and move together in response to contrasting adjectives. For example:

- *Energetic or calm blob*
- *High or low blob*
- *Angry or happy blob*
- *Graceful or awkward blob*
- *Stiff or wobbly blob*
- *Popping, melting or floating blob*

Adjectives may also describe the material from which the blob is made such as *gelatinous, spongy, muddy, crystalline,* or *rubbery.* The sky is the limit for exploration.

Encourage groups to invent their own sound effects to enhance the mood as teams illustrate the adjectives. For example: A popping blob could make explosive sounds while a floating blob might move to light sweet singing.

Extended Activity: Invite participants to originate their own blob skits focusing on adjectives. For example:

- A *frozen* blob turns into a *melted* blob when attacked by a man with a blowtorch or a girl with a hair dryer.

- An *energetic* blob turns into a *tired* blob after dancing for hours to a lively rock band.

- An *expanding* blob *contracts* (and jiggles) when poked and tickled by inquisitive children.

- An *angular* blob is rubbed until it becomes *rounded.*

To add new definitions to the blob shapes, experiment with safe objects beneath the cloths to extend shape possibilities such as:

cardboard boxes   *basketballs, beach balls*
umbrellas   *brooms and mops*

Credit: Nancy Frazier, co-author of IMAGINATION: At Play with Puppets and Creative Drama
Published by Nancy Renfro Studios

Exploring adjective blobs with scarves

SYLLABLE RHYTHM

Objective: To learn how words are divided into syllables by exploring the rhythms which are in part formed by the syllables in songs, rhymes, and poems.

Getting Started: Open up a group discussion about how syllables in a song lyric, poem, or rhyme create the rhythm pattern.. Clap or stamp out the rhythm formed by the syllables, then have the participants copy it. A nursery rhyme or one of the sound-oriented poems found in the Language Arts section make good examples.

Warm-up: Introduce staccato movement through the "Staccato/Legato Locomotion" exercise, page 29 .

Next, have participants spread out in the space. Repeat a pattern of quick, sharp claps or drumbeats. Ask the participants to make a quick, sharp movement to each beat in the sound pattern. Challenge them to explore the use of different body parts, (head, eyelids, shoulders, elbows, fingers, hips, knees, legs, feet) to see which body parts work best for accurate quick movements. The movement may be a single movement repeated, or a series of interesting changing movements. In all cases, emphasize concise movement that has a distinct beginning and ending. "Jump/Freeze", page 23 , is very helpful for practicing stops.

Conduct the "Name Game", page 43 .

Activity: Ask participants to spread out in the space and respond with a quick, sharp movement for every syllable, as a rhyme or well-known poem or song is recited. The leader can maintain the rhythm for the group to follow with a hand clap or drum beat. The following are rhyme and syllable examples:

HICKORY DICKORY DOCK!

     1 -2-3   1 -2-3   1
Hick-o-ry, dick-o-ry, dock!

     1   1   1 1   1   1
The mouse ran up the clock;

     1   1   1   1
The clock struck one,

     1   1   1   1
The mouse ran down.

     1 -2-3   1 -2-3   1
Hick-o-ry, dick-o-ry, dock!

JOHN JACOB JINGLEHIMER SCHMIDT

     1   1-2   1-2-3-4-   1
John Jacob Jinglehimer Schmit

     1   1   1   1   1   1
His name is my name too

     1-2-3   1   1   1
Whenever we go out

     1   1-2   1-2   1
The people always shout

     1   1   1   1-2   1-2-3-4-   1
There goes John Jacob Jinglehimer Schmit

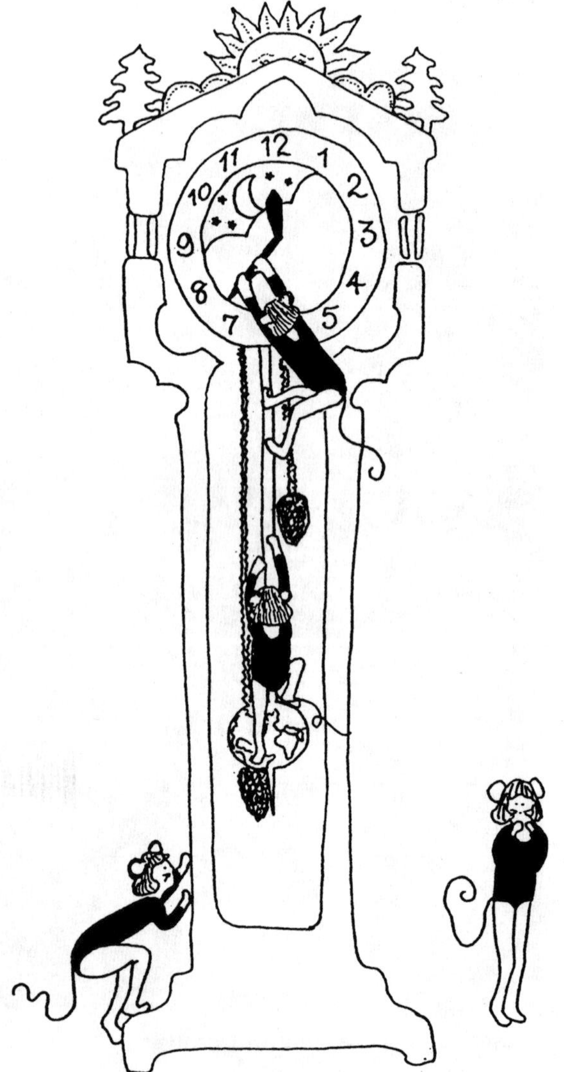

DICTIONARY WISDOM

Objective: To use the dictionary as a source of information for creative drama and for building vocabulary skills.

Getting Started: Ask the group members to brainstorm a list of words they consider difficult to grasp or that some members may be unfamiliar with. List the words on a chalkboard and share meanings.

Word	Interpretation
Obscure	*Hidden, not clear, masked*
Rotund	*Round, fat*
Nimble	*Able, agile*
Pompous	*Stately, proud, stuck-up*
Commotion	*Agitation, disorder*
Resonate	*Vibrate and make sound*
Queasy	*Nauseous*
Tentative	*Hesitant, shy*
Gregarious	*Socially active, to shut out*

Warm-up: Conduct the exercises "Guess-How-I-Feel", page 36 , and "The Magic Ball", page 50 .

Activity: Create a list of words on flash cards for the group to learn. These can be above-grade level words or words useful for the class' specific curriculum study.

Place the cards in a container or paper bag and have each participant draw out one word card and be responsible for researching its meaning in the dictionary.

Afterwards, each participant should then take a turn in a charade to act out his or her word, through movement and expression, for the group to decipher. If the group cannot guess the original word, then write on a chalkboard those guesses which are synonymous or most closely fit the word's meaning. Then, after the charades, write the correct definition above the guesses. For example:

- *Pensive* (guessed words – thinking, reflective, serious)
- *Outlandish* (guessed words – freakish, strange, weird).

Concentrate solely on words that are easy to interpret through movement and expression.

ZIP, ZAP, SIZZLE
Onomatopoeia

Objective: To explore onomatopoeia sound/words through movement.

Getting Started: Tune in participants to listen for sounds in the room or outside as produced by a motor, clock, heater, car, footsteps, etc. Ask for contributions to a word list that imitates natural or machine made sounds and write them on the chalkboard:

gurgle growl boom hiss roar sizzle clip-clop
whirr ding buzz bang wham zap tick-tock

Warm-up: Conduct the exercises "Dancing Words", page 44 , "Pass the Sound", page 32 , and "Pass the Sound and Movement", page 33 .

Activity: Present the sounds or words as listed above, one at a time, and ask participants to demonstrate each sound through *motion* only (no sound allowed!). Be sure to include facial expressions as well as body gestures or movement.

Extended Activity: Proceed to dancing and dramatizing some sound poetry such as "Chip-Chop", "Jabberwocky", and "Row" found in the Language Arts Section of the book.

Exploring onomatopoeia sounds

RISE AND FALL
Synonyms, Antonyms and Homonyms

Objective: To understand synonyms, antonyms, homonyms and their differences.

Getting Started: Compare descriptions of synonyms, antonyms and homonyms with the class and define each on the chalkboard. Focus on one word form at a time and build a sample word list for each category. For example:

Antonyms
(words that mean the opposite)

Hard/Soft	*Straight/Crooked*
Rise/Fall	*Happy/Sad*
Narrow/Wide	*Quiet/Noisy*
Thick/Thin	*Together/Apart*

Synonyms
(words that have the same or nearly the same meaning)

Little/Small	*Difficult/Hard*
Big/Large	*Rough/Bumpy*
Fast/Speedy	*Angry/Mad*
Bashful/Shy	*Assemble/Construct*

Homonyms
(words that sound alike but have a different spelling and meaning)

See/Sea	*Read/Reed*
Hare/Hair	*Wring/Ring*
Peek/Peak	*Flea/Flee*

Warm-up: Explore the exercises "Shapes", page 56 , "Guess-How-I-Feel", page 36 , and "Characterization Locomotion", page 27 .

Activity: Each of the word forms may be presented through drama/dance in the following manner:

Antonyms
Working in pairs, have participants perform actions that depict opposite words. For example:

• *Rise/Fall* – One partner, starting from a low level, stresses rising movements using the arms and body; the other partner falls from a high level. Both partners can repeatedly rise and fall in a variety of ways.

• *Together/Apart* – Partners embrace tightly then depart from one another.

The rest of the group may enjoy guessing the charaded words.

Advance the activity by having partners design short skits based on their words. For example:

• *Rise/Fall* – Two babies learning to walk try to rise, then repeatedly fall, until finally they learn to walk confidently.

• *Together/Apart* – Two friends are strolling along, arm-in-arm. Together, they find a dollar on the sidewalk. They argue over who it belongs to, one grabs the dollar and the other stomps off in a huff.

Synonyms
Have partners work together to pantomime and convey one word in a synonym pair. Each partner may give a slightly different interpretation to reinforce the word's meaning. The class should then guess as many variations (or synonyms) of the word as possible. List these words on a chalkboard until the two original words are quoted.
For example:

• *Angry/Mad* – Partners may stomp around, pretend to argue, show distorted facial expression, shake fists, etc.

Other words that the class may suggest to describe these actions are: *agitated, enraged, displeased, fuming, furious,* etc.

Homonyms
Divide the class into teams of two. Have one partner in each team pantomime a short action sequence or skit, to illustrate one of the words in a homonym pair. The second partner enacts the second word in the homonym pair.

• *Flea/Flee* – Pretend to be a dog scratching *fleas;* run as though *fleeing* from something.

• *Wring/Ring* – *Wring* out laundry; hold up an imaginary *ring* and place it on a finger.

• *Sea/See* – Dramatize the motion of waves in a *sea;* portray a blind person who *sees* for the first time.

THE GOLDEN EGG BOOK

By Margaret Wise Brown
adapted by Kristen Bissinger

This simple story has great appeal to young children. It is an ideal story for simultaneous dramatization because it is a duet in which both characters do the same series of actions.

The dramatization can be incorporated into a unit of study on eggs, spring, Easter, friendship, or the arrival of a new baby, but it also stands on its own very well.

This story is excellent to help develop simple mime skills, beginning characterization and partner cooperation as well as stressing quiet aspects of observation.

Getting Started: If this enactment is used in conjunction with one of the topics stated above, lead a discussion or activity concerning that topic.

Warm-up: Adapt Locomotion exercises found in Primary Tools to explore the actions in the story as follow:

Bunny-hops – Encourage participants to "hop" on all fours as rabbits really do. The teacher can join in the action to demonstrate while suggesting the actions of a rabbit (i.e. hop, stop, eat clover, sit up quickly on hind legs, sniff the air, listen, thump hind feet and scamper quickly to the other side of the room).

Duck Waddles – Have participants waddle forward in a squatting position, quack, ruffle feathers, peck at the ground, flap wings and fly to the side of the room.

Introduce a rolling exercise. Have the group members choose partners. Ask a volunteer to roll his or her partner across the floor to demonstrate rolling actions. Ask the group to point out what helps to make this activity successful. For example:

- The partner being rolled must help, not just lie there like a sack of potatoes.
- The pushing partner must guide the direction of the partner being rolled.
- Those partners being rolled must be careful not to kick others.
- Those being rolled must protect their own heads by putting their weight on forearms or hands to avoid letting their heads hit the floor.

Activity: *Story Enactment* – Have partners sit together and arrange the group in one big circle. Read or tell the story.

Ask: "When we act out the story, how can we jump on top of one another like the characters do without hurting one another?" Caution that fingers, hair, arms and legs should be tucked in and discourage jumping over one's partner. Jumping to

one side or a straddling jump is just as effective.

Announce that the story will be acted out twice so that each person gets a chance to play both characters.

Give partners time to quietly confer with each other to choose parts (the duck or bunny).

All ducks should find locations to curl up on the floor. Group the bunnies to one side of the space. Make sure the eggs have ample space around them so actions can occur without crowding.

Re-tell the story as it is enacted. As part of the narration, talk the bunny through some character establishing actions, just like in the warm-up: hopping, stopping, eating, sitting-up, listening, sniffing. Encourage each bunny to focus intently on its egg when it is discovered.

Emphasize the sounds, "pick, pick, pick", and encourage the eggs to repeat these sounds making pecking actions while in a curled-up shape.

Challenge the bunnies to remain still when asleep and while the ducks are active.

Narrate the duck's dialogue in short segments and encourage the duck participants to repeat after you.

The teacher should feel free to assist any rollers or take part, encouraging action by example.

The playing scene between the characters at the end of the story is a loose improvised ending. After a short time, re-group the participants into a seated circle in order to re-establish control.

Lead a discussion, change parts and re-enact the story.

The Golden Egg Book

By Margaret Wise Brown
Story Enactment

There was once a little bunny who lived all alone. He hopped here and there and he sniffed the air. He sat up quickly and listened with his big sharp ears. He looked about with his bright eyes. He nibbled the clover and hopped around some more. There in the grass lay an egg. He sniffed the egg with his furry nose. He listened to the egg with his big soft ears.

"Pick, pick, pick." Something was inside that egg. The bunny could hear it. What could it be? Maybe a little bunny like himself? Maybe a chick? Maybe a little boy or girl? Maybe an elephant! How could a little bunny know? But whatever was inside the egg, the little bunny wanted to know.

He shook the egg. But the egg did not break. He pushed the egg with his foot. He jumped up and down on top of the egg. But still the egg did not break. So he scampered up a tree and threw nuts at the egg. But, he was a little bunny and the nuts were small and the egg did not break. So he climbed down the tree. He rolled the egg down the hill. But the egg did not break. He listened to the egg with his big soft ears.

"Pick, pick, pick," came the sound from the egg. And then all was quiet. The bunny yawned and he snuggled up close to the egg and there he fell fast asleep.

"Pick, pick, pick. Peck, peck, peck. Crackety-crack!" Out jumped a little yellow duck. He shook himself all over. He waddled around on his little webbed feet.

All of a sudden he saw the bunny. He came close and took a look.

"When I was inside the egg I was in a small dark world. All alone. Now I'm alone with a bunny in a big bright world and the bunny won't wake up!" He shook the bunny. He pushed the bunny with his little webbed foot. He jumped on top of the bunny. But the bunny was very sleepy and the bunny did not wake up. The duck looked around and flew up into a tree with his new little wings. He threw nuts at the bunny. But the bunny did not wake up. He flew down and rolled the bunny down the hill. At the bottom of the hill the bunny woke with a start!

"Who are you?" said the bunny, "and where's my egg?"

"Never mind," said the duck. "Here I am." And neither was ever alone again for they became close friends and they played and played!

THE RAINY DAY RAINBOW
by Kristen Bissinger

Objective: To enjoy the free use of scarves and practice a sequence of locomotor movements through a fantasy adventure story.

Getting Started: Discuss the colors of the rainbow and, if your group is ready for such information, how a rainbow is formed.

Ask each person to share what he or she might find as a special gift at the end of the rainbow. Encourage individual answers by giving a variety of suggestions: a puppy, a baby brother or sister, a pony, etc.

Start with "Jump/Freeze", page 23 , and narrate the participants through a slow melt, as in the story.

Warm-up: Have the group sit in a circle. Set the mood by saying, "We're going on an adventure hike today! It will be pretty rough territory, so let's get on our hiking boots." Sit down with the group and pretend to pull on big boots using exaggerated gestures while pulling laces and tying a bow.

Do a trial run of some of the actions in the story. Line up the participants single file to walk along the road (edge of space). Continue by telling them , "Now, we must cut through the cornfield. Push back the leaves as you go...Oh! Here's a field of mud! Got your boots on? This stuff looks thick and sticky!" (Slowly take big steps, pulling up feet as though the mud is sucking down the boots. Make slurphy, sucking noises.)

Continue with the hike going through other terrain experiences in "The Rainy Day Rainbow" story: a lake, a thicket of stickers, a mountain. Participants may wish to add ideas for new terrain (sandy desert, ice pond, etc.).

Conduct "Basic Scarves", page 51 .

Activity: *Story Enactment* – Tell the story, "The Rainy Day Rainbow". Strive to use varied voice intonations to build drama and excitement while telling the story. Cue the participants to yell, "No!", when the sun asks for the rainbow the first two times.

The leader can represent all of the mothers or fathers and play the part of the sun, if desired. The leader may also lead the hike to the rainbow.

Before enacting the story, lay out the scarves (or use colored ribbons, strips of fabric or crepe paper) side-by-side in the center of the space in order of their position in the rainbow. When acting out the story, conduct the hike sequence single file around the outside edges of the space. When enacting the rainbow, allow each child to pick up one scarf and dance with it throughout the space. When the rainbow is given back, each scarf may be laid down side-by-side, in any color order. Finally, with everyone on one side of the scarves, each participant walks across, on top of his or her scarf and halts at the top of the rainbow (the middle of the scarf) to look down.

This is an opportune time for the participants to share what they see from the top of the rainbow, looking down at the landscape below. Then, pretend to slide down the rest of the scarf to the other end and find a gift.

All participants return directly to sit in a circle and share with the "mother" (leader) what gifts they found.

THE RAINY DAY RAINBOW
By Kristen Bissinger

One week it did nothing but rain! It rained and rained and rained! The children had been inside for days. They had played with their toys. They had watched TV. They had read books. And now they were bored. They wanted to get outside and play so they all went to their mothers and said, "Can we *please* go outside and play in the rain?"

To their surprise, their mothers said, "Yes, go ahead but put on all your raingear. It's cold out today."

So they ran to the closet. They put on their red boots. They pulled on their orange rainpants and their yellow raincoats, snapping them up the front. They put on their green rainhats and put up their blue umbrellas. They dashed outside. They ran and splashed in the rain. They waded in the deep puddles. They stamped and splashed with their feet. They opened their mouths wide and caught raindrops on their tongues. They squatted by the road and sent leaf boats down the gutter.

They ran and slid in the puddles and fell down and got all wet. Just as they leaped up, a cold wind blew and froze them stiff. The sun came out from behind a cloud. Slowly their fingers melted and their wrists melted and their arms melted. Their heads melted, their backs melted and their knees melted until they were all melted down in a puddle on the ground. They looked up in the sky and there, overhead, was a rainbow! The rain was falling and the sun was shining and a rainbow filled the sky. "Let's go find the end of the rainbow!" they cried. "We've heard that at the end of the rainbow, there's a special gift."

So up they jumped and walked single file along the road toward the end of the rainbow. Then they turned and went through a cornfield, pushing the stalks aside with their arms. At the edge of the cornfield stood a field of thick mud. "We have our rainboots on. Let's go!" they cried. So they slogged through the mud pulling their feet slowly out as the mud sucked on their boots.

Once they reached the other side, they found a lake. "Can you swim?'" they asked each other. "Yes, of course," all replied. So they dove in. And swam and swam till they reached the shore. There they were confronted with a thicket of stickers. "Ow! Ooo! Ooo! Oww!" they cried as they picked their way through, pulling the thorns from their clothing and jumping from the sharp stickers.

On the other side of the sticker patch stood a large mountain. They climbed and climbed and climbed and climbed till they reached the top. There shone the rainbow! Within a moment, each had grabbed a favorite color and then they all danced with the rainbow, leaping and waving it in the air. They danced with the rainbow and they danced with the rainbow and they danced with the rainbow.

Then out came the sun and it called down, "Give me back my rainbow!"

All the children said, "No!" They danced with the rainbow and they danced with the rainbow and they danced with the rainbow!

"Give me back my rainbow!" said the sun.

All the children said, "No!" And they danced with the rainbow and they danced with the rainbow and they danced with the rainbow!

Then the sun said, "*Please* give my back my rain-

bow. If you do, I'll let you climb up to the top of the rainbow. From there you can see far and wide. Then you may slide down to the other side and there will be a gift for each of you. Something very special: maybe a puppy, maybe a baby brother or sister, maybe a pot of gold. Maybe a beautiful dress or a pony. Something just for you."

So the children agreed. They threw the rainbow back into the sky and they climbed to its top. At the top they looked down and they could see the cornfield they had walked through. They could see their mothers hanging out the laundry. They could see cars as small as ants traveling along the road. Then they slid down the other side and each found a special gift just for him or her. All ran home to show the gifts to their mothers.

THE LION AND THE MOUSE
An Aesop's Fable

Objective: To explore a thought provoking story with an action plot involving characters with contrasting character dynamics. This is a perfect story for a group to act in unison as described in the introduction, and for inexperienced leaders and participants as well as those more advanced.

Getting Started: Aesop's fables are great fun for enactment. Concealed in interesting animal characters, human concerns are addressed. This fable includes a large range of emotions, plus a character, (the lion), for those who enjoy an expression of brute strength and a mouse to develop confidences in "being little".

Warm-up: Stand with the group members in a circle and conduct "Bend and Stretch" and "Cat and Dog Backs", pages 18 and 19 , to prepare the group for the lion's stretching episode.

Line the participants up for locomotion and rehearse some of the characters' actions across the floor as in "Animal Walk", page 29 :

- *Lion*
  - *Show claws.*
  - *Shake mane.*
  - *Roar!*
  - *Slow walk with big powerful legs. ("Let's see those muscles ripple!")*

- *Mouse*
  - *Scamper across the floor quickly. (Emphasize tiny tip-toe steps.)*
  - *Pick up a seed in little front paws.*
  - *Nibble. (Bare teeth and make quick little nibbling sounds.)*
  - *Look around with sharp little eyes.*

Divide the group into partners of equal weight and conduct the pull segment of the "Push/Pull" exercise on page 63 . After the warm-ups, tell the story, pausing for participants to mimic the dialogue of the lion and mouse characters. Break the sentences into short segments when necessary. Encourage use of voice characterization, stressing contrasting voices – tiny and squeaky for the mouse, loud and low for the lion. (See "Who's Speaking", page 67 .)

Inject some simple pantomime that can be done in place for the participants to mimic. This helps familiarize the group with the actions in the story. Discourage full physical enactment during this preliminary storytelling session as full enactment can be done at the second reading.

Activity: *Story Enactment:* Divide the group members into pairs. Within each pair one participant will enact the part of the lion, the other will act both the parts of the mouse and the hunter. This works well, for the parts of the mouse and hunter never overlap, making everyone always active, eliminating the need to supervise an inactive group. All pairs enact the story at the same time with partners interacting with each other when appropriate.

Set the Stage. Separate partners, have all the lions find a place in one half of the room where they are not close to anyone or anything. Situate the mice on the other side of the room and establish a location for the hunter's pit (an area big enough to accommodate all the lions).

Some simple musical accompaniment can re-enforce the movement of the characters. For example, a strong slow drum beat for the lions, a quick rattle shake for the mice, and a sharp marching beat with rhythm sticks for the hunters.

Re-tell the story pausing for appropriate movement and dialogue by the characters. Call a freeze to the action at any point when: 1) it would be fun for the participants to witness themselves in mid-action, 2) the enactment becomes too rowdy, or 3) when it is necessary to remind the participants to stay in character.

Some sample actions follow:

- In unison, lions slowly walk through the jungle, then separately lie down in a patch of sunshine.
- Each mouse scampers over to his or her lion partner and runs fingers up and down the lion's tummy, tickling.
- Each lion catches his or her mouse, etc.

Emphasize the lion's big hearty laugh that shakes the jungle, the shaking fear of the mouse, the lion's leaping, clawing rage at being caught in the pit and the strong pulling displayed by both the hunter and the lion with the rope. Encourage exaggerated movements so that the emotions and actions are clearly displayed but caution the participants to stick to the script, for example, the lion does not bite the hunter or run after the mouse.

The fable's ending in which the lion goes one way and the mouse the other will help calm participants after the climax.

Discussion. Spend some time sharing the story's moral. Ask the group to verbally share favorite segments of the story or story enactments.

Emphasize that even though the mouse appears unimportant to the lion because of its size, he does not have that view of himself and is capable of solving problems.

For further discussion, share experiences in which group members have helped someone bigger or seemingly more important than themselves. Illustrate that even small deeds of helpfulness in a problematic situation can make a big difference.

Extended Activity: The group may wish to develop further scenarios of cooperation between characters with differing characteristics, such as small and large, weak and strong, old and young. Have teams of two or three members each act out original scenarios based on one character assisting the other. For example, a feeble old duck saves a young know-it-all duck from being devoured by a vicious crocodile by patiently luring away the crocodile.

THE LION AND THE MOUSE

adapted by Kristen Bissinger
from Aesop's fable in *My Book House*

Once a great big Lion lay fast asleep in the woods. By-and-by a teeny, tiny Mouse came along. Now the Lion was lying so still, the Mouse thought he was only a big heap of dried brown grass. So the Mouse began scampering up and down on the Lion's body, tickling the Lion's stomach. The Lion squirmed and growled. He opened one eye and then the other. He saw the teeny, tiny Mouse, reached out and trapped the little Mouse under his big paw.

"You woke me!" he roared, "and I'm going to eat you for my breakfast!"

Well, the Mouse was terribly frightened. He was shaking all over but he squeaked in a little voice: "O mighty King of the Beasts, please don't eat me up! I'll never forget your kindness if you'll let me go!"

But the Lion opened his great big mouth and began to smack his lips. "Yum, yum, little Mouse," he said. "I think you will taste very good!"

Trembling all over, the Mouse began to coax harder and harder. "Please let me go! If you let me go, I might even be able to help you some day."

"You help me?!" cried the Lion. "A teeny, tiny thing like you help the great big King of the Beasts? Hah hah! Haw haw! Ho ho!" He laughed so loud and so long that all the forest rang and this made him feel very jolly. "Well, after all," he said, "you're far too small to be even one bite for me. I'll catch something better for breakfast!" And he opened his great, big paw so the little Mouse slipped out and scampered as fast as he could to hide himself in the grass.

Not long afer this, the Lion was wandering in the woods when he suddenly fell in a deep pit that had been dug by some hunters who wanted to catch him. These hunters meant to put the Lion in a cage to show him off in the palace yard of the King.

The Lion leaped and scratched at the walls of the pit but he could not get out. He was finally groaning in the hole when the band of hunters found him. They lassoed him, drew him up out of the trap and left him tied to a tree. Then off they marched to get a wagon to carry the Lion to the palace.

The Lion tugged and tore at the rope but he could not get himself free. So at last he lay down and cried.

As he was crying and sighing, the teeny, tiny little Mouse came by.

"Friend Lion," he squeaked, "What has happened to you?"

"The hunters have bound me fast," the Lion groaned. "I cannot break this great, strong rope. I shall end my life in a cage. I shall never roam this great big, beautiful forest again!"

"Is that all, friend?" the Mouse laughed cheerily.

"You needn't seem so glad about it. It's a very sad end for me!" the Lion began to grumble.

The little Mouse went straight up to the rope and began with his sharp teeth to gnaw it. He gnawed and he gnawed and he gnawed. And pretty soon, split, split, split, the rope began to break. Bit by bit, the Mouse chewed until all at once - snip, SNAP! the rope broke and there stood the Lion free!

The Lion was surprised and delighted.

"I'm free!" he roared. Then he stopped and looked at the tiny Mouse. "You've shown me that, no matter how small one is, he can always be helpful to others, although they are larger than he. Goodbye, little friend! I thank you!"

The Lion ran with a bound off into the forest, and the little Mouse scampered off happily in the other direction.

SHINGEBISS AND THE NORTH WIND

A Chippewa Native American Tale

Children will quickly find this story one of their favorites. It has a great theme focusing on overcoming difficulty with ingenuity, cheerfulness and bravery. The two characters and their actions are very clearly presented and each has an interesting part.

Getting Started: Practice the song from the story. Add a tune if you wish. Have the group repeat the song several times with a drumbeat. Encourage participants to beat the rhythm on their thighs as they sit cross-legged and chant along. Repeat the verses until the participants are familiar with them. Discuss the meaning of the song, and of the words "fierce" and "feature".

Warm-up: Begin with "Jump/Freeze", on page 23 . Add and demonstrate a slow melting sequence starting from the top of the body down to the bottom, calling out each body part as it melts: fingers melt, then wrists, arms, heads, shoulders, backs and legs, all the way down to a puddle on the ground.

Gather in a circle and enact with the particpants a variety of emotions using "If You're Happy and You Know It', page 35 . Be sure to cover the feelings stated in the story: cheerful, sneaky, brave, angry and cold.

Next, explore "Basic Scarves", page 51 . Add a variety of wind and weather movements with the scarves; swirling around to represent the sharp biting wind (caution against hitting each other with scarves, especially in the face), throwing the scarves up in the air and catching them to represent snow, etc.

Next have the group explore the scarves as wings. Ask volunteers to demonstrate a duck waddle. Mention the fact that ducks do not have hands, and must, therefore, perform many actions with their bills.

Activity: *Story Enactment* – Sit in a circle and tell the story encouraging the particpants to join in the song. Assign half the class to play the North Wind and the other half the duck, or have the participants choose parts. Designate the location of the two ponds, the lodge and the north. Group the ducks in a circle around "the fire" in the lodge and choose a location at the opposite end of the space as the North Wind's home. Have each North Wind choose a scarf and stand, ready to enter and begin action.

First, Shingebiss is introduced in the story. Encourage the ducks to waddle, preen, ruffle feathers, quack, or tend the fire inside the lodge area. Pause in the narration as they try some of these actions. Introduce the North Winds. Direct them to use the full space and use their scarves to run, leap, swirl and whip. Pause in the narration, giving the North Winds a chance to express their character.

Continue with specific action: ducks waddle to the pond, catch fish and return home. (Fullest enactment occurs when all the actions are mentioned in the narration: waddle, pull reeds with beak, make a hole, dive in, swim, catch fish, swim back, pop out, shake, waddle home, warm toes and cook fish.)

North Wind voices his anger (and shows it with his face and body), heaps snow and ice on the pond and returns home, etc.

The action alternates between the two characters. Each remains in his home while the other takes center stage with action and dialogue. At the climax they come together, parting again at the end.

Those playing the North Wind tend to creep into the lodge *during* the song, so clearly identify the lodge area and instruct the actors to wait until after the song to tiptoe in and sit down. As the North Wind melts, call out the body parts from top to bottom, as in the previous warm-up exercise. Before the legs are melted the North Wind should dash out of the lodge with a loud bloodcurdling cry of "Aiiiii!"

Finish with a repeat of the song for a very satisfying effect.

SHINGEBISS AND THE NORTH WIND

A Chippewa Native American Tale
Adapted by Kristen Bissinger

In his lodge, on the shores of Lake Huron, lived little brown duck, Shingebiss. When the fierce North Wind swept down from the glittering land of ice and snow, four great logs for firewood had brown duck, Shingebiss. No matter how the North Wind blew, brown duck, Shingebiss, was brave and cheerful. Each day he waddled out to his pond, and pulled up the reeds and rushes, breaking holes in

The North Wind voices his anger

the ice. He dove down through the holes and caught fish for his supper. All the other animals feared the North Wind. They hid in their homes or they went South for the winter. But brown duck, Shingebiss, heeded not the ice and the snow.

'Ugh, I do not like brown duck, Shingebiss. All other creatures fear me, save Shingebiss. I will show him who is chief. I will cover his pond with ice and snow and I will starve him!" said the North Wind, his face fierce with anger.

So the great North Wind heaped ice and snow on the pond of little brown duck, Shingebiss. He blew his sharpest breath. Shingebiss waddled out to his pond and tried to pull out the reeds and rushes with his bill but he could make no holes in the ice. He straightened up. He did not grumble or complain. Brave and cheerful as ever, he flew on to the next pond, and there he pulled up the reeds and rushes, dove down under the ice and caught fish for his supper. He swam back, popped out of the hole and shook himself all over. He flew back to his lodge and there he warmed his little webbed feet by the fire and cooked his fish.

"Ugh, I do not like brown duck, Shingebiss," said the North Wind. "I can not scare him. I can not starve him...I will freeze him!"

So the North Wind tiptoed quietly up to the lodge of brown duck, Shingebiss. Now Shingebiss could not hear the wind. But he could feel his icy breath and he shivered. He began to sing this song:

> "Ka-neej, Ka-neej,
> Bee-in, Bee-in,
> Bon-in, Bon-in,
> Ok-ee, Ok-ee,
> Ka-weya, Ka-weya!"

And the North Wind knew he was saying:

"North Wind, North Wind, fierce in feature,
You are still my fellow creature;
Blow your worst, you can't freeze me;
I fear you not, and so I am FREE!

Then the North Wind was furious and his face grew fierce with anger.

"I will slip into the lodge of brown duck Shingebiss and breathe my iciest breath till he freezes."

So he tiptoed into the lodge of Shingebiss and sat down next to him and breathed his iciest breath. Just at that moment, little brown duck, Shingebiss, picked up a stick and stirred the fire. Sparks shot up and the logs glowed a ruddy gold. The North Wind leaped away from the heat throwing his arms in the air. Slowly his fingers melted and his arms melted. Great tears rolled down his cheeks. His shoulders

drooped. He dashed out of the lodge and jumped headfirst into a snowbank, yelling, "Aiiiiii!"

"Ugh," he said weakly. "I do not like brown duck, Shingebiss. I can't scare him. I can't starve him. I can't freeze him. I will leave him alone. The Great Spirit must be with him!"

So the North Wind flew up to the glittering land of ice and snow and danced with the Northern Lights.

Little brown duck, Shingebiss, lived brave and cheerful in his lodge by the shores of Lake Huron. He warmed his little webbed feet by the fire and cooked his fish and lived happily ever after.

Taken from *My Book House, Vol. 3*
by Olive Beaupre' Miller.

HUGIN AND THE TURNIP
By Isabel Wyatt

Here is a story centered around Halloween and involving repetitive dialogue.

Getting Started: Discuss the origin of the jack-o-lantern which started in Europe with the hollowing out and carving of large turnips to make Hallowe'en lanterns. Explain that Hallowe'en is a contraction of "Hallowed Evening".

Warm-up: Conduct "Animal Walk", page 29 . Make up a distinctive walk for each animal character in the story, such as:

> *Lion* – Slow walk on all fours with chest out
> *Bear* – Slow heavy walk on hind legs
> *Fox* – Zigzag walk on all fours with nose to the ground
> *Hare* – Bunny-hops
> *Mouse* – Quick tiptoe scamper
> *Caterpillar* – Worm crawl on tummy.

Prepare the group for the story's climax by discussing how to "fall down" in a line without hurting each other. Practice this a few times, then add getting up and saying "Sorry", one after another. The getting up helps inhibit excessive giggling and tumbling on the floor.

Read or tell the story to the group and encourage participation in the repetitive dialogue. Emphasize voice inflection when telling this story to set the tone of the enactment and to aid the children to find variety within their own voices. Recite the short repetitive refrain with an imploring tone as you ask the turnip to grow and the animals to pull. Let the radiance and awe be expressed in an expansive gesture as you say, "The *finest* lantern ever seen." Then the words, "I want-to-put-a-candle-in my turnip," is matter of fact and reminds us of just what is to be done.

Do not rush the words, even though they are repetitive, they are an important part of the story and will be experienced with interest if they are not sloughed off.

Make sure the participants understand what a gnome is.

Allow participants to choose parts. More than one participant may play each part, if necessary. As parts are selected, group the characters along the side of the space in the sequence of their entrance in the story: Lions, Bears, Foxes, Hares, Mice and Caterpillars. Arrange turnips and Root Gnomes in the center of the room with the Hugins.

Activity: *Story Enactment* – Retell the story while participants act it out. Encourage older participants to use different voices as they carry out the actions. Have each animal repeat after you as the story is read, or recited one phrase at a time. Drop out as you see a child able to say the words without coaching.

The group may all be asked to join in the repetitive phrases: "... but that turnip did not budge *one inch*" (gesturing with thumb and finger showing an inch).

During the pulling actions, the tendency is for the actors to pull and fall down after each animal adds on. This is acceptable unless it becomes distracting or dangerous. The animals can pull in a standing or sitting position. The latter tends to be safer and less raucous, but also less dramatic. A good suggestion here is to save the falling down sequence until the very end of the enactment.

It is also helpful for control to require all animals to form a sit-down circle around the turnip as Hugin carves it out and puts the candle in. This re-establishes order and takes the enactment to a participatory conclusion.

"HUGIN AND THE TURNIP"

By Isabel Wyatt
From the *Seven-Year-Old Wonder-Book*

Once upon a time there was a little boy named Hugin, and he wanted a turnip to make a Hallowe'en lantern, so he went out into the garden and planted a turnip-seed; and he said:

> "Turnip, turnip, grow for me;
> Grow as big as big can be,
> That I may make for Hallowe'en
> The finest lantern ever seen.

> I-want-to-put-a-candle-in-you, Turnip."

So the turnip grew as big as big could be, till it was so big that it *nearly* filled the garden.

Then Hugin went out to pull the turnip up. And he pulled and he pulled; but the turnip did not budge an inch.

Just then a lion came by, and asked:
"What are you doing, Hugin?"
And Hugin replied:
"I'm pulling up a turnip.

> Lion, Lion, pull with me;
> Pull as hard as hard can be,
> That I may make for Hallowe'en
> The finest lantern ever seen.
> I-want-to-put-a-candle-in-my-turnip."

So Lion pulled Hugin, and Hugin pulled the turnip; they pulled and they pulled, but the turnip did not budge an inch.

Just then a bear came along, and asked:
"What are you doing, Lion?"
And Lion replied:
"I'm helping Hugin to pull up a turnip."
And Hugin said:

> "Bear, Bear, pull with me;
> Pull as hard as hard can be,
> That I may make for Hallowe'en
> The finest lantern ever seen.
> I-want-to-put-a-candle-in-my-turnip."

So Bear pulled Lion, and Lion pulled Hugin, and Hugin pulled the turnip; they pulled and they pulled, but the turnip did not budge an inch.

Just then a fox came by, and asked:
"What are you doing, Bear?"
And Bear replied:
"I'm helping Lion to help Hugin to pull up a turnip."
And Hugin said:

> "Fox, Fox, pull with me:
> Pull as hard as hard can be,
> That I may make for Hallowe'en
> The finest lantern ever seen.
> I-want-to-put-a-candle-in-my-turnip."

So Fox pulled Bear, and Bear pulled Lion, and Lion pulled Hugin, and Hugin pulled the turnip; they pulled and they pulled, but the turnip did not budge an inch.

Just then a hare came by, and asked:
"What are you doing, Fox?"
And Fox replied:
"I'm helping Bear to help Lion to help Hugin to pull up a turnip."
And Hugin said:

"Hare, Hare pull with me;
Pull as hard as hard can be,
That I may make for Hallowe'en
The finest lantern ever seen.
I-want-to-put-a-candle-in-you, Turnip."

So Hare pulled Fox, and Fox pulled Bear, and Bear pulled Lion, and Lion pulled Hugin, and Hugin pulled the turnip; they pulled and they pulled, but the turnip did not budge an inch.

Just then a mouse came by, and asked:

"What are you doing, Hare?"

And Hare replied:

"I'm helping Fox to help Bear to help Lion to help Hugin to pull up a turnip."

And Hugin said:

"Mouse, Mouse, pull with me;
Pull as hard as hard can be,
That I may make for Hallowe'en
The finest lantern ever seen.
I-want-to-put-a-candle-in-my-turnip."

So Mouse pulled Hare, and Hare pulled Fox, and Fox pulled Bear, and Bear pulled Lion, and Lion pulled Hugin, and Hugin pulled the turnip; they pulled and they pulled, but the turnip did not budge an inch.

Just then a caterpillar came by, and asked:

"What are you doing, Mouse?"

And Mouse replied:

"I'm helping Hare to help Fox to help Bear to help Lion to help Hugin to pull up a turnip."

And Caterpillar said:

"But does Hugin know the right way to pull up a turnip? Did he first ask its root-gnome if he might?"

Then Hugin bent down and put his mouth close to the ground, and called:

"Gnome, Gnome, good Root-Gnome,
May I take your turnip home,
That I may make for Hallowe'en
The finest lantern ever seen?
I-want-to-put-a-candle-in-your-turnip."

And at once a little root-gnome popped up his brown head out of the ground, and said:

Good gracious me, Hugin, why didn't you *tell* me? All this time I've been pulling the other way, when there's nothing a root-gnome likes better than a candle put in his turnip! Now pull again!"

And he popped back his brown head into the ground.

So Caterpillar pulled Mouse, and Mouse pulled Hare, and Hare pulled Fox, and Fox pulled Bear, and Bear pulled Lion, and Lion pulled Hugin, and Hugin pulled the turnip. And suddenly Mouse sat down backwards with a bang on Caterpillar, and Hare sat down backwards with a bang on Mouse, and Fox sat down backwards with a bang on Hare, and Bear sat down backwards with a bang on Fox, and Lion sat down backwards with a bang on Bear, and Hugin sat down backwards with a bang on Lion, with the biggest, whitest, chubbiest turnip in his hand that ever anyone saw!

Then Hugin got up and said "Sorry" to Lion; and Lion got up and said "Sorry" to Bear; and Bear got up and said "Sorry" to Fox' and Fox got up and said "Sorry" to Mouse; and Mouse got up and said "Sorry" to Caterpillar. And nobody was hurt, and everybody laughed, and Hugin put-a-candle-in-his-turnip.

HOW THE RHINOCEROS GOT HIS SKIN
By Rudyard Kipling

Here is a simple action-packed story perfect for simultaneous enactment.

Getting Started: "How the Rhinoceros Got His Skin" is an endearing story for enactment featuring two strong main characters with contrasting movement qualities. The rhinoceros can be visualized as heavy, lumbering and powerful, while the Parsee man is tall, thin and spry.

Warm-up: Before enactment, explore the varied movement qualities needed by the characters through "Staccata/Legato Locomotion", page 29 . Emphasize the hot sand and mud actions as these dynamics are central to the two main characters.

Follow this up with "Emotion Locomotion", page 27 , to draw out an overt expression of emotion. Make sure to include the expressions: scared, hot, angry, gleeful and sneaky, and encourage exaggeration.

Assemble the group members in a circle and have them pantomime the cake baking segment. Involve the group in discussion, "Imagine the most delicious cake … What would you put in it?"

Demonstrate the cake making action step-by-step, as told in the story while the group copies the actions, then pretend to eat a slice.

Pantomime the rhinoceros's skin removal sequence with the group. Open discussion with "If you could take off you skin without hurting yourself, how would you do it? What fastenings could you use to get it on again? (Buttons, zipper, hooks, Velcro, etc.)" Ask everyone to pretend to unfasten and take off their skins. Have those willing to share, show the others how they took off their skins, and what fastenings they used.

You may choose to work on this story for several sessions which will encourage work in greater depth. In this case concentrate on one of the pantomime exercises only (cake baking or skin removal) as a warm-up for each session. In this way, the basic story is repeated with fresh, creative dramatic emphasis each time.

Activity: *Story Enactment* – Tell the story in your own words, yet maintain some of the original repetitive phrases such as "a stove of the type you most particularly must not touch", and "a golden hat that shone with more than oriental splendor". Ask the group members to repeat and learn the magical incantation of the Parsee man.

Work in pairs and have partners decide whom will be the rhinoceros and whom the man.

Establish one portion of the room as the jungle, one portion as the Red Sea (possibly a rug area), and one portion as the Parsee man's camp. Have all pairs work simultaneously, acting out the parts as the story is narrated. For example, all the Parsee men bake cakes at the same time, each in his own camp space; all rhinoceroses remove skins at the same time.

Encourage pantomime actions by mentioning specific detail such as, "He cracked three eggs, one … two … , and beat them up." "The rhinoceros, Strorks, slowly came out of the jungle with *big heavy* steps."

Caution the actors, if necesssary, to stick to the story. For example, the rhinoceros does *not* chase the Parsee man or Parsee man attack the rhinoceros.

For embellishment, consider using a strong, slow drum beat when the rhinoceros moves; use a lighter quicker drum beat, a penny whistle, bells or

"The Parsee Man was very angry"

some other contrasting instrument when the Parsee man moves.

Once the story has been enacted, sit the group down and share what worked, what did not and how the enactment could be improved.

Maintain the same partners but reverse roles.

HOW THE RHINOCEROS GOT HIS SKIN

By Rudyard Kipling
Adapted by Kristen Bissinger

There was once, oh, Best Beloved, a tall thin Parsee man who lived by himself on an island in the Red Sea. Among his few possessions was a tall golden hat that shone with more than Oriental splendor and a cookstove of the type you most particularly must not touch.

One day, he decided to make the most delicious cake he could imagine. He heated up his cookstove of the type you most particularly must not touch, and got out his ingredients. In a large bowl he mashed his butter and sugar. He cracked two eggs and stirred it up. Next he added his flour, a pinch of salt and all his most favorite flavorings. He took a taste. MMmmm! It was delicious!

He poured it into his baking pan. Next he opened his stove, of the type your most particularly must not touch and slid in the cake. He climbed up to the top of his palm tree to catch a bit of a breeze and to wait for his cake to cook. After awhile he

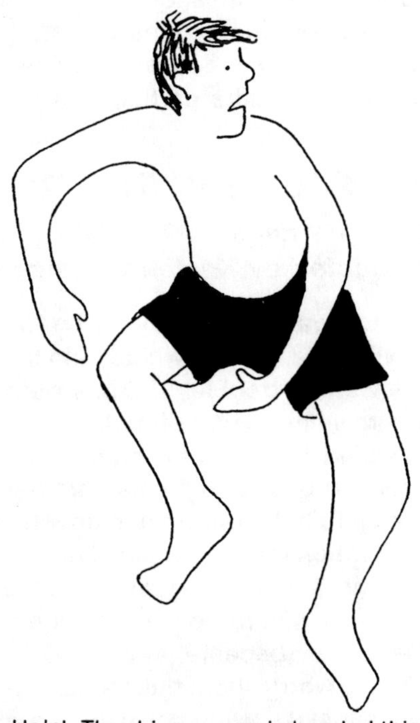

Help! The rhinocerous is headed this way.

sniffed the air. Mmmm! It smelled like the cake was done.

He climbed down the tree, opened the stove of the type you most particularly must not touch, and tested the cake with his finger. It was done. He slid it quickly out of the stove. Oooh, it was hot! He set it in the shade and squatted down next to it, waiting for it to cool.

As he squatted there, who should come out of the jungle but Strorks, the rhinoceros. Slow and heavy, Strorks wandered into the clearing. He sniffed the air. He gave a snort and ran headlong toward that cake. He speared the cake upon his horn and went thundering back into the jungle. The Parsee man jumped up and down with anger. He ran after the rhinoceros shaking his fist. But when he got to the jungle, Strorks had broken the cake and eaten the whole thing.

The Parsee man jumped up and down in fury and he yelled,

> "He that takes cakes
> that the Parsee man bakes
> makes dreadful mistakes!"

Now you might think this was a simple poem but it was a magical incantation and three weeks later a heat spell hit the Red Sea. Everyone took off their extra clothing. The Parsee man took off his hat that shone with more than Oriental splendor. He climbed to the top of his palm tree to catch a bit of a breeze.

Whom should he spy, lumbering out of the jungle, but Strorks, the rhinoceros. Now, in those days, the rhinoceros had a smooth, gray skin that fit him like a glove. He could take off his skin without hurting himself, with three great big buttons down the front. Strorks lumbered down to the edge of the Red Sea, and there he took off his skin and laid it on the beach. He wallowed into the water. He blew bubbles with his big nose. He snorted; he rolled over, he floated and he swam, cooling himself in the Red Sea.

The Parsee man spied that skin and a grin went around his face three times. A sneaky idea lit up his eyes. He slid down the tree and went to his camp. There he took his golden hat that shone with more than Oriental splendor and filled it with old burnt cake crumbs, dried burnt raisins and sand. He tiptoed over to the rhinoceros's skin, and sprinkled the skin full of old burnt cake crumbs, raisins and sand. Then he danced around the skin three times with glee. He chanted,

> "He that takes cakes
> that the Parsee man bakes
> makes dreadful mistakes!"

He scampered back to his camp and climbed up his tree.

By this time old Strorks was cooled off. He lumbered out of the water and put on his skin, buttoning the three big buttons up his tummy. He *itched* and he *scratched* and he rolled on the ground! He bellowed, "HuHUHHH!" He ran right toward the Parsee man's tree. He rubbed up against it, rubbing the buttons right off his front, rubbing great wrinkles into his smooth skin. The Parsee man clung to his tree for dear life as the palm tree swayed this way and that. Strorks crashed back into the jungle.

The Parsee man climbed out of his tree grinning from ear to ear. He picked up his golden hat that shone with more than Oriental splendor, dumped out what was left of the cake crumbs, and placed it upon his head. He picked up his cookstove of the type you most particularly must not touch (but now it was cool and he could touch it), and he danced off to another part of the Red Sea where he never saw that old rhinoceros, Strorks, again.

And that, oh, Best Beloved, is the story of how the rhinoceros got his wrinkly, wrinkly skin.

THE STONE IN THE ROAD
An English Folk Tale

Here is a story with the moral "Those that help others will be rewarded", or "Do unto others as you would have others do unto you". It is a delightful story to use as a base to explore characterization through action and improvised dialogue.

Getting Started: Tell the story and discuss the setting and plot. How did the duke help the villagers? What effect did the stone have on them?

Warm-up: Conduct "Character Locomotion", page 27 , centered around the village characters. For example:

- Grumpy, fat person
- Thin, nervous person
- Old or young shepherd with confused sheep
- Horses pulling a carriage
- Military men on horses
- Person carrying produce to market

Have the group explore some pantomime exercises based on some of the following character ideas:

- Scholar reading and tripping over the stone.
- Scientist inspecting the stone with a magnifying glass.
- Cart driver showing anger that the stone is in the way.

- Children thinking the stone is funny and dancing around it.
- Miller's son carrying a sack of flour.
- Duke pushing the stone onto the road.

Also introduce the push segment in the "Push/Pull" exercise, page 63 . Concentrate on first pushing with medium intensity and then pushing with "all your might".

Activity: *Story Enactment* – Let participants choose parts. If necessary, more than one part can be given each actor. For example, the person playing the scholar may also play a sheep.

Establish the setting: the duke's mansion, the town, roadway, and the bush where the duke hides. Indicate which characters travel into town and which go out of town, then arrange the sequence of their entries.

Begin the narration and encourage the participants to improvise dialogue while enacting the characters as practiced in the locomotion and pantomime warm-ups. For example, participants may add their own appropriate grumbling and complaining. Only the duke and the miller's son have prescribed dialogue at the story's end.

An alternate, simpler approach to acting out this story is for the leader to narrate the entire story without action and stop short of the ending. Then have pairs simultaneously enact the duke and miller's son episode only. Each pair may give its own interpretation.

Or, the group could focus entirely on the parade of villagers and their reactions to the stone.

Encourage dialogue appropriate for the characters and historical setting rather than modern slang. *Anno's Journey* By Mitsumasa Anno is an excellent picture book to help participants visualize the people and activities of this period. Some Shakespearean or other stories, or historical books on the Middle Ages or the Renaissance, may also be shared to inspire the participants.

THE STONE IN THE ROAD
An English Folk Tale
Adapted by Kristen Bissinger

There once was a kind Duke, who lived on the edge of a village. Often he would help the villagers when they were in trouble. If crops were poor, he helped in providing food. If floods washed away a home, he would send over his men to help rebuild. If a fence was broken and animals strayed, he sent his horsemen to help round them up. His kindness and consideration for the people of his neighboring village were great. So kind was he, that the villagers began to rely on him rather than on themselves or each other. They became lazy.

"No need to worry about this fence. Just run and tell the Duke that it's fallen down and he will handle the work."

"No need to conserve. If we run out of potatoes the Duke will surely feed us out of his great store."

The villagers became so lazy, that the Duke began to question the wiseness of his kind acts. "I can see that the villagers no longer rely upon themselves. They have grown lax. I doubt that there is one man or woman that would put forth effort for another. But I still have hope. I will devise a plan that will reward that person who is willing to make an effort for the good of others."

So early one morning, before the sun had risen, the Duke snuck out of his mansion and crept quietly down to the road that entered the village. There, with great effort, he pushed a huge stone into the middle of the road. It took him a long time, but as the sun rose, an enormous boulder blocked the way in and out of town. There was no way that a cart could get past it. No carriage could get in or out of town without the removal of the stone.

Under the stone, the Duke had placed a bag of gold, then he hid in the bushes beside the road. As the first rays of sunlight touched the stone, a man and his son came down the road into town leading a herd of sheep. Spying the stone, the father called out to his son, "Run ahead, boy, see what that is in the middle of the road. Maybe a sack of meal has fallen off someone's cart. We shall be all the richer if that is so."

The boy ran ahead and discovering the stone, he called back to his father, "It's a stone, Father, a huge boulder."

"Drat," said the father, "now the sheep are going this way and that! What a nuisance this boulder is. Someone should tell the Duke. His men will pull this boulder off the road."

On they went into town, scurrying this way and that as they attempted to round up the divided sheep.

The Duke waited.

Next came two women with baskets of eggs and produce. As they approached the stone, they took little notice,. Then one sat down on the stone emptied some gravel from her shoe. "I'm weary," she said. "It's a long way to town. But it will be worth the trip if my produce sells well. I am hoping to buy some beautiful material to make myself a dress. Ah, but I wish I were the Duke's wife, for she has all the fine dresses she could wish for. She doesn't have to wake early in the morning and walk miles and miles into town. She just snaps her fingers and she gets what she wants!"

"Come along," said the other. "We will be late and then no one will want our goods."

Off they went down the road.

Next came a regiment of soldiers on their fine steeds. Thundering down the road, the horses reared and bucked as they came upon the stone in their way. The men hollered and whipped their horses and shook their fists at the stone.

"This is dangerous and a disgrace! A large boulder in the middle of the road? It's a wonder the Duke hasn't done something about this!" But did they stop and work together to free the path? No, off they rushed out of town, shouting and complaining of the nuisance it caused them.

Following them, in a fine carriage, were two ladies on their way to the countryside for a day visit. They coughed and fanned themselvs as the dust from the horses flew up into the air. Then their carriage stopped with a jolt. And they shrieked and complained. "Now my hair's a mess! Can't these horses be controlled?"

One called out the window, "What is it, George? What has stopped us so abruptly? If we don't keep moving, we shan't get to Lucy's by noontime. And you know, such sudden stops upset Elizabeth's stomach!"

"It can't be helped," said George. "There's a large stone in the road, ma'am, and our carriage just can't get by."

"Oh, fiddle!" said Elizabeth. "Now the day's spoiled! I've a mind to go up to the manor house and tell the Duke how displeased I am with the way he's keeping the roads these days. Well, we shall just have to turn around. What a shame!" And off they went, back to town, complaining all the way.

That day, a stream of travelers came in and out of town. A group of girls, surprised and delighted by its placement, danced around the stone. A scholar, reading a book as he walked, tripped over the stone. A gypsy stopped and inspected the stone for magical properties, but finally had to turn around for her cart would not fit past. Many commmented and complained but no one took the effort to move the stone.

As the sun lay low on the horizon, the Duke was about to give up, he was stiff from crouching and disappointed.

Then in the dusk, he heard a cheerful whistling tune. The miller's son came around the bend with a large sack of flour on his back. He stopped when he came to the stone, setting his sack down on the ground. He wiped the sweat from his brow. "Whew! There's a big stone," he said, "and right in the middle of the road to town. What a nuisance for those with carts and carriages." And in no time he set his shoulder to the stone and pushed it aside.

As he returned for his sack, he was astonished to see a small sack that had been beneath the stone. He picked it up and gave it a shake.

"Someone must have dropped this, sounds like gold to me. I must take it to the Town Hall. The owner will surely be relieved to have it back again."

"You are its owner," said the Duke, as he stepped from the bushes. "I placed that gold on the road and the stone on top of it. I have waited all day to find one person willing to move the stone; one person kind enough to make that effort for the good of all. This gold is for you, my boy, it is your reward for the thoughtfulness you have shown toward others."

"Oh, thank you, thank you, sir," said the boy. "Moving the stone was a small thing to do." And with that he picked up his sack, put the gold in his pocket and hurried home to share his good news.

Villagers spying the stone in the road

WATCH ME!
SEQUENCING

Objective: To teach observation, memorization and sequencing skills through pantomime action.

Getting Started: Discuss with the group the term "sequencing", and why it is important in story presentation.

Prepare beforehand a quiet activity that individuals in the class can work on, such as identifying and outlining the sequence of events in a given story or two, to occupy them as other members perform the sequencing enactment.

Warm-up: Conduct the "Bend and Stretch" exercise, page 18 and the "Magic Ball", page 50 in preparation for pantomime activities.

Spread participants out in the space or in a circle formation by other participants to practice a variety of pantomime movements, including ones to be useful for the sequencing scenarios that follow.

Assign the quiet activity to the class as a whole.

Explain that each person will have a chance to play the part of a "spectator", observing a pantomime sequence in *private*. He or she will then copy the pantomime for the next participant to watch. Point out that it will be important for each person to observe and remember the sequence as carefully as possible in order to repeat it. Everyone will eventually be called upon and no spectator should look at the pantomime until it is his or her turn. The goal is for each spectator to pantomime the sequence as *exactly* as possible without adding or subtracting material. Emphasize that all actions should be kept as clear and simple as possible.

You may allow class members who have already pantomimed and completed their quiet work to observe the rest of the pantomiming.

Activity: Select a volunteer to locate in the hall or back of the room. Give him or her a written or oral sequence of events, such as the ones that follow, to pantomime. Watch the volunteer pantomime the sequence to make sure every section has been included. Then call on a second volunteer to observe the first volunteer's pantomime version. The original volunteer may now sit down to the quiet assignment.

The spectator now becomes the actor and pantomimes the sequence over again for a third spectator.

This process continues until all class members have observed and pantomimed the sequence.

The last person repeats the actions for the entire class to observe. Then the first person repeats, his or her original version and/or the original sequence is stated for all to hear.

The class then discusses and compares the differences, if any, between the two sequence versions.

The following is a starter suggestion for this sequence game and may serve as a sample for participants to make up other original simple sequence skits:

The Apple Tree
- *Walk down a country road.*
- *Climb a tree.*
- *Pick an apple.*
- *Climb down the tree.*
- *Walk away while eating the apple.*

BAG OF PROPS

Objective: To develop a story or skit centered around a prop.

Getting Started: Ask each participant to bring in a safe object from home to put in a community pile and share with the group, such as:

music box	*paper bag*
egg beater	*pillow*
toy robot	*vacuum cleaner nozzle*
cardboard tube	*hand mirror*
pliers	*rag doll*
rope	*soccer ball*
broom	*hammer*
unusual gadget	*book*

Discuss logical uses and illogical, imaginative possibilities for the use of some props brought in. A cardboard tube, for instance, can be a telescope, sword, spy glass, rolling pin or a unicorn horn. Ask the participants to suggest what sort of conflicts might arise over some of these objects.

Using a tube prop

Warm-up: Allow everyone to choose a prop and explore its use in a solo scene. Encourage ingenuity by making suggestions that the props be used with imagination. Allow a short period of exploration time and then have everyone switch to another prop exploration.

Return the props to the pile and prepare the class for creating characters with "Characterization Locomotion", page 27 and "Who's Speaking", page 67 .

Activity: Divide the class into teams of two to four members each. Invite each team to choose an object, then design a short skit around the object. Work with the class in developing strong conflicts and satisfying resolutions. For example:

A *vacuum cleaner nozzle* has magic powers to clean a room with one sweep of the nozzle in one's hand. Each of the characters in the cast wants to possess this magic nozzle and claims it belongs to him or her.

Who are the characters involved? Tenants of the same apartment house? Co-workers in a house cleaning company? Some animals in a zoo? Some hair shedding creatures who live in an environment requiring a great deal of vacuuming? How does this conflict begin? How does it build? Do the characters contest each other with reasoning or battle? In what way does it end? Do they find the rightful owner and is the magic nozzle finally used?

Using props as imagery

NEW ADVENTURES FOR FAMOUS CHARACTERS

Objective: To inspire short story writing and enactments centered around famous characters.

Getting Started: Focus on a popular, historic or tall tale character whose attributes will generate enthusiasm from your class, such as Spiderman, Mary Poppins, Paul Bunyan, John Henry, Calamity Jane, Jack the fool (as in "Jack and the Beanstalk"), or Iktome or Coyote (tricksters from Native American stories).

Familiarize the group with one of these characters by reading several chapters or short stories involving his or her adventures. Discuss the character's distinguishing characteristics such as smartness, foolishness, bravery, cowardice, honesty, or deceit and list them on the chalkboard.

Activity: Ask each participant to create a story centered around the character, and his or her characteristics. Point out that stories must include a:

- *Beginning* which introduces the character and setting.
- *Middle* which involves a series of events resulting in a dramatic change of events or conflict called the climax..
- *Ending* in which the climax reaches a conclusion.

Participants may write, draw , recite, or tape record their story ideas, depending on abilities and the aim of the assignment. Have participants share their stories with the rest of the class.

Extended Activity: In a follow-up session, divide the class into smaller groups to work in various parts of the room on brief enactments of each participant's story. Or, if the group is comprised of young children or too many participants for the above suggestion, choose a few stories and direct the entire class in the enactments.

Hah, Heh, Heh! I'll cast a spell on you

SPECTACULAR SPEECHES

Objective: To become aware of and utilize some components of a successful speech.

Getting Started: Ask participants what they believe composes a good speech. Write their suggestions, along with those listed below, on the chalkboard.

SPEECH HELPERS

- *Quality of voice (upbeat and varied as opposed to monotone)*
- *Good diction*
- *Pacing (rushed, languid, use of pause)*
- *Humor*
- *Conviction (eye contact, projection, dynamics)*
- *Gestures (too many, too few, appropriate, distracting)*
- *Visual aids*
- *Rich vocabulary (variety, appropriateness to audience)*
- *Appearance*
- *Generalities and particulars (detailing)*
- *Interesting topic*
- *Length of speech*

Compile, with the aid of the participants, a list of interesting speech topics, such as:

- A dog or cat's viewpoint on how humans should behave.
- Why should we recycle materials?
- What makes the best amusement park or fast food restaurant?
- The best and worst things about being the age of ten (or whatever age the participants are)

Warm-up: Ask a few volunteers to choose and demonstrate only one of the Speech Helpers (or the distinct lack of a helper) listed above in a one to three sentence speech sample. When the speaker is reseated the other participants may raise their hands to guess which Speech Helper the speaker had in mind.

Activity: Form small teams of participants. Give approximately five minutes for each team to decide on a topic for its speech and to list a few points they wish to make within the speech.

Whisper one Speech Helper (or present them on flash cards) to each team. Explain to the teams that they may:

(1) Use this helper,
(2) Show the lack of it, or
(3) Demonstrate a contrast of its use and non-use, such as using both poor diction and good diction in the same speech.

Have all teams work quietly and separately, for about ten to fifteen mintues, to develop short speeches on their topics using (or purposely not using) the Speech Helper assigned to each team. The goal is for each team to develop a speech but just one of its team members will actually present the speech to the rest of the class. The class is to guess which helper has been represented. Or, if desired, individuals in each team may work in tandem and all participants become involved in presenting the speech.

Extended Activity: Have each participant choose a topic and work on a two to three minute speech choosing two or more of the Speech Helpers as guides. After these decisions have been made, divide the participants into pairs so that they may be helpful to each other. Give each participant five to ten minutes to practice his or her speech out loud, but quietly, in front of the partner. That partner acts as "coach" and timekeeper. Switch roles so that each member receives a chance to try a speech. Afterwards, have members present speeches to the whole class.

DINING OUT

Objective: To strengthen both acting and writing skills through improvisations based on settings, character, and plot development.

Getting Started: Brainstorm a list of restaurant types: fast food, seafood, French cuisine, truck stop, etc. Focus on one of these settings and briefly discuss examples of food and decor, props and characters in this setting. For example, an Italian restaurant:

- *Food* – ravioli, antipasto, spumoni ice cream, etc.
- *Decor* – National colors, green and red, dimly lit by candlelight, small crowded tables, photographs of famous people on the walls.
- *Props* – Wallet, purse, napkins, table cloth, grated cheese, salt and pepper, silverware, candle, menu, order pad and pencil.
- *Dining characters* –

Customers: A belligerent boxer, beautiful boisterous socialite, feeble old man, hungry construction worker, persistent tramp, angry businessman, cool gangster, lovers, picky woman, sloppy man.

Waitperson: Clumsy, slow, fastidious, narcissistic, sly, frazzled or overeager.

Discuss the motivation of the diners may have in choosing this particular restaurant. Is it romance, business, hunger, to impress, for revenge, to waste time, routine, surprise party, good food.

Warm-up: Conduct an adaptation of "Characterization Locomotion", page 27 . Suggest characters appropriate to the setting and ask participants to locomote across the space as specific characters would (draw from the character suggestions listed above and the group's compiled list). Encourage conscious characterization through physical expressions by mentioning emotions or specific body parts and how these aspects might be utilized to convey character. For example, walk:

• With the broad shoulders of a boxer, hunched shoulders of a a feeble old man, the high tense shoulders of an uptight waitress.
• With small uneven steps as though tense or frightened or slow swinging limbs as though relaxed.
• Energetically or lethargically.

Ask participants to spread out in the room for a short time to envision a character and practice walking and sitting the way that chatacter might walk and sit. They are not to interact with each other, but work individually within the space. Guide the exploration with questions and directives such as: "What is a characteristic gesture of your character? A shrug, a punch, a twitch, a laugh, a yawn? Are his or her movements fast or slow? Are they large and dramatic? Controlled? Naturally relaxed? How does this person stand or sit? Heavily? Casually, awkwardly, slumped, straight?"

With an abbreviated version of "Who's Speaking", page 67 , guide the participants in exploring voice qualities. Have participants divide into pairs. One member in each pair is to be the waiter, the other, the diner. Have pairs work individually at the same time. The pairs are to improvise dialogue centered around dining. Give the diners an opening line such as, "Waiter, there is a fly in my soup!" or, "What is the specialty today?" The waiter must respond and the conversation go back and forth for several minutes.

The leader is to walk among the pairs helping those who are having trouble achieving dialogue..

Activity: Divide the participants into teams of two to four members each. Each team is to work individually to create a short skit centered around a restaurant episode involving at least one waiter or waitress and one customer. The customers need not be eating together but all of the characters in each team's scene must relate to each other in some way. First each team must define their characters, for example:

• An overworked waiter, a fussy eater at one table, a sloppy noisy eater at another.

• A loud, explosive cook, an oily well groomed waiter, a feeble older dining couple.
• Two businessmen in conflict over a business transaction, a slow dreamy waitress.
• A boxer and a girlfriend he wishes to impress, a clumsy waitress.

Each team finds its own space in the room. Call out a question and give the team members some time to discuss their ideas with each other. Use a drum, a bell or other cue to quiet the conversations when ready to pose the next question. Some questions asked are:

• What type of restaurant is this?
• What does it look like?
• Who are the people in the scene and how do they relate to each other?
• Why have the diners come to the restaurant? (see Getting Started: Motivation)
• How is the service? The food?
• What conflict or crisis occurs? (The steak is burned to a crisp, the service is horrendous, a customer is overly loud, etc.)
• How is it resolved?

After discussion allow ten to fifteen minutes for the teams to improvise the action and dialogue for a two or three minute skit.

Culminate by having each team share its scene with the rest of the class and/or having the participants write down the action and dialogue as they remember it.

Dining Out

SOCIAL STUDIES

Elves trying on new clothes in a skit on "The Shoemaker and the Elves"

INTRODUCTION TO SOCIAL STUDIES

There are a multitude of topics in the existing Social Studies curriculum suitable for drama/dance enactment. Social Studies in the early grades must deal directly with the social issues that arise in the day-to-day school setting. At the teacher's fingertips are stories from ancient cultures through today which are full of lessons centered around social and personal behavior. Chosen well these stories lend themselves amicably to the drama/dance arena providing a most effective and valuable means for teaching socialization skills.

For example, the activity in this section "Carry Your Own Weight" uses the humorous folk tale, "The Cock, the Mouse and the Little Red Hen" to focus on the theme of accepting responsibility within a group. The lessons learned through the story's improvisation are both enjoyable and memorable.

Historical events alone include an array of fascinating and vivid characters and potential dramatic material. Explorers finding new worlds, politicians building nations, inventors providing tools and artisans making cultural impact offer motivational material for classroom study. What better way to assimilate history than to bring memorable events to life through the enactment of Columbus' voyage, Ben Franklin's kite flying experiment, or Harriet Tubman's contribution to the Underground Railroad. When approached dramatically, history lessons can generate thought, involvement and research.

This section also includes a small selection of foreign folk tales to expose the participants to other cultures or periods of history. The classroom itself, can create a globe of goodwill for understanding many cultures as these stories are enacted.

To round out the Social Studies curriculum, drama/dance activities are included in this section which study the comparing of communities, supply and demand, archaeology, geography, and numerous other topics. The manner of approach is aimed to enliven Social Studies lessons, strengthen rapport among students, and demonstrate to the teacher the endless possibilities of adapting drama/dance into the global classroom.

CARRY YOUR OWN WEIGHT
(Group Responsibility)

Objective: To raise awareness in accepting responsibilities of group membership.

Getting Started: Discuss the various social groups that the participants are part of: family, school class, church, sports, clubs, etc. Find out what contributions they give to these groups, such as participation in activities, emotional support, work efforts, financial support, communication, and discussion. What other groups are they aware of? (National, political, work, volunteers, etc.)

Warm-up: Concentrate on the emotional aspects in the story (cheerfulness, boredom, hunger, fear, and grumpiness) through some "Locomotion Emotion" exercises.

Conduct "Locomotor Lift", page 30 .

Pantomime specific housekeeping skills found in the story - cooking, sewing, sweeping, etc.

Read or tell the story "The Cock, the Mouse and the Little Red Hen". an English folk tale (an alternate story suggestion is "The Hen and the Grain of Wheat"), for the class to enact.

Activity: *Story Enactment* — Ask the group to establish locations for the two houses, pathway taken by the fox between them, and the stream.

Divide the group in half. One half are to play the foxes, the other half the occupants of the neat house – either cock, hen, or mouse. Have participants choose parts within these two categories. (All the foxes will take the role of Father Fox in the latter part of the story enactment.) Assign each fox to "carry" a cock, a hen or a mouse in the latter part of the story.

Have each group retire to its respective house and begin the narration. Participants may copy the narrator's dialogue or initiate their own, when appropriate. The narrator should pause for action and suggest character action through narration, such as : "The little foxes jumped for joy. They all held hands and danced in a circle, licking their lips."

Emphasize staying in character and following the story line. For example, the chase scene before the fox catches his victims is not lengthy, but short.

When arriving at the rock-carrying segment of the story, remind the actors that they are carrying and pushing rocks *equal* to their own weight.

When the story has been completely enacted, discuss the enactment with the group. If time permits, or in your next session, switch roles and re-enact the story.

THE COCK, THE MOUSE AND THE LITTLE RED HEN

An English Folktale

There was once a cock, a mouse, and a little red hen who lived in a neat little house on a hill. On the other side of the valley was a ramschackled old house wherein lived a big bad fox and his five little hungry foxes.

One morning the hen arose, she built up the fire and set on the kettle to boil. Then she woke the cock and the mouse who grumbled and groaned. "Who will help me fix the breakfast?" asked the little red hen. "I'm too tired," complained the cock. "I'm not hungry," replied the mouse. So the little red hen made breakfast herself. When it was ready they all sat down and ate. The cock and mouse quarreled and complained throughout breakfast then they propped up their feet by the fire to rest. "Who will help wash the dishes?" asked the hen. "Not I," said the cock and mouse, so the little red hen did it herself. When that was done the little red hen asked, "Who will help me make the beds?" The cock and mouse complained and made excuses refusing to help, so the little red hen went upstairs to make the beds.

Back at the foxes' house the little foxes were complaining that they were hungry. "Daddy, we haven't had anything to eat for days," they whined. "Alright," said the big bad fox, "I'll go over to the house across the valley and see what I can bring home for supper."

The little red foxes held hands and danced with glee, licked their lips and rubbed their tummies. Mr. Fox headed out with a sack across the valley, across the river and up the hill where he knocked on the door of the neat little house.

"You get it," said the cock to the mouse. "Maybe it's a friend come to visit me," said the mouse, as he opened the door without even checking to see who was there.

In jumped the fox. He grabbed the mouse and stuffed him in his sack. Then he grabbed the cock and stuffed him in as well. Up the stairs he bounded, then grabbed the hen and stuffed her in and tied up the sack. He left for home carrying the heavy sack on his back.

Down the hill he trudged with his heavy load. When he came to the river he was quite tired and stopped to rest under a tree. There he fell asleep. As he began to snore the little red hen pulled out her sewing kit from her apron pocket. With her scissors she snipped a hole big enough for the mouse to crawl out.

"Go find a rock as big as yourself and push it back here into the sack," she whispered. The mouse did just that. Then she snipped the hole a bit bigger and said to the cock, "Go find a rock the same size as yourself and roll it over here into the sack." So the cock did just that. The little red hen then slipped out of the sack, she rolled a rock her size into the sack and sewed the sack back up. The three of them ran home as fast as they could and bolted the windows and doors shut with a sigh of relief.

When the big bad fox awoke, he stretched, yawned and lifted the sack to his shoulder. "It must be late!" he exclaimed and he hurried down to the river. He stepped into the river with the heavy sack on his back, slipped on a stone and down into the river he fell. The stones were so heavy that the sack sank to the bottom of a deep pool and those little foxes went hungry again that night.

While back in the neat little house, the cock and the mouse fetched the water, heated the kettle, made the meal and straightened the house as the little red hen took a rest by the fire.

The big bad fox never troubled them again and to this day the cock, mouse, and little red hen live happily together. All three help with what has to be done in the neat little house on the hill.

ECONOMICS
Supply and Demand

Objective: To communicate the economic concept of scarcity through the game of musical chairs.

Getting Started: Prepare beforehand a selection of music to be sung, or played on a musical instrument, record, or tape. Arrange two lines of chairs, back to back, allowing one chair for every participant.

Warm-up: Instruct participants in the rules of the traditional game of musical chairs:

All walk in one direction around the chairs while the music plays. When the music stops, each participant is to find a chair and sit down.

From this point on, each time the music is played, then stopped, one chair will be removed.

When the music is played and stopped, the person unable to find a chair is "out" of the game and must watch from the side.

Discussion: Talk with the group about limited resources and unlimited demand or need. First define these words with examples your group can comprehend. Explain that the chairs were used as an example of something that people want or need. Then ask, "If there weren't enough chairs what could we do? Share, substitute, make more chairs, some people do without them, etc." Introduce basic resources such as food, clothing, and shelter.

Activity: Divide the class into small groups of four to ten members each. Select one of the following scenarios, or following these examples, have the groups create their own scenarios depicting scarcity.

For example:

• One group of cave dwellers has fire, the other group does not. Possible solutions: fighting, stealing, sharing, bartering.

• A shortage of oil results in : higher prices, lines at the gas stations, government money and effort going into oil prospecting.

• Crop failure causes: price hikes, shortages, black market sales, more small home gardens, importation of crops from foreign countries.

• A shortage of housing causes: families to live together, a boom in construction business, higher prices for smaller housing units, people moving to other areas.

COMPARING COMMUNITIES

Objective: To study how communities differ from one another in serving basic needs through their resources and technology.

Getting Started: Discuss with the group some diverse community resources, such as:

Fishing
Farming (cotton, tobacco, soybean, citrus fruit, dairy, etc.)
Ship building
Textiles
Furniture building
Iron and steel drilling
Manufacturing (chemicals, paper, etc.)
Mining/quarrying
Electronics (TV, motion picture, computer, radar)

Ask questions such as what tools and technology each of these communities adopt? What effect does this make on their overall living environment? Are location and natural resources important factors in determining community technology?

Warm-up: Conduct "The Magic Ball", page 50 , adapted to concentrate on tools, equipment and activities characteristic of a community and the use of its resources. Explore "Machine Madness", page 66 , concentrating on what the participants imagine would be involved in a machine to process certain natural resources.

Activity: Depending on size, divide the class into three to five teams. Assign each team one community resource as listed above and have each team research information about its resource and technology. Ask each team to establish a fictitious community and its location. Have each team present a skit to the group showing the basic resource, the technology being used in its acquisition, processing, and how the final product is used. For example: Corpus Christi is a fishing town located on the Gulf Coast of Texas. Fishing is a main industry around which technology is centered. Team members can act out both the machinery and human power involved in:

   – *Fishing from a fishing boat, or using nets*
   – *Hauling fish to a fish processing plant where it is cleaned, packed and frozen*
   – *Distribution by truck or plane*
   – *Cooking, serving, and eating the fish.*

Extended Activity: Discuss interdependence with the class and how people across the country depend on one another for products; people who live in the north cannot grow oranges, thus depend on Florida or California for oranges. These resources are shared through shipping, buying, and selling. This is called "trade".

As a final activity in this project, ask each participant to draw a picture, large and bold, of a resource item he or she would enjoy harvesting. Bring the pictures to the front of the room to display, forming an impromptu marketplace and have students exchange and barter these items with one another.

THE IMPORTANCE OF TOOLS

Objective: To understand the way people change their environment by the tools they use.

Getting Started: Open up discussion about simple tools (with few parts) and how they affect the environment and lifestyle of a society. Explain that without tools people would not be able to change their environment. Using these tools to serve human needs is what is known as "technology".

Some examples of simple tools:

Hammer	Fishing net	Chisel
Shovel	Bow and	Surgeon's
Mortar and	arrow	scissors
pestle	Plumb line	Rope
Writing tool	Weaving loom	Cooking vessel

Discuss what societies use these tools and how they affect living conditions. For example, the fishing net allows coastal peoples to include fish as a mainstay in their diets and to convert into fertilizer for raising improved crops. The surgeon's scissors allows for operations which help prolong the life of individuals in that society.

Discuss some more complex tools:

Automobile	*Bulldozer*
Sewing Machine	*Pneumatic drill*
Tractor	*Washing machine*
Mixer	*Water pump*

Warm-up: Ask each participant to choose a simple tool and pantomime a short skit using the tool for its intended purpose. For example: chopping down a tree with an ax or hunting for prey with a bow and arrow. Let the class guess the tool being used.

Activity: Have each member of the class bring in a safe tool from home (spatula, hair dryer, comb, clothespin, screwdriver, can opener) to display on a community table. Discuss the diverse uses of these modern day tools and what tasks they make possible. Divide the class into teams of three to four members each. Ask each team to choose a tool and create a short story skit (fantasy or real) around that tool, including a conflict and resolution of the conflict.

For example: A lion, monkey and an afghan hound all have important appointments at the same time. After washing their hair, they each want to use the hair dryer so that they will look impressive for their appointments. They argue and fight over whose appointment is most important; and who should be first to use the dryer. Finally, they draw straws to decide who will first use the hair dryer.

Exploring tools in a skit on The Shoemaker and the Elves

SATISFYING BASIC NEEDS

Objective: To help participants understand and identify the basic needs for survival.

Getting Started: Lead a discussion on where and how the participants in your group get food, shelter, and clothing. Identify these items as the basic needs and concentrate on each division, one at a time. Guide the discussion towards the original source of each commodity as well as some of the processes required to obtain the final product.

Share some specific information on a community or communities with a fundamental lifestyle, such as traditional Eskimo, Samoan, or African groups.

Discuss the staple foods, shelters and clothing of these or other lifestyles. If your group is able to spend time in research, divide the groups into three teams. Each team is to choose a native group to research, concentrating on food, shelter, and clothing. Or, take each of these categories one at a time and work in greater depth. An example follows:

Clothing Example

Discussion – Cotton is planted, tended, picked, cleaned, spun, woven, dyed, cut and sewn to create a T-shirt. It is also shipped several times during this process.

Field Trip – Projects and field trips may also be conducted to support facts. Research what is in your area and visit a weaving mill, clothing factory, sheep farm, or other. Or, teach the group, with the aid of a parent or volunteer, to finger crochet, knit, embroider, or weave.

Warm-up: Conduct the costume aspect of the "Scarves" exercise, page 54 .

Ask everyone to bring in pictures and clothing from different countries, stressing native dress. Pass out scarves, one to each participant. Ask participants to explore all the variety of clothing or costumes and related characters, that they can dream up by wrapping, tucking, folding, and tying their scarves into garments, such as: turbin, diaper, cloak, shirt, veil, eye patch, arm sling, pantaloons, Indian sari, Samoan sulu, leg wrap, vest, belt.

Activity: Divide the group into teams. Each team must create a skit , with or without dialogue, centered around the topic of clothing in some context. Factual information can easily be presented in pantomime form as a lead person narrates information of interest. For example, a fashion show, quality control in a factory, sheep shearing, silkworm farm, etc. Have teams work together in researching facts and creating a plot.

ROBERT FULTON
Inventor and Boy Wonder of the American and Industrial Revolutions

Objective: To present interesting scenes and characters of both the American and Industrial Revolutions for enactment.

Getting Started: Read aloud the story of Robert Fulton and briefly discuss the American and Industrial Revolutions, clearly stating that the Industrial Revolution came considerably later than the American Revolution.

Warm-up: Start with the "Jump/Freeze" exercise on page 23 . Conduct the "Guess-How-I-Feel" exercise, page 36 , with emphasis on emotions needed in the story: surprise, delight, disappointment and others. Conduct "The Magic Ball", page 50 , with emphasis on pantomiming work needed in the story, such as shopkeepers' activities, sawing, hammering, etc.

Familiarize the group with sculpting techniques through "Shapes", page 56 , "Positive/Negative Sculptures", page 58 , and "Group Sculptures", page 61 , concentrating on group sculptures needed in the enactments of the story such as a town shop, bonfire, paddle boat and steamboat. Also, conduct the firecracker portion of "Staccato/Legato Locomotion", page 29 , to be used when participants enact the firecrackers exploding on July 4th.

Activity: If time is limited decide which of the three scenes the group will enact: the 4th of July, the paddle boat or the "Clermont". Ask the participants to cast themselves in one of the following four categories. Position those in each category in one of the corners of the room.

    1) Robert Fulton
    2) His friends, including Christopher Gumpf
    3) The shopkeepers, townspeople and witnesses of the paddle boat and the first voyage of the "Clermont"
    4) The fireworks, bonfire, paddle boat and "Clermont" achieved through sculpting techniques. Aspects of the scenery may be done through body sculpting, as well.

In each scene the actual parts involved in each of these four categories will vary. For example, in the scenes around the 4th of July story those playing Category Two will enact Fulton's friends. In the paddle boat scenes Category Two will play the part of Christopher Gumpf, and then in the "Clermont" scene they will enact friends on the steamboat along with Fulton.

The following is an example of what is involved in preparing for and enacting the Fourth of July scenes.

• In their corner of the space have those members enacting Robert Fulton practice the pantomime they will need for the scene: working at a job, reading a book, constructing the rockets.

• Have those members enacting shopkeepers decide on an occupation appropriate to the era such as blacksmith, storekeeper, carpenter, farmer, dressmaker, town council member, mother and children, printer, brushmaker, stable owner, etc. When this is decided each member must practice pantomime of the tasks involved.

• Those members enacting friends of Fulton must choose or be assigned a shopkeeper to assist at the beginning of the scene and practice the pantomime involved.

• Those members enacting the fireworks and bonfire must practice their group bonfire enactment and their individual rocket explosions. During the actual enactment they should first enact the bonfire as a group then go out, one by one, to enact a rocket explosion. If desired, this group may body sculpt shops, the flag, bell and town post board, etc.

Allow these four groups to practice elements of their parts for five or ten minutes.

Stop the action and have everyone sit down and establish the locations of the shops in town, town square, and Robert Fulton's home in the space. Arrange the townsfolk, shopkeepers, and boys, including Robert, in their designated shops and work places. Have those body sculpting create aspects of the scene with their body shapes or sit aside until the firework episode.

Start the action with a short improvised scene of everyone at work, including the town council members in their meeting. The town council adjourns and the council members enter the square and ring the bell. The townspeople and boys put aside their work and gather in the square where the procalamation is read by a council member. The people react in dismay and concern as they talk of the war and return to work. The boys act disappointed and gather to talk of the spoiled plans for a July Fourth celebration. Give the cue for all action to freeze. Those participants not involved in the next episode may sit aside as audience.

Robert runs home, finds and reads his book on the construction of fireworks. Robert goes to the shops where he makes his transactions with the shopkeepers using improvised dialogue and action.

The boys gather at Robert's house, improvise dialogue about the fireworks and make the rockets. At this point the participants enacting the fireworks will be sculpted into the shape of rockets by those enacting the boys. Once this has been achieved give the cue to freeze the action then regroup for the bonfire scene in the town square.

Start this scene with the townspeople building those participants in Category Four into a bonfire. The use of scarves may enliven the bonfire enactment. One by one, those enacting the bonfire stand alone on the square in the shape of a rocket and are lit, exploding like fireworks. The townspeople react with surprise and delight as the boys and Robert hoot and dance with enthusiasm.

This scene completes the first portion of the story. At this point sit down and discuss what went well in the enactment and how it could be improved.

When time permits proceed to enact the paddle boat and "Clermont" scenes in a similar manner using any positive suggestions to improve the enactment.

ROBERT FULTON

Inventor and Contributor to the
American and Industrial Revolutions
Adapted by Kristen Bissinger

Robert Fulton was an imaginative boy from Lancaster, Pennsylvania who was always designing remarkable things. He was thirteen years old when the Fourth of July drew near in 1778. The men of the town were still fighting in the American Revolution. Robert and the other boys were planning to light the whole town splendidly with candles in honor of the second anniversary of the Declaration of Independence.

On July first a number of boys were delivering groceries, sweeping stores and walks, whitewashing fences and other odd jobs in exchange for extra candles. They all were eager to contribute to a jubilant celebration of liberty. At noon that day the bell rang in the town square and everyone gathered to listen to the reading of the proclamation the town council posted on the signboard.

> It is decreed by the council of the town of
> Lancaster, Pennsylvania, that in these
> trying times of war the people must save
> all that they are able for the use of our
> brave army. The following items, being
> scarce, must be conserved.

On the list was tallow and tallow is an important ingredient for the making of candles. The council ordered that no one should light a candle to celebrate Independence Day.

What a disappointment for the boys! They stood with sad faces before the signboard announcing the order of the council. But Robert Fulton did not waste time in regrets. He stood for a few moments lost in thought, then hurried home and searched the bookshelves until he found what he was looking for. He got down a large book and studied it carefully. Afterwards he gathered his candles and went to the brushmakers and exchanged them for gunpowder. At a second shop, he bought cardboard.

"What are you going to do with cardboard?" asked the clerk in the second shop.

"We are forbidden to light the street with candles," Robert answered eagerly, "so I'm going to light the sky with rockets!"

"Light the sky! Why, that's impossible!" The man laughed heartily for fireworks were at that time almost unknown in America, though they had long been used in China.

"Nothing is impossible!" Robert replied, and he marched off home with his purchases. There he fully worked out the making of the rockets from the general description in this book. Under Robert's direction the boys made cylinders, taking the utmost care to have them the right length and thickness, with the stick just the proper length in proportion to the size of the cylinders. The rockets were filled with gunpowder and a number of little balls, made by Robert himself out of such stuff as he knew would produce colored fire.

When darkness came on the Fourth, the boys gathered in the square and a gigantic bonfire was built. Their shouts and the leaping flames summoned everyone to the square. A row of cardboard cylinders attached to sticks lay on the grass.

The boys set off the rockets. A loud report, then a streak of fire shot hissing up in the air to burst gloriously in the sky with a great bouquet of stars! Everyone cried out in amazement and delight.

The townspeople thanked Robert Fulton, who had worked out that celebration; and the boys, themselves, felt that rockets far exceeded candles as a means of expressing their exuberance in celebrating the Fourth of July. After this, Robert continued experimenting with things and haunting the factories where arms were made for the Continental Army. He had many ideas and drew his plans so well, that he often gave older workmen valuable suggestions.

In 1779, when Robert was fourteen, he met, among the factory youths, a lad named Christopher Gumpf. Now Christopher liked to fish and he kept an old flatboat padlocked to a tree on the banks of the Conestoga Creek. On holidays, he and Robert would set out with bait and lunch for a glorious day upstream. The flatboat was pushed by a pole, and the boys took turns at poling. It was a hard and tedious task to push the clumsy, old scow upstream, so Robert's active mind began to work on how men could make a boat move through the water more easily. He made a model of a boat propelled by paddles at the sides and showed Christopher his plan for moving a boat by means of paddle wheels. The two boys secretly sawed and hammered in the woods by the river making a set of side paddles, to move the old flatboat. The paddle wheels were joined by a bar and worked by a crank. One boy, standing in the center of the boat, turned the crank, which turned the bar, which turned the paddle wheels, which made the boat go forward!

When the work was done, Christopher himself could hardly believe it would work; but Robert, with no doubts at all, stepped into the boat, took hold of the crank and turned it. Off went the scow gliding along upstream. Christopher leapt on the boat with an oar for a rudder to steer the craft.

In delighted triumph, the boys enjoyed their success and the astonished faces of the spectators who stopped, open-mouthed, to watch them form the banks of the Conestoga Creek. Up and down, round and round they took turns turning the crank to make the paddles go. Very little efforts was needed to send the boat a long distance. It was much faster and easier than the old-fashioned poling method.

In this way Robert Fulton, as a boy, began to plan easier ways to propel boats in the water, little dreaming to what it might lead.

Years later crowds of people lined the banks of the Hudson River in New York, to witness the launching of the first successful steamboat. They cheered and stood along the shore talking with excitement about Robert Fulton and his incredible new invention, the steamboat, "Clermont".

This success ended the day of sailboats and ushered in the day of steamboats, steam engines and machines, the Industrial Revolution.

Through imagination, experimentation and determination Robert Fulton had harnessed the powerful might of steam, demonstrating what he proclaimed as a boy, "Nothing is impossible!"

Adapted from "The Boyhood of Robert Fulton" by Olive Beaupre' Miller, *My Book House*, **Vol. V, page 48.**

CHRISTOPHER COLUMBUS

Objective: To share some basic information about Christopher Columbus, his voyages and the prevailing theories of his day, and how these theories differed from our current understanding of the Earth and the oceans.

Getting Started: Introduce the topic of Christopher Columbus and share some basic facts: He was born in Italy over 500 years ago. At the time, the Earth was thought to be flat, not round. It was commonly believed that dragons and sea monsters existed.

Read the following poems with your group.

"All About Columbus"*

*Columbus sailed the ocean blue
In fourteen-hundred and ninety-two.
He said: "I think the earth is round,
And I'll sail round it, I'll be bound!"
 But the wise men said: "The earth is flat,
You'll fall off the edge if you sail like that,
You'll meet strange monsters in the sea,
And what a calamity that would be!"
But Columbus sailed and sailed some more,
Till at last he found America's shore!*

* Olive Beaupre' Miller

"In Columbus' Time"**

*Supposed you lived then, do you think that you
Would believe what Columbus said was true
Or would you be like the wise men who
Laughed in his face and said "pooh, pooh?"*

** Annette Wynne

Columbus believed that the Earth was round. He wanted to sail to the West in order to get to India and the trade centers in the East. He finally was able to convince Ferdinand and Isabella, the King and Queen of Spain, to finance his trip West. It was very hard to convince a crew to go with him because most people believed the Earth was flat, that no land would be found to the West and that they would fall off the edge of the Earth or be attacked by sea monsters in the big, dark, unknown ocean.

On his first voyage to the West, fights broke out on the ships and the leading mutineers had to be imprisoned. The sailors sailed West for over a month when they finally spotted land and discovered what is now called the West Indies (the New World, not India at all) which is south of Florida.

Share any other information you may have on hand about Columbus.

Warm-up: Conduct any variety of basic stretches to stretch bodies, such as "Bend and Stretch", page 18 , "Cat and Dog Backs", page 19 , and "The Clothes Washer", page 21 .

Proceed to "Positive/Negative Sculptures", page 58 and "Instant Scenery", page 61 .

Activity: *First - Third Graders:* Divide the group into teams of three to ten members. Give these teams five minutes to create a group sculpture sea monster using the positive/negative and group sculpture techniques as a guide. Have each team share their make-believe sea monster, first in shape and then in movement, with the rest of the class.

Fourth - Seventh Graders: Give each team one section of the Columbus story to enact:

• Columbus trying to find someone to sponsor and financially support his trip to the West. Being turned away by John II of Portugal.

• Ferdinand and Isabella granting Columbus money, ships and supplies, plus rights to a percentage of treasure, or such things of worth, discovered in the land he is to find in the West.

• Trying to find a crew willing to undertake the voyage and stocking the ships.

• The voyage and mutiny on board.

• Discovering land, anchoring, getting onto the land and giving thanks to God. Claiming it for the King and Queen of Spain. Capturing native West Indians and forcing them into the ship along with food, birds, and animals native to the islands.

• Columbus and crew re-entering the court of Spain with specimens from the West Indies. An enthusiastic reception by the King and Queen and people of the court. Honors given to him and his brothers.

Allot about 10-15 minutes discussion and improvisation time. Have each team meet separately and discuss the sequence of events in each team's section of the story, choose characters and act it through. After the teams (working at the same time in different parts of the room) have completed a rough run through, share the enactments in correct sequence.

Discuss what worked and what did not work in the enactments.

Extended Activity:

• Ask members within each team to discuss and create through movement and sculpting an imaginary land that they might discover. The land can be based on a shape, idea or movement theme (a land of candy or of twisted unusual shapes, a bouncy land, a land with no gravity) or, each individual can create his or her own fantasy part, the sum of which is the teams' ultimate fantasy land.

• Open up discussion centered around the "Age of Exploration". Introduce factual material about other early Spanish, Portuguese, English and

French explorers - Magellan, Balboa, Sir Francis Drake, Hudson, Cartier, etc. What routes did they take? What difficulties did they meet? What did each discover?

Divide the class into smaller teams, assign each team a historical expedition to research and enact for the rest of the class.

*Taken from <u>My Book House</u>, Vol. 5, ed. by Olive Beaupre® Miller, published by My Book House for Children, Lake Bluff, Illinois

**Taken from For Days and Days, permission given by Frederick A. Stokes Co.

IT HAPPENED TO ME!

Objective: To research famous people and present a speech or an enactment of an accomplishment or event that made them historically important.

Getting Started: Introduce an event or period in history with a story and proceed with this theme as the focus of study. Or, open up discussion with the participants on some of their favorite historical personalities. This may include inventors, explorers, artists, politicians, and entertainers. Ask what character traits might be needed to make a person famous, such as imagination, artistic or physical talent, inquisitiveness, patience, strong will, endurance, beauty, humor, etc.

Warm-up: Conduct the exercises "Characterization Locomotion", page 27 . "The Magic Ball," page 50 , and "Who's Speaking", page 67 .

Activity: Assign or have participants select a famous person or event to research in the library. Magellan, Martin Luther King, Jr., Cortez, Thomas Edison, Florence Nightingale, Michelangelo, Ben Franklin, and Madame Curie are a beginning list of interesting and diverse people from which to choose. Ask each participant to create a short speech titled, "It Happened to Me!", highlighting a historical event that happened in that famous person's life. Or, if working in a team format of several participants, have them prepare a short skit centered around one of these events to present to the group. For example, the dumping of tea at the Boston Tea Party, the court scene as Christopher Columbus asks Ferdinand and Isabella to support his voyage to the spice world, or the first American astronauts stepping onto the moon. Encourage actors to express the personality of their characters, through action, posture and use of the voice.

GEOGRAPHICAL TOURS

Objective: To identify and compare the various geographical regions around the world - deserts, jungles, plains, polar caps, oceans, mountains, foothills, river valleys.

Getting Started: Focus on one classification of region at a time and build a word list on the chalkboard with the group. For example:

The Desert

Cactus	Century Plant
Sand Dunes	Sidewinder Snake
Oasis	Sandstorm
Nomads	Arroyos
Intense Heat	Camel
Horned Lizard	Addax

Discuss some of the conditions of a desert that make it unique: long periods of dry weather, sandstorms, flash floods, elevation from sea level, etc.

Name some deserts such as: the Mojave, Kalahari and Death Valley; and the people, flora and fauna which live on these deserts. Or, have participants research some of the twenty-one deserts, individually or in teams, guided in their research by a list of questions such as: Where is this desert located? What are some important natural resources in this desert? What causes deserts to occur or expand? How can a desert be reclaimed?

The team's tour guide or archaelogist takes the other half of the class on a walk through this desert explaining and pointing out its special features along with pertinent facts. The guide may wish to embellish facts with some imaginative but plausible history, such as a sandstorm that wiped out a colony of bandits sleeping near a particular sand dune, a famous explorer that trekked across the desert and met a certain fate, an old gold mining camp , oil discoveries that made the country very wealthy, or the discovery of some ancient bones of a prehistoric animal.

Extended Activity: The same tour guide approach may be applied to other regions. For example, teams may wish to act out: the two polar regions (Arctic and Antarctic); diverse bodies of water such as the Great Salt Lake and the Mississippi River, or a tropical rain forest and an African plain.

SEARCH FOR LOST WORLDS

Objective: To involve participants in a make-believe archaeology excavation to discover artifacts that help to explain ancient lands and history.

Getting Started: Open up discussion about digs and how they are organized to uncover ancient objects or artifacts that give clues to a society's culture or history. Provide some examples such as the Dead Sea Scrolls, Egyptian tombs, dinosaur bones, etc. If you are studying a specific culture or period of history, share information that will familiarize the participants with possible artifacts from that period. Explain also that an expedition to a site designated for excavation usually consists of a team of surveyors led by a director and that they all must work hard together to mark the site, prepare it and study the environment before carefully digging up layers of soil in patient search for artifacts.

Warm-up: Conduct "Instant Scenery", page 61 emphasizing various environments. Also practice pantomime through "The Magic Ball", page 50 . Center the exercise around objects that might be found in an archaeological expedition.

Activity: Focus on a specific aspect of history or culture such as Native American, Greek, Egyptian, Incan, African, Eskimo, or pre-historic animals.

Ask some participants to form an environment appropriate to the site: forest, desert, ocean floor, mountain or other region, include weather, and animal and plant life. Have other members be the survey team or lay people enacting the expedition. The team members might follow a map (drawn up by the teacher or class artists) through difficult terrain before reaching the site. They might stumble upon their discovery while bulldozing the site; exploring caves; scuba diving to search a sunken ship; or come upon a temple hidden in the jungle.

Have the team work as a whole, asking each survey team member to stake out an area and to pantomime some of the techniques used in excavating to come up with an appropriate object or artifact of his or her choice, such as a pot, statue, tool, bone, toy, coin, jewelry, etc. Through pantomime the member uncovers and cleans off the artifact, defining its shape and form with the hands. Afterwards, sit the group in a circle and ask each participant to share his or her pantomime briefly. The artifact can be further defined by showing it in use, such as a vessel pouring water or a knife carving wood. Or, several bones may be fitted together to form a specific animal. In this manner the rest of the class can quess what the artifacts are.

An excellent book for supporting this activity is *Digging To The Past* by W. John Hackwell, Charles Scribner's Sons, 1986.

JOHNNY, JENNY AND THE GOATS
A Norse Tale
Adapted by Kristen Bissinger

Objective: To explore emotional and physical characterization, sequencing and repetitive dialogue.

Warm-up: Perform, "Run, Skip, Jump" and "Animal Walk", pages 27 and 29 . Practice a characteristic walk and sound for each animal in the story in order of their appearance. For Example:

Little Girl and Boy - Skip along or trudge laboriously up a hillside.

Goat - "Trot" on all fours, occasionally stop to chew and to make "maaaa" goat sounds.

Wolf - Walk slowly on all fours, sit down and howl.

Fox - Walk quickly on all fours, in a zigzag pathway across the floor with nose to the ground; make "yip, yip, yip" sounds.

Hare - "Bunny-hop" on hind legs, or mimic a realistic rabbit hop using first the front then the back legs; sit up straight on hind legs and look alert while "sniffing"; thump with hind legs.

Bee - Tiptoe and move hands quickly at shoulder height like wings, while "buzzing".

Have participants stand in a circle and sing "If You're Happy and You Know It", page 35 . Emphasize both body and facial actions including laughing and crying emotions. Point out how our shoulders shake when we laugh or cry hard.

Activity: *Story Enactment:* Read or tell the story. Set aside a portion of the space as the woods and another portion as the turnip field. Establish the fencerow, between the woods and field, either with a strip of tape, yardstick, blocks or other safe indicator which the goats can jump over.

Ask participants to choose parts and as they do, line the animal characters up in order of entrance along the side of the woods. If you wish to set limits, establish how many participants may choose to be each character. One may state limits such as, "There may be no more than four of any one character."

Narrate the story as it is dramatized.

Jenny, Johnny and the Wolf sat down and cried

Encourage all characters to establish who they are with the previously practiced actions and voice characteristics (i.e., the wolf may "howl", the fox "yip", hare "sniff" and thump back legs to express crying and laughing.).

Caution the goats beforehand that head butting must be done very gently or without actually touching. Encourage a variety of actions from the animals and varied reactions from the goats. For example, the goats might huddle when the wolf howls, scatter when the fox nips at their heels, and kick up their own heels (using great care that they do not kick one another) when the hares thump. The leader can direct these actions by including them in the narration.

Discussion – Sit and discuss the enactment when completed. Did the characters remember to use their voices, their bodies? Did they say the words? What actions made a particular character convincing? Were there any actions or comments out of character? Any dangerous actions? If time allows, re-choose parts and re-enact the story with these suggested improvements in mind.

JOHNNY, JENNY AND THE GOATS

Adapted by Kristen Bissinger from the Norse tale
"Johnny and the Three Goats"

There were once a little boy and girl named Johnny and Jenny who lived in the mountainous land of Norway. Every summer their job was to take care of the goats. Each morning Johnny and Jenny herded the goats up the hill where the grass was thick and there the goats fed and Johnny and Jenny watched them. Every evening all came down home again. One evening Johnny and Jenny were guiding the goats along the path homeward with their shepherd staffs, the goats jumped into a neighbor's turnip field and happily began to eat the turnips. Johnny and Jenny leapt into the field after them. They chased the goats this way and that but they could not get them out of that turnip field. So they sat down beside the road and began to cry. As they cried, out of the woods came a wolf.

"Why are you crying little boy and little girl?" asked the wolf in a deep voice.

"We're crying because we can't get the goats out of the turnip field," wept Johnny and Jenny.

"Oh, *I* can get the goats out of the turnip field," boasted the wolf. So he leapt over the fence and howled at the goats. The goats huddled together but they did not leap over the fence and they did not jump out of the turnip field. The wolf sat down next to Johnny and Jenny and began to cry. As he cried, he howled as wolves do. The three of them sat there crying and out of the woods came a fox.

"Why are you crying?" said the fox in his high yippy voice.

"I cry because the boy and the girl cry," howled the wolf, "and the boy and girl cry because they can't get the goats out of the turnip field."

"Oh, *I* can get the goats out of the turnip field," said the fox. He slid under the fence and ran this way and that, yipping and nipping at their heels. But he could not get the goats out of the turnip field. Exhausted, he sat down next to the wolf and he began to cry with his high whining yips. As they sat there crying, out of the woods came a hare.

The hare hopped up to the fox and asked, "Why are you crying, fox?"

"I cry because the wolf cries, and the wolf cries because the boy and the girl cry, and the boy and the girl cry because they can't get the goats out of the turnip field."

"Oh, I can get the goats out of the turnip field," said the hare as she thumped her back legs. She hopped over the fence and ran around the goats thumping her back legs and dodging this way and that. The goats kicked up their heels but did not jump out of the turnip field. So the hare sat down next to the fox and she began to cry. She sniffed with her whiskery nose and wiped her eyes with her paws. As the five sat there crying, who should come out of the woods but a bee.

The bee flew up to the hare and asked, "Why are you crying, hare?"

"I cry because the fox cries, and the fox cries because the wolf cries and the wolf cries because the boy and the girl cry. The boy and girl cry because they can't get the goats out of the turnip field."

"Oh, I can get the goats out of the turnip field," buzzed the bee.

Everyone stopped crying and looked at the bee. They all began to laugh.

"You can't get the goats out of the turnip field! We're big and we couldn't do it! How could you possibly get the goats out of the turnip field, you're so small?" And they laughed all the harder.

"Just watch and see," said the bee. The goats were quietly munching on the turnips. The bee flew into the turnip field. He flew over to one goat and buzzed in her ear. The goat leapt over the fence and trotted down the road. The bee then flew over to the rest of the goats and buzzed in each of their ears in turn. The goats immediately leapt over the fence and trotted home as fast as they could.

Johnny and Jenny jumped up with delight and relief. They thanked their friends and skipped down the hill after the goats, bringing them safely home.

THE LITTLE SNOW MAIDEN
A Russian Folk Tale

Objective: To introduce Russian culture through story enactment and native folk dance.

Getting Started: This story includes a multitude of wonderful dramatic and dance material. It is suggested that the story be enacted in at least two drama/dance sessions with emphasis on different aspects of the content in each warm-up.

Music to inspire movement can be found in the soundtrack for the Nutcracker Suite and the ballet opera "The Snow Maiden" by the Russian composer Rimsky-Korsakov.

Warm-up: *Warm-up Session #1* — Stretches such as "Juice", page 16 , "Cat and Dog Backs", page 19 , and "Twinkle, Twinkle, Little Star", page 17 , are recommended, but optional.

Adapt "The Copy Hop", page 31 , by requiring that the shared movement be centered around activities in the snow, such as snowball throwing, fort, and snowman building, sledding, skating, pathways in the snow, and snow angels.

Conduct "Jump/Freeze", page 23 , and add to it the action of melting slowly to the ground.

Divide the group into pairs and conduct "Partner Sculpting", page 56 . Introduce the idea that snowmen are sculpture in snow. Roll, shape, and pat the sculptures as if making a snowman.

Warm-up Session #2 — (Optional warm-up for a second enactment session.)

Ask participants to make their movements either quick and sharp, or floaty while dancing to "My Hands Say Hello", page 43 . This exercise in dynamics will assist in the moonlight snow dancing scene as well as the Troika folk dance and snow-play scenes.

Teach the "Troika", a Russian folk dance found on page 126 .

Activity: Ask what the participants know about Russia: What is it? Where is this country located? What is the weather like?, etc. Share some brief information about Russia and inquire if the participants know the meaning of words such as "maiden" and "porridge".

Read or tell the story and have each participant choose the character he or she would like to enact. All participants will enact the story at once. Begin with the parents grouped in one location, the snow maidens in another, and the village children in another space in the room. Explain that the snow maiden can be played by boys and be called a "snow boy" or a "snow child". Designate a place in the room for the house and the remaining space will be the yard.

Encourage variety in the playing scenes by calling out different activities of the children and maiden to do in the snow. Aim for quick, lively movement during the day then light, floating and snow falling movement in the moonlight.

Add to the story the part about the Troika sleigh ride during the second drama/dance session. Involve all the participants in the folk dance as though they are the three horses pulling sleighs.

Use lively and magical segments of music, such as those suggested previously, to inspire playful movement, sad movement, and snow dancing.

After each enactment allow a time for discussion in which the participants can share favorite story parts or enactments and ideas on how the enactment could be improved.

THE LITTLE SNOW MAIDEN
A Russian Folk Tale

Once there lived in a little village in Russia, a good man named Peter and his wife, Anastasia. Now these two were very sad because they had no children in their home.

One day they saw the children out playing in the snow making snow forts, pelting each other with snowballs, and laughing merrily. The children rolled up the snow into a great snow woman; they put an old kerchief on her head and a little old shawl about her shoulders.

"Now, there's an idea, wife," said Peter. "Let us go out and make a little snow girl. Who knows? She might come alive and be a daughter to us!"

"Good!" says the wife. "It's worth trying at least."

So there in the yard they set to work and the children came to help them. They rolled the snow and began to fashion it into a little maiden and toward evening, she was finished.

"Oh, my little snow maid, speak to us!" said Peter and Anastasia.

Suddenly the little maid's eyes opened and she smiled. All at once, she skipped from her place and began laughing softly, dancing like snowflakes whirled in the wind.

Peter and Anastasia were so happy that they laughed and played in the snow with their new daughter and the other children. At night-time the other children went home. The new little family went inside and the mother and father sat their daughter down near the fire to warm her.

"It is too hot in the cottage. I must go out in the cold," said the snow maid.

"No, no," said Anastasia, "it is time I tucked you in in a warm and cozy little bed."

"Oh, no!" said the little snow maiden, "I am a daughter of the Snow. I cannot be tucked up under a blanket. I will play by myself in the yard all night." And out she danced in the moonlight. She leaped and floated like the snowflakes.

For a long time Peter and Anastasia watched her.

Then at last they went to bed, but more than once that night they rose to look out of the window and make sure she had not run away. Each time she was just as before, dancing about in the moonlight or curled up in a snowbank.

In the morning she ran into the cottage and her eyes were shining. Her mother brought her some hot porridge to eat.

"Oh, no!" she said. "I'm a child of the Snow. I can't eat hot food. This is the porridge for me," she cried, and she showed the good woman how to crush up a little piece of ice in a wooden bowl, for that was all she would eat.

After breakfast the snow maiden ran out and joined the other children at play. How she played and how the children loved her! They ice skated, made snow angels, footprints and paths in the snow. Peter got out the three big horses, hitched them to the troika and took all the children for a sleigh ride in the snow.

Thus it went all through the winter. The little snow maiden made Peter and Anastasia very happy. She was forever singing and laughing and dancing in and out of the house. She was very good, too, and she did everything Anastasia told her. Only she would never sleep indoors. She seemed happiest and most at home when the snowflakes were dancing about in the air.

But, when there began to be signs of spring in the air and the snow melted, then the little snow girl seemed to be drooping and longing for something.

One day she came to Peter and Anastasia and said,

> "Time has come when I must go
> To my friends of Frost and Snow.
> Good-bye, dear ones here, good-bye.
> Back I go across the sky!"

Peter and Anastasia began to weep and lament very loudly. They wished to keep her all to themselves and share her with no one else.

"Ah, my darling, you must not go!" cried Peter and Anastasia.

And Peter ran and barred the door while Anastasia put her arms about her darling and held her close up beside the stove.

But even as Anastasia held her tight, she seemed to melt slowly away. At last there was nothing left but a pool of water by the stove. Yet it seemed to Anastasia and Peter as though they saw her still before them with her bright eyes shining, her long hair streaming.

"Oh, stay, stay, stay!" they begged, but all at once the very door that Peter had barred burst open. A cold wind swept into the room; and, when Peter had pushed the door shut again, lo! the little snow maiden had vanished!

Then Peter and Anastasia wept and thought they should never see her again. Often through the summer they longed for their little child and watched sadly as the neighbors' children played. But, when the first snow of winter had come again the two heard a silvery peal of laughter just outside the window.

"That sounds like our little snow maid!" cried Peter, and off he hurried to open the door. Sure enough! Into the room she danced, her eyes shining as she sang:

> "By frosty night and frosty day,
> Your love calls me here to stay,
> Here till Spring I stay and then
> Back to Frost and Snow again!"

So Peter and Anastasia clasped the little snow maid in their arms; so happy were they to see their daughter again. And that is the way it was for them: each Springtime the snow maid went northward to play through the summer with her friends on the frozen seas, but every winter, she stayed in Russia with Peter and Anastasia and they came not to mind her going for they knew she would come again.

Adapted from *My Book House* by Olive Beaupre' Miller, Vol. 4

TROIKA
A Russian Folk Dance

Objective: To learn a folk dance from a foreign country and practice cooperation and coordination with two other partners.

Getting Started: Music for the Troika and other simple folk dances, plus instructions for those dances, can be found on the record "International Folkdance Mixer", by Gateway Records, Stereo GSLP 3528. If this or other records containing the Troika are unavailable, it can be danced to music with a lively count of fours accompanied by the tambourine, drum or other instrument. Explain to the group that a "troika" is a Russian sleigh drawn by three horses and this dance was inspired by such sleighs. The following is an explanation of steps involved in the Russian folk dance as well as possible simplification for younger participants.

Teach the dance, one segment at a time, working through the more difficult movements carefully. Do not have the teams run in different directions as in Segment I (below), unless the teams of three can

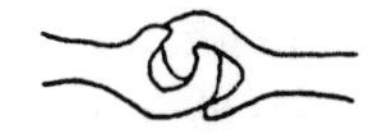

Proper hand holding

Troika dance

first run together in one direction. Allow teams that have mastered the bridges in Segment II (below) to help other teams that may be having difficulty. Regroup teams so that the center dancer can lead the team, if necessary.

Practice Segments I and II a number of times before adding Segment III.

Activity: Have participants divide into teams of three members each. These members stand side by side all facing counter-clockwise the direction that they will travel in a large circle with the other teams. Traditionally each team consists of two women on either side of one man, but teams in this version can be formed with any three participants holding hands. (Note simplified versions at the end of each segment.)

All teams progress around the floor counter-clockwise in a large circle and perform the following dance steps:

Count	*Segment I*
1 - 4	• Starting with the right foot, run four steps forward, diagonally to the right.
5 - 8	• Turn left and run four steps forward, diagonally to the left.
9 - 16	• Run eight steps forward following the large circle pathway.

Simplified version: In teams of three, run or prance counter-clockwise around the circle in time to the music for sixteen counts (with no diagonal pathways).

Count — **Segment II**

1 - 8 • The three members of each team remain holding hands. Both the center member and the member closest to the inside of the circle raise their arms and make an arch or "bridge" while the outside member runs *forward, under* the arch, and *around* the center member to return to his original place. The center member completes the motion by also passing *under* the arch to his left and back to his original position. Team members continue to hold hands throughout this segment.

9 -16 • Center and outside members raise arms and make an arch while the inside member runs *forward, under* the arch. The center member follows again *under* the arch as before and returns to original position.

Simplified version: Practice this "under the bridge" move several times prior to the dance. Continually encourage participants to hold fingers gently and loosely so that they can let their hands slide around each other during this part. If they hold hands too tightly, arms and wrists will be twisted and the move will appear awkward.

Count — **Segment III**

1-12 • Each team of three joins hands in a small circle and takes twelve little running steps to their left.

13 - 16 • Stop and stamp feet three times while standing in place.

17 - 28 • Each team turns and circles to their right with twelve running steps.

29-32 • Again stamp feet three times while each team opens out their small circle into their line of three in the big circle ready to repeat Segments I and II.

THE RIGHT TIME TO LAUGH
An Australian Folk Tale

Objective: To explore humor through dance and mime while enacting an Australian tale involving many of the unusual animals of that country.

Getting Started: Discuss with the participants what animals live in Australia and this country's location on the globe.

Have a discussion about what makes for a humorous situation. Some participant suggestions have been: surprise or the unexpected, falling down, funny faces, funny body posture or positions, wiggling, fat tummies or bottoms, feet in the air, tying oneself in knots, imitation and contrast.

Warm-up: Follow "The Copy Hop" format, page 31 , but focus on funny movements and substitute the words: "Here's to __________ and the way she does The Funny (or Silly) Hop."

Have participants sit down in a circle formation and ask volunteers to share a funny face for others to copy.

Practice "No Bumping", page 23 , and "OK Bumping", page 23 and then divide the group into partners to practice bumping and falling down. Encourage variation with suggestions such as, "Do a silly walk and a silly bump and fall. Do a snooty or uptight walk then bump and fall. Try a backwards walk, then surprise bump and jump."

Activity: Read or tell the story "The Right Time to Laugh". Have participants choose the part they wish to play or have the group remain in partners and ask each pair to decide which one of them will play the frog and which the lyrebird. In this situation ask each lyrebird to also enact another funny animal during the scene when all the animals try to get the frog to laugh.

Enact the story with narration, discuss what worked and what did not. Switch parts and re-enact. The narrator may incorporate appropriate funny activities suggested by the participants.

If large scarves are available they may be used to represent the water swallowed by the frog. The scarves may then be stuffed under the shirts of those enacting the frog to give the funny puffed-out effect of all the water he has swallowed.

If time and interest permit, one half the group may watch as the other half performs the story and vice versa.

THE RIGHT TIME TO LAUGH
An Australian Folk Tale

In a dense Australian thicket, a lyrebird scratching in the ground, once found a choice bit of food. So he spread his tail and rejoiced.

Just then along came a frog. "Good morning, friend," said the frog, and he sat very solemnly by, waiting to be invited to eat a share of the feast. But the lyrebird took his food and flew up into a tree.

"My friend," said the frog, feeling injured," yesterday you dined with me, haven't you one morsel to spare for me today?"

"Certainly!" said the lyrebird, for he did not wish to appear so greedy as he was! "You may have a bite of my food. Just come right up and get it!"

"I can't come up," said the frog. "I've no wings with which to fly, and my feet were not made for climbing."

But the lyrebird, looking about, spied a vine trailing down from the tree with one end on the ground.

"Take hold of the vine," said he, "and I will pull you up." So the frog caught hold of the vine and the lyrebird pulled him up slowly until he was on a level with the branch where the lyrebird was sitting.

"I thank you, my friend," said the frog, and he was about to hop down beside the food he desired, when the lyrebird let go of the vine and dropped the frog – plump! – to the ground. Then the lyrebird, thinking he had played a very fine joke on his friend, laughed and laughed and laughed and he ate his dinner up all by himself.

But the frog was very angry. He sat down below and sulked, thinking of nothing but the trick which the lyrebird had played on him.

"Well, I'll pay him back!" the frog told himself. "I'll pay him back, I will!"

So he hopped to the neighboring river, where the lyrebird got his water, and he drank and drank and drank. He drank till he swallowed not only all the water in that river, but all the water in all the rivers and all the lakes in Australia! Then he sat, quite puffed out with the water he had swallowed, and

solemnly blinked his eyes.

Soon the lyrebird wanted a drink, but where was he to get it? There wasn't a river to turn to! The lyrebird got thirstier and thirstier until he was half crazy for want of a drink of water. At least he was sufficiently punished for the wicked prank he had played to be very sorry for what he had done. And alas! He wasn't the only one who suffered; for not a beast or a bird in all Australia could get a drink of water. One by one, they went to the frog and begged him to give out the waters. Dingo, the wild dog, went; Spiny, the anteater, went; Flying-fox, the great bat, went. And they said:

"Great frog, the lyrebird has done you wrong, but now he is very sorry and you are making us suffer who did you no wrong at all. Give forth the water, we pray you."

But still the great frog sulked and would not answer a word. Then the lyrebird himself went before him and humbly begged his pardon. But the frog held, stubborn as ever, to the memory of his wrongs and he would not forgive the lyrebird. He sat as puffed up as before and solemnly blinked his eyes.

Then the great black swan went before him, and the white eagle, and emu, and all the other birds and beasts. But no matter how they besought him, he would not give back the water. So at length the birds and the beasts all got together and said:

"If the old frog only knew how ridiculous he is sulking away like that, he would laugh at himself; then the waters would gush from his mouth."

"Ah!" cried the anteater. "If that is the case, let us *make* him laugh and give up the rivers."

So they all stood in a circle about the solemn old frog and performed their funniest antics. First, they brought out the duck-billed mole, and a funny enough fellow he was! They backed him up to the frog and from the mole's furry back, Mr. Frog expected, of course, to see the face of a beast. Then they turned the mole around quickly. Lo, there was the face of a bird with a flat, absurd bill like a duck's in the place where his snout ought to be! But as funny as this looked it did not make the frog laugh. The koalas bumped into each other and fell down, the flying-fox flew in dramatic circles nearly colliding with the frog himself. Still the frog would not open his mouth. The kangaroo hopped this way and that, the dingo dog chased his tail, the emu walked his funny walk with his neck moving forward and back but the frog never smiled the least smile.

At last they brought out an eel, and that was a happy thought. The eel stood up on the tip of his long, long tail and he danced. He wiggled and wriggled and twisted. At that the frog's mouth began all at once to turn up, his lips began to twitch, his nose began to wrinkle, and all of a sudden – Hah! He opened his mouth big and wide and he let out a mighty laugh. He laughed and he laughed and he laughed; and, as he laughed, the waters gushed forth from his mouth and filled up all the rivers and all the lakes in Australia.

"I was a silly old frog to sulk like that!" he cried.

Then the lyrebird, and the wild dog, and the anteater, and the flying-fox, and the koalas, and the black swan, and the white eagle, and the emu, and the duck-billed mole, and the kangaroo all hurried to get the drink which they so sorely needed.

Adapted from *My Book House*, Vol. 3, by Olive Beaupre' Miller

THE STONECUTTER
A Japanese Folk Tale

Objective: To develop the use of the chorus by exploring group scene creation through body sculpting and scarves.

Getting Started: The leader may wish to hear the participants' ideas on what the word "power" brings to mind. This story may be linked to a study of power, nature, appreciation, geology, etc.

Warm-up: Give a preliminary reading of "The Stone Cutter", then conduct some stretches with participants to limber up bodies and get them into a physical mode.

Adapt the use of scarves as described in "Multipurpose Scarves: Environments", page 54, to illustrate the wind, rain, clouds, and sun.

Conduct "Characterization Locomotion", page 27, and include in the study the Spirit of the Mountain, members of the prince's procession (dancers,

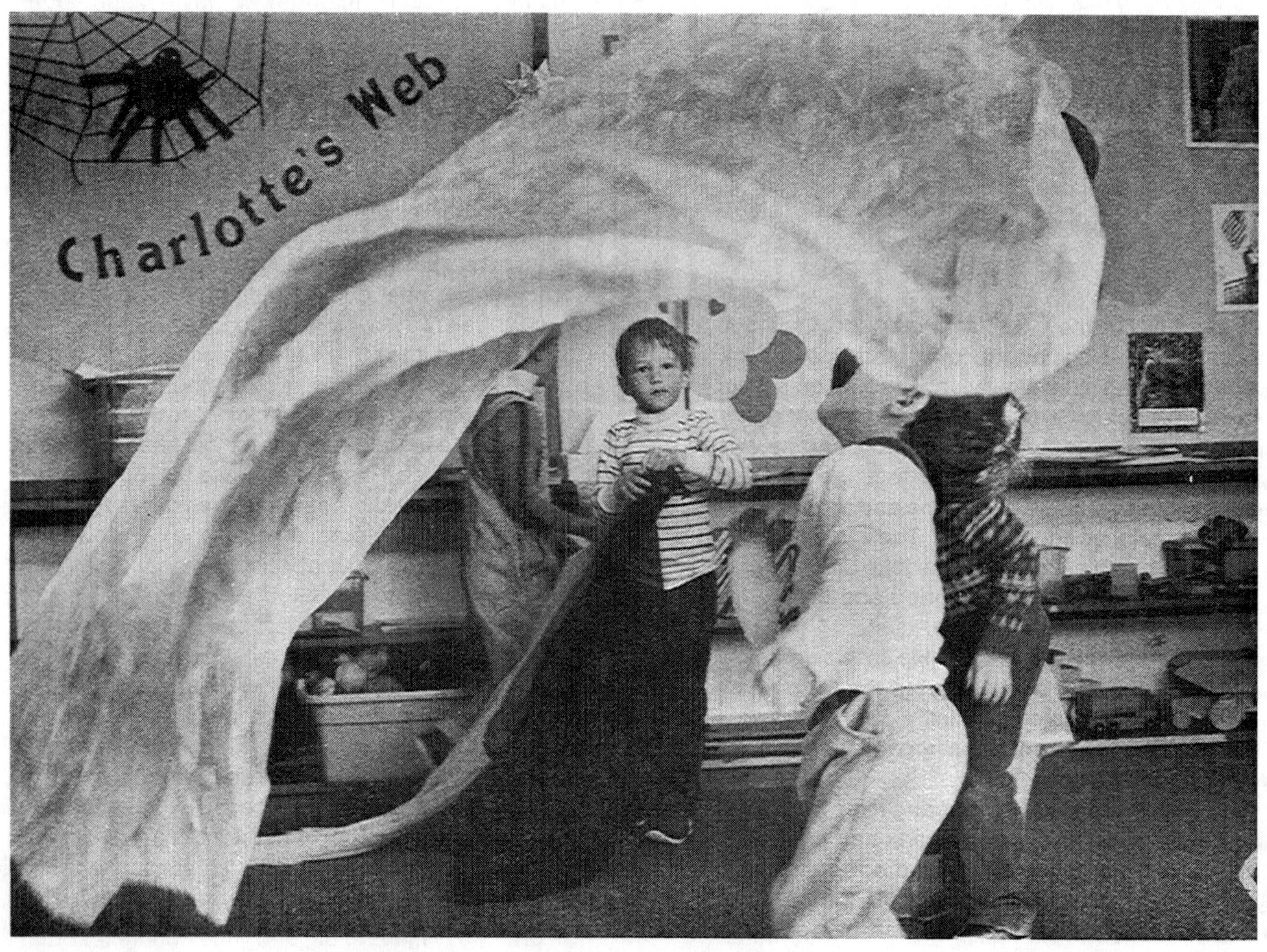

"Tasaku became the cloud...

soldiers, courtiers), the prince's stately walk (use scarf for costume — turban, sash, cape, etc.). This may be done at random in the room, or from one side of the room to the other as in locomotion exercises.

Adapt "Instant Scenery", page 61 , to the story. Separate the participants into several groups. Whisper to each group an environment or aspect of climate needed in portraying the story: garden of flowers, farmers tending crops, desert, flood, and mountain. Ask each group to create and share with the class a still group sculpture based on these ideas to bring to life with movement, such as plants sprouting or a flood sweeping away crops and cattle.

Activity: *Story Enactment* – Start by enacting the first scene in the story. Ask the participants to form into three groups:

- *Group 1* – Enacts the stone cutter, Tasaku
- *Group 2* – Plays the chorus
- *Group 3* – Represents the Spirit of the Mountain

Have the members of the chorus choose among: the prince, soldiers, servants with fans, dancers, acrobats, musicians, and horses. Arrange the procession in groupings of similar role types, first the soliders, next servants and the prince, dancers , musicians, etc.

In the space, establish the location for the mountain, and Spirit of the Mountain, Tasaku , and the route that the prince and his procession will take. For example, around the perimeter of the room, or diagonally from one corner to another.

Pass out scarves for each member to use as he chooses, to help establish his character.

Begin the narration with all the Tasaku actors performing stone cutting actions.

Consider adding live or recorded music to announce each of the groups in the procession as they go by Tasaku. Pause with each part of the procession to allow time for the group members to perform. They can also perform when: Tasaku wakes up as the prince; the dancers dance; the soldiers march and stand guard; the musicians sit or dance while they play; and the servants fan, clothe and feed Tasasku.

At this point have participants stop activity to sit down and discuss what worked and how to better the enactment. Either re-enact the story or con-

...with his new power he made violent storms."

tinue narration as Tasaku, now a prince, walks in his garden and enjoys the flowers. Enact the scene with the strong sun wilting the blossoms. (Both the sun and the flowers are enacted by the chorus.)

Each time, after Tasaku asks to become the prince, the sun or other powerful form, he lies down to sleep. As he sleeps the Spirit of the Mountain dances, weaves his magic spell and transforms Tasaku. Play some live or recorded music to inspire movement. After each dance the Tasaku characters wake up as a new form.

Continue the story as Tasaku goes through various stages and the Spirit of the Mountain dances to transform him. With each transformation the chorus plays all the parts needed, whether representing scenery or characters, such as the sun and garden, the flood victims, etc. Stop the action at any time with a freeze to help establish order or to share the fun of seeing the action as a still tableau. If the participants are not staying in character, these still moments can serve as reminders.

Have the chorus members play the final stone cutter(s) as they chip away at Tasaku, the mountain. To help make a strong ending, have the stone cutter chip and then freeze in an action pose as the mountain (Tasaku) trembles in his realization that his original position of "lowly" stonecutter was a position of great power after all.

Call for discussion. Ask, what worked well? What convincing characterizations did you see or hear? How could the enactment be done better next time?

THE STONECUTTER

A Japanese Folk Tale
by Gerald McDermott

Tasaku was a lowly stonecutter. Each day the sound of his hammer and chisel rang out as he chipped away at the foot of the mountain. He hewed the blocks of stone that formed the great temples and palaces.

He asked for nothing more than to work each day, and this pleased the spirit who lived in the mountains.

One day, a prince went by. Soldiers preceded him, musicians and dancers followed him. He was clothed in beautiful silk robes, and his servants carried him aloft. Tasaku watched until the magnificent procession had passed out of sight.

Tasaku cut no more stone and returned to his hut. He envied the prince. He looked up into the sky and *wished* aloud that he might have such great wealth. Then he slept. The spirit who lived in the mountains heard him ... and that night transformed the stonecutter into a prince.

Tasaku was overjoyed! He lived in a palace and wore robes of the finest silk. Musicians played for him and servants bowed low. He commanded great armies and ruled over the land.

Every afternoon Tasaku walked in his garden. He loved the fragrant petals and graceful vines. But the sun burned his flowers. He knelt over the withered blossoms and saw the power of the sun.

Tasaku wanted to be as powerful, so he *asked* the spirit who lived in the mountains to change him into the sun. The spirit heard him. Tasaku became the sun, and he was happy for a time. To show his power he burned the fields and parched the lands. The people begged for water.

Then a cloud came and covered him, and the bright rays of the sun were obscured. Tasaku then knew the cloud was even more powerful than the sun. He *told* the spirit to change him into a cloud. The spirit heard him. Tasaku became the cloud. With his new power he made violent storms. Thunder rolled across the sky, rivers overran their banks, fields were flooded, huts and palaces were washed away.

But the mountain remained. Tasaku was angry because the mountain was more powerful than the cloud. "Make me into the mountain!" Tasaku *demanded.* The spirit obeyed and then departed, for there was nothing more he could do.

Tasaku became the mountain. He was more powerful than the prince, stronger than the sun, mightier than the cloud.

But Tasaku felt the sharp sting of a chisel. It was a lowly stonecutter, chipping away at his feet. Deep inside, he trembled.

Published by Viking Press, New York, 1975.

GLUSKABYE AND WATER GUARD

A Penobscot Native American Tale

Objective: To expose the participants to a Native American myth that can be enacted in conjunction with studies of water, conservation, dam building, amphibians, fish and aquatic life, drought, sharing, and Native American tribes.

Start by telling the tale so the participants can envision the characters and action as they prepare with the warm-ups and discussion.

Getting Started: Discuss the ages and occupations that might exist in an ancient Native American village. There are babies, children, teens, adults and older people. Activities might include hunting, water carrying and food gathering, cooking, clothing construction, weaving, pottery and basketry, tool making, dancing, joking, story telling, etc.

Discuss what animals live in a creek or river, such as fish, frogs , and turtles.

Warm-up: Start with a locomotion exercise to fit the story:

- *Run joyfully*
- *Run weakly*
- *Walk proudly and bravely*
- *Walk frightened*
- *Hop like a frog*
- *Roll and tumble downstream*

Adapt "Guess-Who-I-Am, page 37 , to concentrate on pantomiming activities in a Native American village. Ask for volunteers and have others guess each pantomimed activity. Finish by having everyone try a widemouthed, bulgy eyed, tongue flicking, giant frog face.

"Action/Reaction", page 63 , will be invaluable for the fight scene. Focus on some of the actions mentioned in the tale: Water Guard thrusting out his tongue or powerful legs, Gluskabye swinging a tomahawk or shooting arrows which Water Guard must deflect. Have the group work in teams of two, each team experimenting with its own action/reaction strategy for the Gluskabye and Water Guard fight. Remind the participants that though Water Guard reacts, he does not move from the spot where he is holding back the water. Share some of the fight sequences with two or three couples performing at once, while the others watch.

Activity: *Story Enactment* – Plan the locations of the village, the forest in which Gluskabye travels, the direction of the river, and Water Guard's territory.

Have particpants choose parts and gather in the proper locations. Those who choose to be Indians must establish the ages and activities of their characters and whether they intend to be transformed into a water creature or remain human. Encourage participants to group themselves in lodges, family units, or activity groups (hunters or weavers in one spot, a family in another, etc.). Encourage establishment of character through pantomime and actions.

Gluskabye expressing anger at Water Guard

Pair the Gluskabyes with those playing Water Guard. If there is more of one character than the other, indicate the order of action, such as: Gluskabye #1 will fight the first round of the battle, Gluskabye #2 the middle section and Gluskabye #3 the final fight sequence. Only the fight sequence will need this order, the rest of the story can be played in unison by those that choose main parts.

Retell the story as participants enact it. Actions such as using the tomahawk and other props can be pantomimed. For control, the leader may freeze the action in the fight sequence, the transformation by water sequence or whenever necessary.

Finish the enactment with a mid-action freeze.

Discuss and, if time allows, re-enact. Consider two one-hour periods or one two-hour period. This will give plenty of time for the warm-ups, some character development and re-enactment. You may, of course, take more time and work in greater depth or prepare it for presentation to parents or other classes. If you can allot only a one-hour session, choose the locomotion and action/reaction exercises and don't plan to re-enact it.

Extended Activity: Have paticipants together to form group sculptures of various imagery related to this tale: Water Guard, totem pole, canoe, lodge.

"GLUSKABYE AND WATER GUARD"
A Penobscot Native American Tale adapted by Kristen Bissinger

Gluskabye, the hero of the Penobscot Indians of Maine, traveled far and wide in the lands of his people. One day on his journeys he came upon a village where the people were sad and weak.

"Why are you so sad and why are you so weak?" he asked them.

"There is a giant, monstrous frog named Water Guard who has blocked up the source of our water and will not let us drink."

Then Gluskabye spoke: "This is not right. No one can keep water for themselves alone. It must be shared. I will go speak to this Water Guard. I will reason with him. If need be, I will fight him. I will right this wrong." And Gluskabye headed out in the direction that the villagers indicated would lead him to Water Guard.

When he came upon the site he found a monstrously large frog holding back the river's flow. "Why do you keep this water for yourself alone? My people are in need. It is not right that one should have the use of water, leaving others to die of thirst." said Gluskabye.

"I'm big. I need all this water for myself. I care not for your people. I care only for myself," croaked Water Guard.

"Then we must fight," said Gluskabye. And he prepared his weapons. The battle was long and hard. Gluskaybye used his bow and arrows. Water Guard used his long and sticky tongue.

Gluskabye used his tomahawk. Water Guard used his powerful legs. At one point Gluskabye broke the neck of Water Guard but still Water Guard did not budge. So Gluskabye cut down a mighty birch and it fell on Water Guard.

With that blow Water Guard was defeated. He rolled down the riverbed, pushed by the onrushing water.

The villagers who had come to witness the fight leapt with joy. They dashed into the water. They drank; they splashed; they swam. Then suddenly, those who had touched the water were transformed into water creatures. Those that had not yet reached the waters' bank, gasped to see their relatives: mothers, fathers, sisters, brothers, grandparents, transformed into frogs, fishes, snakes, and salamanders.

"What is this?" they cried. "How can this be? What are we to do? Gluskabye you are great, you must tell us what to do."

"These magical powers come from Water Guard, but the power of good has defeated him and the waters will naturally purify themselves. We must wait as the river flows and I will be the first to test the purified waters." After awhile Gluskabye stepped forward and took a long drink. He remained human and timidly the villagers tested the water themselves. They, also, remained human and are today the Penobscot Indians. Their river: the Penobscot River.

PANDORA'S BOX
A Greek Myth

Objective: To introduce one of the Greek myths and inspire further research of this fascinating culture.

Getting Started: First conduct teh Warm-ups found below, then proceed with the following:

Familiarize the participants with background information about the characters involved in Pandora's story. Read or tell the story of Pandora to the group. An excellent source book for Greek mythology is the award-winning *D'Alaire's Book of Greek Myths*. Discuss the various miseries that may have come out of Pandora's box or jar.

A large cardboard appliance box may be used as Pandora's box. Make openings on both ends of the box and lay the box on the floor so that participants may crawl in one end and out the other when the front flap or door is opened by Pandora. The jar or box may also be represented by a scarf covering each misery, or all the miseries collectively. Or, it may be represented by a designated spot or corner of the space from which each or all the miseries are unleashed.

Warm-up: Conduct "Shapes", page 56 , "If You're Happy and You Know it", page 35 , or "Guess-How-I-Feel", page 36 , to help prepare for misery enactments.

Discuss various miseries and evils of this world.

Brainstorm a list of words describing forms of misery or evil. For example:

Greed	*Distrust*	*Accusation*
Thoughtlessness	*Fear*	*Cruelty*
Vanity	*Lies*	*Spite*
Slander	*Drudgery*	*Teasing*
Envy	*Gossip*	*Prejudice*

Participants will also suggest specific examples which may be listed under these more general titles. Examples of this might be: "When someone trips you" (teasing), "When Joe took four of the five cookies" (greed or thoughtlessness).

Combine the shapes and emotions exercises by asking participants to depict the miseries through appropriate body shapes and facial expressions. As teh leader calls out some examples from the compiled list the participants must strike an instantaneous pose depicting the misery. The shapes may be abstract or may utilize pantomime characterization. Effective examples can be shared individually or in small groups for teh class to see.

Continue by taking these shapes into action with the "Characterization Locomotion" exercise, page 27 . Practice strong and powerful, as well as gentle, graceful movements through this exercise, to be utilized in depicting the fire god and the love goddess characters.

Next, have each participant find a partner and proceed with the "Partner Sculpting" exercise, page 56 . Contrast contorted shapes with beautiful and graceful poses.

Activity: Have participants choose partners and spread out in the space. One partner in each pair will enact Pandora and the other will enact all the other characters as they take action in the story: Hephaestus, Athena, Aphrodite, Zeus, Hermes, Epimetheus and one of the miseries. For enactment of the story's climax, each misery can work individually with his or her partner or those playing the miseries can group together to come out of a large box, scarf, or one spot in the space designated as "the box".

If males express embarrassment or difficulty in playing the female roles, mention that in Greek theatre, all roles, male and female, were played by men and boys. If they find it easier, males can ignore the maleness or femaleness of the character and concentrate on a character's other qualities such as "curiosity" for Pandora or "wisdom" for Athena. This may, of course, be applied to females playing male parts as well.

Challenge those participants with multiple roles to create gestures, movements and voices to match

Distrust

each character they play. Between each new role, they may walk away from their Pandora and re-enter the scene with the walk and demeanor of the new character to be portrayed. These transitions may be cued with a musical instrument such as a drum, cymbal or rattle.

Scarves may be used as impromptu costuming to aid in developing characters (see "Multipurpose Scarves": costumes, in the Primary Tools Section).

Narrate the story of Pandora from her creation to the releasing of the miseries while it is enacted by all the partners.

After one enactment, discuss what worked well and why it was successful. Then discuss what did not work so well and how the enactment could be improved. Re-enact the story with partners changing roles, those who played Pandora enacting the multiple roles and vice versa.

Extended Activity: If interest is high, Pandora's Box may be re-enacted as a group, rather than partner formation, with participants taking the individual roles in the story.

PANDORA'S BOX
A Greek Myth

Greek mythology involves a large and complicated array of gods and goddesses. The stories of their adventures answered for the Greek people such questions as "Who created humankind?" and "How did evil originate?" The following story addresses both these questions.

Zeus, the main god of the Greeks, gave Prometheus and Epimetheus, two brothers who were minor gods, the task of creating living beings. Epimetheus formed animals quickly out of clay and gave them the strongest attributes: teeth, strength, speed, sharp eyesight and warm fur. Prometheus modeled humankind from what was left, and feeling sorry for his creations he stole fire from the gods to aid the humans.

Zeus was very angry at Prometheus for this act and set about to teach him and his human beings a lesson. Zeus ordered Hephaestus, the god of metal smiths and fire to form a beautiful woman named Pandora. The strong Hephaestus modeled Pandora in the likeness of Aphrodite, the beautiful goddess of love, then he called on Athena, the goddess of wisdom, to breathe life into this new woman.

Zeus endowed Pandora with insatiable curiosity, gave her a sealed jar and warned her never to open it. Then Hermes, the mischievous and merry herald of the gods, brought Pandora to earth and offered her in marriage to Epimetheus. Epimetheus was dazzled by this beautiful woman but soon after their marriage Pandora could not resist opening the jar for just a peek. Out swarmed a horde of evils that were as yet unknown to humankind. Horrified, Pandora replaced the lid in time to keep Hope from flying away thereby protecting Hope from destruction by the evils. Mortals were stung and bitten by these miseries and became infested with evil attributes rather than chastened into good behavior as Zeus had hoped.

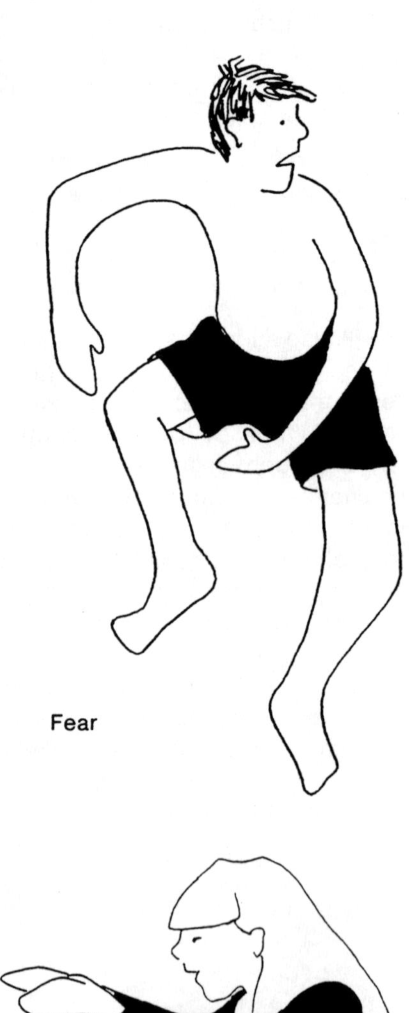

Fear

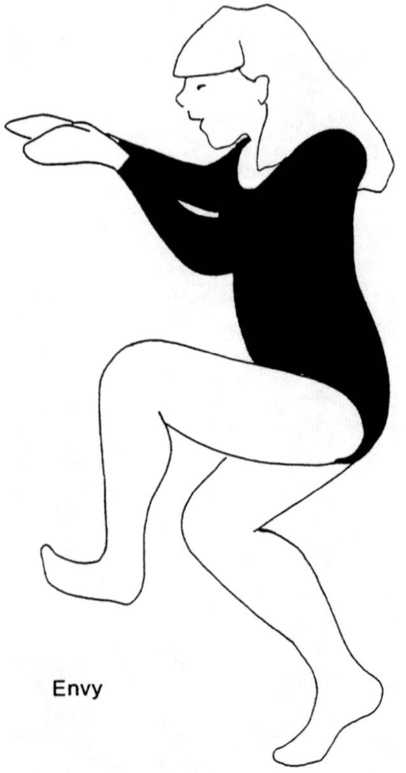

Envy

SCIENCE

A class field trip

Introduction To Science

Science, with its marvelous diversity and dynamics, offers great material for interpretation through drama/dance enactment. Science concepts are particularly suitable for movement activities because many scientific principles intrinsically involve motion and transformation, as do drama/dance. The "dance of life" is found everywhere as we study the nature of our universe. Atoms, for instance, have structured movement patterns similar to the structures found in folk dance: traveling, coupling, separation, re-coupling, spinning, circling, etc. Because movement manifests the laws of physics it follows that elementary physics such as levers, action/reaction, friction, inertia, can be meaningfully and playfully taught through dance activities.

The authors of this book feel a sense of elated discovery in realizing how compatible Science and movement activities are in their interconnectedness. Students can interpret through drama/dance such ideas as the motion of orbiting planets or molecules, animal behavior, shifting land masses and flowing air currents, to name a few. Through these mediums, participants can illustrate everyday Science concepts such as the transformation of a seedling to a fully bloomed flower, a boulder eroding over eons of time into small stones, water evaporating and condensing, or the alignment of iron atoms in a magnet.

With warm-ups, factual data and imagination, these ideas and others can be easily enacted through drama/dance. Science lessons can thus become highly energized, reinforced and internalized. The activities in this section are designed to clarify scientific facts and processes using a kinesthetic approach.

Not only are movement and physics inextricably connected, but it is through the medium of drama/dance that humans have historically strengthened the feelings of "becoming one" with nature. Through drama, dance, and ritual, early peoples enacted and communicated an understanding of their natural environment, those in it, and the universe as well. They stressed the importance of maintaining a balance with all beings and with the forces of nature. As teachers, we can learn by this example and can help nurture this feeling of connectedness in present day students. By "becoming" the active factor – the caterpillar spinning its cocoon, the plant giving off oxygen – the student dances and enacts, through conscious use of the basic elements of dance, these Science lessons. Once the students experience this "becoming one" through movement and become familiar with this exciting method of working, new avenues for learning open in the Science classroom.

This Science Section is divided into three major categories: *Life, Physical,* and *Earth* Science, and within each category the activities are arranged according to difficulty. Please note, that it is very important for the participants to become familiar with some of the simpler games and warm-up exercises as found in Primary Tools in Section One before moving on to the Science activities.

The teacher will soon note that some of the warm-ups found in the Primary Tools are particularly well matched to Science lessons. For instance, the "Push/Pull" exercise is highly suited to illustrate lessons as magnetism, friction, fission, simple motors and gravity. "Body Sculpting" techniques can be employed to create instant and exciting natural environments such as jungles and deserts as well as illustrate an interesting array of scientific topics such as molecular and rock forms, machines, insects, dinosaurs, and other Science related material. However, it is important that the teacher first convey fact curriculum related information prior to conducting Science activities in which the participants must accurately imitate a form as complicated as say, a grasshopper. Prepared with anatomical information, such as the description of a grasshopper's body parts, plus "Group Sculpting" techniques, the grasshopper can be re-created kinesthetically and accurately in the classroom.

Note, also, the use of colorful scarves, vividly incorporated in numerous Science activities. "The Elements" activity, through which the four elements; earth air, fire, and water, can be effectively and dynamically portrayed with scarves is an excellent example. Nature's forces of flowing air currents, flickering fires, shifting continental plates and or undulating waves are learned about through scarves with enthusiasm.. Scarves add a magical touch and an enriching dimension to teaching and the leader should feel free to introduce them from time to time for color alone or, as an extension of movement possibilities.

Thus, through a multi-media drama/dance approach, the study of Science can be an involving and energizing learning experience. The ideas explored in this section on Science are meant to be "eye-openers" and express only a partial list of the diverse topics that can be taught through drama/dance techniques. It is hoped that the individual teacher will quickly discover how additional Science concepts can be taught using these mediums.

Some topics are best taught by more traditional methods, but, for those areas that are suitable, this approach can encourage interest and observation, facilitate information retention, and provide a challenging way for students to learn Science concepts.

INSECTS

Objective: To enact the caterpillar, cocoon and butterfly metamorphosis through the popular story *The Very Hungry Caterpillar,* by Eric Carle. It may be used along with a study of insects or adapted to an activity on healthy eating habits.

Warm-up: Conduct the exercise "Juice", page 16 . Instruct participants that while picking and squeezing the fruits in this exercise that they are also to pantomime eating them. Have participants show the size and shape of the fruit with their hands. Ask them," Is the fruit hard to bite or soft and juicy? Is it bitter or sweet? Did you find any worms in your apple?"

Follow this up with some locomotion exercises based on those found in Section One. Include various caterpillar crawls, such as: Wriggling on the floor from side to side; with bottom in the air

- Walking with tiny hand and foot movements
- Walking forward with hands, and then forward with feet to meet the hands "inch-worm" style
- Roll across the floor as though very fat

- Fly and flutter like a butterfly

Activity: Tell the story *The Very Hungry Caterpillar* by Eric Carle. Have everyone find their own spot in the room. Ask all participants to act out the part of the caterpillar, individually, and while in unison as you retell the story.

Start actions with: "Show me how teeny you can all be curled up inside your egg in the moonlight." In the text, when the sun comes up make a broad gesture to indicate the sun – warm and big. Encourage action with comments such as: "How do you look when you are very hungry?", and "As you start on your journey to look for food use your caterpillar walk. Sway your head and use your feelers to sense food." Continue the text as participants act out all the eating segments, then concentrate on how a caterpillar would squiggle and squirm with a bellyache.

After caterpillars eat through their leaves prompt participants to show how fat they have gotten. Continue to emphasize action with directives such as: "Now, show me how you spin or make your cocoon. Do you use your fingers? Nose? Toes? Within your

Butterfly group sculpture

cocoon show me how you are changing. Now, nibble your way out of your cocoon, unfold and pump your wings up, dry yourself off and try out your wings."

Extended Activity: Add scarves and music to this story enactment for additional enrichment. Place the scarves in the room while the caterpillars are eating. One scarf can be "eaten" by each participant. To achieve this illusion, the eaten scarf is stuffed in each participant's shirt to help make him or her appear fat. Later it may be transformed into the cocoon and then finally, the wings.

Plan a field trip early in the fall or in late spring. Arrange to have the group go on an outing to look for and gather various *safe* insects. The leader must familiarize him or herself with the local insects in order to conduct an insect search with the least amount of fear yet proper respect for local insect life. Carefully overturn rocks, logs or other places where they might be hiding, if these are considered harmless locations for children to search in your area.

Be prepared with jars with perforated lids and small insect nets for capturing live insects for observation and to release later.

Observe and point out to the class the differences and similarities among diverse insects and also between spiders and insects. After discussing insects' various body parts, such as legs, feelers and mouthparts, divide the class into smaller groups. Have each group decide on an insect to portray and create an insect sculpture as described in "Group Sculptures", page   . The rest of the class can observe and guess what insect is being represented with its accompanying actions and formation.

• Other popular stories that include insects may be enacted in a similar manner as described above:

– *The Grouchy Ladybug, The Very Busy Spider,* and *The Honeybee and the Robber,* by Eric Carle.
– *Clickety Cricket,* by Garry and Vesta Smith.
Scenes from *Charlotte's Web,* by Garth Williams.

Also books that include factual information for children make appropriate study, such as:

– *When Insects Are Babies,* by Gladys Conklin.
– *Ladybug, Ladybug, Fly Away Home,* by Judy Hawes.

ANIMALS AND HABITATS

Objective: To study animals and their habitats through story enactment.

Getting Started: Discuss with the class what animals live in your local area (woods, fields, water, buildings, etc.) or in a particular habitat under study (arctic, jungle, ocean, Australia, etc.).

Warm-up: Conduct the "Animal Walk" exercise found on page 29 . Concentrate on animals discussed or in habitat being studied. Stop the action partway across the floor and direct the participants through various animal pantomime such as: finding food, eating, sleeping, self-cleaning, listening, watching and playing. Direct the action with a scenario built around fast and slow locomotion such as, "The rabbit stops, he sits up on his back legs and sniffs the air, he stands alert, he slowly hops (first front legs and then back legs), then nibbles some clover, sits up, then dashes in a zigzag pattern across the field."

Prepare other warm-up activities appropriate to the individual story to be enacted, such as fast and slow locomotion for "The Tortoise and the Hare", specific pantomime activities or emotional exploration as found in Primary Tools.

Activity: Choose a story for the group to enact that includes some natural aspects of, or qualities attributed to, an animal you wish the group to study.

Tell the story, enact, discuss and re-enact it with the group. Discuss the characteristics of the animal characters in the story and how they may or may not reflect scientific reality, if factual information is part of your goal.

Animal story suggestions:
> *Dreaming Bunny* and *The Golden Egg Book*
> (rabbit and duck) both by Margaret Wise Brown

> Selections from *Aesop's Fables,* such as:
> "The Tortoise and the Hare"
> "The Fox and the Crow"
> "Wolf in Sheep's Clothing"
> "The City Mouse and the Country Mouse"
> "Brer Rabbit and the Tar Baby"
> by Uncle Reemis
> "Fox Went Out One Chilly Night",
> traditional song
> *Who Speaks for Wolf?*
> by Paula Underwood Spencer
> "Peter and the Wolf"
> Russian folk tale
> *Bombal Das,*
> Pakistani story told by Ashrat Siddiqui

"The Right Time to Laugh"
Australian tale found in *My Book House,* vol. III
by Olive Beaupre' Miller.

Studying habitats

PREDATOR AND PREY

Objective: To use sound to introduce the concept of predator and prey within the study of animals.

Getting Started: Discuss predators and prey with the group. Have the group name some examples of this relationship.

Warm-up: Conduct "Share-A-Sound", page 32 . After this exercise, concentrate on exploration of animal sounds. Determine four predators to be used for this activity and select one prey for each predator. Choose a sound from participants' suggestions to identify each of these eight characters. Call out each animal's name and have participants respond with a the appropriate sound. For example:

Predator	*Prey*
1. Fox (yip)	Chicken (cluck)
2. Wolf (howl)	Duck (quack)
3. Hawk (squawk)	Mouse (squeak)
4. Snake (hiss)	Frog (croak)

Activity: Divide the class in half, one half represents predators and the other half, prey. Divide each half into four subgroups representing animals as listed above. Assign each predator animal with a corresponding prey animal and have each animal use one identifying sound.

Mix the groups together and have participants close their eyes as they begin moving randomly about the space.

Give the cue for all participants to simultaneously start making their sounds.

The goal is for the prey to avoid their designated predator while predators strive to hear and tag their designated prey among the chorus of all eight sounds. If a predator tags its prey, the prey must sit down on the edge of the space. Without peeking, the predator must continue to seek prey with eyes closed.

If two or more prey of the same type, such as two mice, find each other, they may huddle together, stop making sounds and be safe from being caught. In all other cases, those still playing must continue to repeat their identifying sound.

The activity is complete when all prey have huddled or been tagged by their designated predator.

Conclude with a discussion of how predators find prey and how prey elude their predators. Are there any predators that are also prey themselves? Do humans fit either of these categories?

DISCOVERING DINOSAURS

Objective: To visualize the age of dinosaurs through sculpting techniques.

Getting Started: Present a study unit on dinosaurs, sharing as many pictures as possible of diverse types of dinosaurs as well as their environments. Emphasize also the distinctive shapes of dinosaurs and their methods of moving and obtaining food.

Warm-up: Conduct the "Partner Sculpting" and "Group Sculpting" exercises, pages 56 and 61, if your group is unfamilar with sculpting techniques. Proceed to the "Instant Scenery" page 61.

Activity: Several dinosaur related activities follow:

• *Form prehistoric environments.* Begin by prompting the entire class to compose, through sculpting methods, an imagined setting of the Mesozoic Era, appropriate for dinosaurs to inhabit. Tantalize imaginations to include lush fern-like plants, swampy plains, tall conifers for long-necked leaf eaters, shallow waters for wading creatures, stubby palm-like plants, and exotic rocks.

• *Explore dinosaurs in action.* Disband the scenery and ask the group to spread out and work individually, but in unison, to re-create the actions of some of the smaller dinosaurs. Call out the name and description of a dinosaur as well as some of its probable actions:

- *run in fear*
- *eat high or low plants*
- *creep up and pounce on a rival*
- *wallow through a shallow swamp*
- *hide from a rival*
- *rest in the sun*

• *Create large group dinosaurs.* Begin this activity with smaller groups, and, as the participants become more comfortable with the technique, the participants rearrange into larger groups depending on the size of the dinosaur being depicted. For example: One or two participants can represent the head and neck, several the back, one or two each set of legs, and several the tail.

Once created, share these dinosaur sculptures with the class. Encourage enactment of the believed characteristics of these creatures, their actions, and methods of locomotion. Provide ample space such as a gym or playground for maximum results.

The following are a few dinosaurs to get your group started:

Brontosaurus — This dinosaur was among the largest, weighed as much as twelve elephants, and was several school buses in length. This particular beast is most fun as an entire group project, with various members choosing to be components for its parts. Some participants can represent the heavy body; others can group in four locations to represent thick legs, while another can ride piggyback and form a long, snaky neck with an overly small head, balanced by an equally long tail.

These peaceful creatures were plant eaters who relished treetop leaf nibbling. Challenge the group to synchronize movement *slowly* as a unit, with head nibbling and tail slowly swishing.

Tyrannosaurus — This heavy creature measured thirty-nine feet long and weighed as much as an elephant. It can be sculpted by several participants crouching to form the huge back legs and massive claw-tipped toes, while other participants sit on their shoulders or stand between them to represent the upper body and smaller arms. Additional participants can stand right in front of the arms and sculpt the huge jaws and teeth with their arms and fingers.

As for movement, some experts think they waddled like ducks.

Extended Activity: Practice the "Action/Reaction" and "Mock Battle" exercises, pages 63 and 64, to prepare for improvising dinosaur scenarios involving sculpted scenery and dinosaurs involved in battle action.

Divide the class into four groups:
1. *Scenery*
2. *Dinosaurs not involved in battle*
3. *Predators*
4. *Prey*

Have the first group form a prehistoric environment using sculpting techniques.

Let the second group begin action with everyday dinosaur activities such as egg laying, feeding young, browsing, roaming the countryside, and eating.

Set up the third and fourth groups in a clearly defined conflict situation such as one dinosaur stealing another's egg or competing for food. This can lead to staging a controlled fight that reaches culmination (prey escapes, one dinosaur retreats, or is killed), and ends with regular everyday activity resumed.

Sit down and discuss the enactment and possible changes or improvements. Reenact the scenario, shifting the roles by groups to allow opportunity to play other parts.

Cast the class members to act out the following script from "A Day in the Life of Stegosaurus". The class can be divided into three character groups.

One third plays stegosaurus dinosaurs, one third the baby "stegos" and the remainder, allosaurus. Pinpoint the locations of the river valley and bush areas, and lead the action through narration of the story.

A Day in the Life of Stegosaurus
By Rick Strot

Stegosaurus: "Hello. boys and girls. Get ready for a trip to dinosaur land! I'm going to take you with me in our imaginations to spend a day in my life. That's right, a day as a Stegosaurus! So relax, close your eyes and listen. Here we go.

"It's morning. You're lying on your stomach as the morning light warms the blood in your bony back plates. You begin to move - first a few twitches of the heavy tail, then lift your head for a look around. Stretch stegosaurus backs. The rest of the herd is starting to wake up. You stand up. Your small stegosaurus babies are up, too, and bumping into your sides as they stumble around. Time for breakfast!

"Slowly, you move with the herd, spread out along a river valley, munching leaves from the low bushes and ferns scattered in clumps on the hard soil. You grind the green fibers with your flat teeth. Bite, chew, gulp. Over and over. The little stegos are eating close by. One comes over for some free lunch. You drop a mouthful of chewed leaves and the little stego snorts loudly as it eats.

"The day is getting hotter. Your small stegos are walking toward the water. Cool liquid splashes down your throat when you raise your head high. Sniff that smell. Danger nearby! Where are the babies? Where is the herd?

"You turn and run through the bushes. The little stegos are eating bushes near a grove of palm trees. There it is! Allosaurus, the meat eater, moving around the trees! Quickly, you push your little stegos toward the herd, snorting the danger call. The babies run fast. You turn your back and swing your tail as Allosaurus rounds the trees. Wham! Allosaurus is thrown into a tree, a scratch on his side from your spike.

"You start running toward the distant herd, but Allosaurus is faster. He snaps at your back, but his teeth are no match for the bony plates. As Allosaurus moves for the head, you turn and swing your spiked tail. Wham! Allosaurus is thrown into a small ravine. You run and run. Finally, the herd is there, gathered in a circle, stamping feet, twitching thorny tails, raising a cloud of dust. In the middle, little stegos snort in terror. You join the defense circle.

"But Allosaurus won't face the whole herd. He roars and stomps away. Slowly, you turn and begin to eat again. Bite, chew, gulp, over and over. When the sun begins to sink, you settle down on the rocky soil, surrounded by your herd, your little stegos at your side and close your eyes to sleep."
The End

A tree sculpture

A group leaf sculpture

TO BE A TREE

Objective: To observe and learn to identify leaves and trees by their individual shapes and characteristics.

Getting Started: Have the group members gather leaves from the school or neighborhood environment. In the process have members look at the shape, size and texture of the trees themselves, smelling, feeling and looking at both the leaves and trees for a full sensory exploration.

Ask participants to form into small groups, each with a resource book to assist identification and labeling of leaves.

Display one leaf from each variety of tree on a large table. Have the group gather around the table and discuss characteristics of contrasting leaves. Share information on the trees themselves mentioning characteristics such as the shape of the leaf and tree, texture of the bark and leaf edge; flowers, nuts or fruits that grow on the tree, or other pertinent information.

Warm-up: Conduct "Shapes", page 56 , and "Partner Sculpting", page 56 .

Activity: Assign or have each team choose a leaf or tree to enact through body sculpting techniques. Allow five minutes for exploration time, then have everyone sit in a circle formation. Each team can share its enactment as others observe and guess which leaf or tree is being enacted. For example:
Guessing Trees - An individual or group of individuals can recreate the shape of a specific tree through body sculpture, such as:

- Stand of poplars – Bodies tall, legs together, arms up
- Spruce tree - Faces looking up, legs wide, arms curved up and out to the sides with wrists flexed.

Tree Group Sculptures – A group can create a sculpture indicating the shape of a specific tree, such as:

- Giant oak tree – Stand close together from the waist down, arms spread up and out in all directions.

Leaf Body Shapes – An individual can recreate a specific leaf shape, such as:

- Sassafras leaf - Arms rounded and clasped over head, knees bent up and to the side to represent a mitten shape.

Leaf Group Sculpture – A group can create a group sculpture to represent the structure of a specific leaf, such as:

- Maple leaf - Five participants lie with their toes toward the middle and heads fanning outward to represent the maple leaf's five points. Arms may be linked to show the curve between each leaf point.

Extended Activity: Enact stories that evolve around trees:
The Fire Stealer, an Ojibwa myth
Why the Evergreen Trees Keep Their Leaves in Winter, by Florence Holbrook
"The Song of Hiawatha", by Henry Wadsworth Longfellow

The Giving Tree, by Shel Silverstein
The Oak Tree, by Laura Jane Coats
Once There was a Tree, by Natalia Ramanova.

• Open up discussion with the group on various uses for trees: furniture, houses, shoes, paper, filler in food products, turpentine, pitch, resin, telephone poles, shade from sun, oxygen for human and animal consumption, bridges, fences, firewood, utensils, bowls, sculptured carvings, toothpicks.

• Play a charade-style game in which each participant or team enacts a use of trees or wood for others to guess, such as:

— *Diners eating a meal using chopsticks and ending up with the use of toothpicks.*
— *Carpenters building a wood frame for a house.*
— *People tobogganing.*
— *Hikers stopping to admire the trees and breathing in the fresh air.*
— *Sculptor, first cutting with a chain saw, then carving with hand tools and sanding a work of art.*
— *Gardener raking and mulching leaves.*
— *Worker scarring and gathering sap for maple syrup or rubber manufacturing.*
— *Musicians playing wooden instruments: guitar, violin, bass, clarinet, rhythm sticks, etc.*
— *Boater paddling a canoe or rowing a boat.*
— *Painter using turpentine with oil paint to paint a masterpiece.*

Other ideas to try:

— *A group apple tree* - A large trunk and many outreaching branches can be formed. Hands made into fists can represent the apples. An additional participant can walk around the group sculpture picking apples from the ground and off the formed tree.

— *A Christmas tree* - Individuals stand in the shape of evergreen trees as described in the previous activity. Other participants come, look at the trees, select one, chop it down, drag it and set it up to decorate with Christmas ornaments.

ANIMAL GROUPS

Objective: To compare through pantomime how animals in the five classification groups vary.

Getting Started: Discuss the characteristics of the five animal groups (vertebrates with backbone) with your group:

    1 - fish
    2 - amphibians
    3 - reptiles
    4 - birds
    5 - mammals

With older participants, extend the discussion to sub-groups. For example: among the mammals, there are pouched animals, rodents, and primates. Ask what characteristics distinguish one animal group from another. Although whales, for example, appear to be like fish, they are not. They are warm blooded, breathe air into lungs, give birth to live young, and feed them milk. Share with the group distinguishing characteristics and list them on the board.

Warm-up: Conduct "Animal Walk", page 29 .

Activity: Divide the class into five groups. Assign one of the animal groups to each of these groups. Have each participant choose (or be assigned) a specific animal in the grouping to research its habits and habitat.

Ask each participant to develop a short skit integrating researched information and mimicking the animal's characteristics. While participants are generally enthusiastic about popular animals such as elephants and giraffes, lesser known animals would be challenging and broadening to introduce. For example, some of the following animals and actions could be attempted.

• *Salmon* – Swims upstream and leaps out of water to climb waterfalls.
• *Frog* – Has life cycle from tadpole to fully developed frog.
• *Opossum* – Carries young in a pouch, plays "possum", hangs upside down, and is very docile.
• *Macaw* – Lives in tropical forests, feeds on large seeds and nuts that are broken by strong curved beak.
• *Ostrich* – World's largest living bird, too heavy to fly, so runs at top speed with long legs.

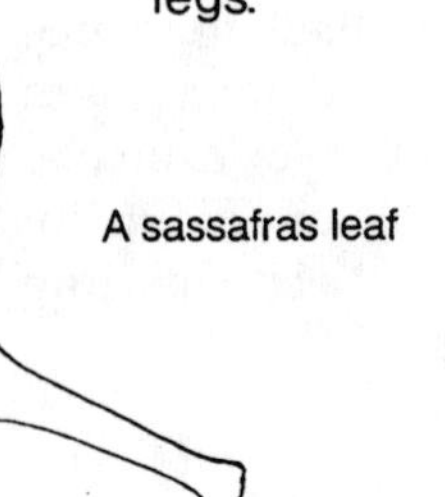

A sassafras leaf

PHOTOSYNTHESIS

- *Walrus* — Uses long ivory tusks to dig for shellfish in the sand and mud, cannot swim fast, and moves clumsily on land.
- *Dolphins* – Strong swimmers that leap out of the water and do tricks.

Have each participant share his or her skit with the rest of the class. Give class members the task of determining the characteristics expressed by the performer in each individual skit.

An animal in locomotion

Objective: To share a basic understanding of photosynthesis and what it involves.

Getting Started: Here is some information to clarify what happens in photosynthesis. Share the definitions with your group in a way that they can understand. The basic concepts will get across, whereas the terminology retained will depend on the participants' ages and maturity.

The word photosynthesis can be broken into two words: "photo" meaning "light" and "synthesis" meaning "the combination of parts or elements into a whole". Photosynthesis is a very important cycle in plant life (see the section on cycles in "Environmental Education", page 155) involving sun energy and two elements of our environment: air and water.

It is a process that occurs in green plants which creates both the food and air that we need in order to survive.

Plants take in sunlight, water and a portion of the air called carbon dioxide. In photosynthesis the light from the sun provides the energy to break down water (H_2O) and carbon dioxide (CO_2). This light energy, with the help of cholorophyll found in all green plants, recombines these elements to form carbohydrates. Some oxygen is left over from this process and is breathed out by the plants.

Animals, including humans, eat carbohydrates (starches and sugars) found in plants. They use this food to build and maintain their bodies. They breathe in oxygen and breathe out carbon dioxide which, in turn is used by the plants.

Warm-up: If the group is relaxed with each other and familiar with creative dramatic activities, no warm-up is necessary. If not, warm up with some locomotion exercises such as "Run, Skip, Jump", page 27 , and the movement game "Do Your Ears Hang Low?" found on page 45 .

Activity: During this activity it helps to set a playful mood. Divide the class into two groups on either side of a circle formation, facing each other. One side represents plants, the other side, animals. The plants state the dialogue on the left, while performing the adjacent actions:

Dialogue	**Actions**
• Take in carbon dioxide (CO_2)	*Reach arms way out in front and pull them in toward the chest while audibly and enthusiastically drawing in a breath.*
• Take in sunshine	*Throw arms up, smile upwardsand emit a loud "Ahh!" as though totally enjoying the sun's rays.*
• Take in water (H_2O)	*Bend down and draw hands from toes up legs making loud slurping sounds.*
• Make carbohydrates	*Move and shape hands to represent leaves all around oneself.*
• Breathe out oxygen	*Motion with arms away from body and out toward the animal group while audibly blowing out air.*

Now the animals state the phrases and perform the accompanying actions:

Dialogue	**Actions**
• Take in oxygen	*Suck in air audibly while reaching out toward the plant group and pulling arms back toward the chest.*
• Eat carbohydrates	*Make exaggerated eating motions with hands and mouth.*
• Use oxygen and carbohydrates	*Jump and wiggle around in an energized fashion or mimic movements of specific animals.*
• Breathe out carbon dioxide	*Blow out air with a loud "whoosh" sound and move arms away from body and toward the plant group.*

Repeat these sequences several times, encouraging playfulness, exaggerated actions and loud vocalization of words and sounds.

Have the groups switch places and roles and re-enact.

This can be done with a single class or an entire auditorium full of participants. You may wish to have your groups practice first, the actions and sounds with exaggeration, and then move toward the phrases and action, in sequence.

Plants taking in carbon dioxide, sunshine and water

Animals taking in oxygen

Animals using carbohydrates and oxygen all over their bodies

LEAF COLOR CHANGE

Objective: To teach the processes that occur when a deciduous leaf changes color during the fall season.

Getting Started: Discuss with the group the pigments in a deciduous leaf: chlorophyll, necessary for photosynthesis and responsible for the green color of leaves; carotin - orange color; xanthophyll - yellow; lycopene and anthocyanins - red; anthocyanins - blue and purple.

Note that chlorophyll dominates all the other pigments when the leaf is green.

Explain that with the changes of light and temperature during the fall, blockages form inside the plant that stop the flow of water and sap, causing chemical changes in the leaf. These changes cause the chlorophyll to break down revealing the other pigments. Further chemical changes stimulate the production of the anthocyanins. Thus the color of the leaves changes dramatically.

If you are working with a younger group (second to fourth graders), emphasize chlorophyll but do not concern the group with memorizing all of the pigment names.

Warm-up: Make sure the group has previous experiences with "Instant Scenery" and "Basic Scarves" exercises, pages 61 and 51 .

Activity: Identify the characters involved in the enactment of leaf color change: sun, water, chlorophyll (green plant), carotin (orange), xanthophyll (yellow), and anthocyanin (red).

Use scarves, swatches of color, identifying tags pinned to clothing, and/or identifying movements as in the "Color Spectrum Dance" in the Science section, to represent the pigments as well as the sun and water. It is suggested that the sun be represented by the color white, and the water, by blue.

This activity may be enacted by the group as a whole or in smaller groups of six or more participants. Assign, or have participants choose roles.

To Portray Summer

- Those representing both the chlorophyll and green plants should stand in the center of the space forming plant shapes through body sculpting and scarves.

- All participants representing the color pigments should hide behind or under the green plants.

- Participants representing the sun move toward the plants with radiating movements, bright and strong. Others representaing the water produce rippling scarf movements on a low level, touching the plant roots.

To Portray Fall

- The sun and water move farther away from the plants.

- The plants reach out their roots, but cannot touch the water.

- The chlorophyll in the green plants breaks down (possibly portrayed by a series of quick, short, downward movements).

- As the chlorophyll participants end their movements with low level shapes, the pigments burst forth and show themselves in dramatic displays of color and movement.

The teacher, or a participant, may narrate these changes as they occur, including both the technical names and colors of the pigments for reinforcement.

Discuss the enactment and possibly add more plant or color characters for a re-enactment.

This study of pigment can be paired with related activities also found in this Section, such as "To Be a Tree", "Spectrum Color Dance", and "Why Is the Sky Blue?". The Fire Stealer by William Toye is an adaptation of an Ojibwa tale concerning leaf color change.

THE WORKING EAR

Objective: To visualize the construction and functioning of the inner and outer ear.

Getting Started: Use a diagram of the inner ear to visually explain the ear's working parts. Describe how sound waves travel from a source and funnel through the outer ear to the inner ear.

Warm-up: To better understand vibration concepts, have participants play a sound wave game. Line up participants beside one another holding hands and/or touching shoulders.

Have the person at one end start a vibrational movement such as a slow, back-and-forth sway or a quick, sharp, one-second shake. As soon as the next person in line is sure of the "signal", that person repeats it and it is passed down the line until it reaches the last person. Each person must try to repeat the identical movement in duration, intensity, and quality.

This can be achieved with just movement, or with movement and accompanying sound similar to the "Share the Sound and Movement" exercise, page 33 . Also of value is the "Shapes" exercise on page 56 which will prepare participants formulating body shapes to represent the ear. In this warm-up, ask participants to create a variety of shapes (rounded, angular, bent, straight, spiral; high, middle, and low level), and to mimic shapes of objects in the room such as a clock, desk, plant, or other.

Activity: Ask several participants to sculpt a working model of an ear with their bodies, in group formation. Give leeway for invention. Some suggestions are: several participants form a funnel shape for the *outer ear;* others create a round and flat body sculpture to represent the *eardrum;* others become *hammer, anvil, stirrup,* and *cochlea,* with appropriate body shapes. Additional participants can take on the interesting role of the *brain* itself to which sound travels.

Ask remaining participants to initiate sound waves, one at at a time as described above. Each person's sound wave should include sound and movement which triggers a similar sound and movement (as in the sound wave game, above) within the ear parts as it travels through the sculpted ear, beginning at the outer ear and ending in the coiled tube of the cochlea.

Finally, have the cochlea transmit (pass on) each sound wave and movement to the brain who, for fun, deciphers the represented sound into a bit of information (an actual word, sentence, or idea).

For example:

Movement	Sound	Transmitted Information
Sharp jerk upwards	*Eek!*	*A mouse!*
Waving arms	*Shhh-shh*	*Be Quiet!*
Finger moves right and left	*Tick, tick*	*The clock struck one.*
Slow, steady push	*Mooooooo*	*Milk the cow, someone!*

Extended Activity: Present material or have participants research information about Alexander Graham Bell and the construction of the first telephone. Have those involved with the report, or groups of volunteers from the class, create a group sculpture of the different parts of this first telephone, then enact the movement of sound through its various parts as in the working ear

Group sculpture of a working ear

CELLULAR DIVISION

Objective: To enact chromosomal and cellular division.

Getting Started: Discuss with the group some basic data about cellular division and chromosomes.

When cells divide, they form two identical cells. This process allows organisms to grow. Certain cells always make similar cells, for instance, bone cells make bone cells, while other cells produce many different kinds of cells. The type of division that a cell can make is controlled by genes. When an older cell divides in half, the two new cells will carry on the same traits as the old cell only if they have the same genes. Thus, it is important, before a cell divides, that the cell's genes are duplicated or copied and a code is established. The chromosomes are that part of the cell nucleus that contain the genes.

Warm-up: Introduce the "Mirror Game", page 33 and "Share the Movement", page 32 . The group must also be familiar with symmetrical shapes as described on page   .

Activity: Explore the concept that in simple single-cell division each chromosome makes a copy of itself.

Divide the class up into teams of two members each. Each pair is given the task of creating a closely knit mirror image or symmetrical sculpture involving both partners. In other words, there must be close physical contact, so that the scultpure appears as one unit, and the participants must be mirroring each other's shape so that one side of the sculpture looks like the other. This sculpture is to represent a single chromosome. While remaining in this sculpted shape, each pair is to improvise a characteristic movement that identifies their chromosome. It must be a movement that the two can perform while together as well as each partner do individually (without partner contact) such as a pattern of head nods, rolling the eyes, expanding and contracting the chest, raising and lowering the shoulders, etc.

The pairs are now ready to enact chromosome division. Beat a drum slowly or play some slow music and direct the action to begin. The cell sculptures expand *very* slowly (representing the thickening of the cell), and finally divide into two separate but similar chromosomes. During this entire process, and also after two chromosome partners separate, each chromosome must maintain its characteristic shape, as closely as possible, and continue to make its identifying movement.

Discuss what worked and what did not work then repeat the process. You may wish at this point to change partners, form new sculptures and movements, or simply replay it again with improvements. After exploring changes, divide the class in half so that half can watch and the other half enact. Repeat the chromosome division, so that all members can experience both observing and performing.

Extended Activity: To form a Giant Cell through "Group Sculpting", have a number of chromosome pairs (one half of the entire group) cluster together in their various mirror image shapes to represent the chromosomes in the cell nucleus.

The second half of the class, constructs an outer cell wall by forming a circle around the first chromosome group. Explain that this Giant Cell will be dividing into two parts. About half the nucleus and half the cell wall will be pulled in one direction (indicate which direction they will go), and half in the other direction.

Arrange the chromosome teams so that one partner can go in one direction and the other in an opposing direction, along with their sides of the cell wall.

At the sound of the drum, the entire group *very slowly* expands and divides into two groups involving both nucleus and cell wall participants. Each half-circle of cell wall reconnects to enclose its newly separated chromosomes, forming two new separate, but complete cells.

Discuss what worked and what did not and prepare to re-enact incorporating the suggested improvements.

DOUBLING THE DNA CODE

Objective: To visualize through enactment the division and reformation of the DNA code.

Getting Started: Discuss with the group some basic information about DNA. Precede this study with the activity in this section called "Cellular Division".

Warm-up: Play some music or a drumbeat and have participants improvise dance, or simply walk or move around the space. Stop the music and call out "head to head" as cue for each participant to gently touch his or her head to someone else's head. This can be done in pairs or in groups. Repeat this concept using other body parts.

Finally, call out "Stick together!" as the cue for particpants to find different ways to make group shapes, touching body parts in any formation they wish.*

Conduct a gentle version of "push" from the "Push and Pull" exercise, page 63 , with emphasis on light, floating movement.

Activity: Have half the class represent the DNA ladder and the other half represent the floating individual sections of DNA.

Divide the DNA ladder group into two lines of participants. Arrange the two lines so that they are facing each other. Have each participant in each line place his **right** hand on the shoulder of the person to the right. The ladder rungs connecting the two lines are now formed by each participant holding the **left** hand of the person facing him or her in the opposite line.

Once the ladder is fully formed, the other half of the class enacts the DNA sections that float in the liquid of the cell's nucleus surrounding the ladder. (Some light floating music, a pennywhistle, or a gentle drumbeat may encourage involvement at this point.)

On cue, the ladder rungs (left hands) twist slowly and gently this way and that until hands all split apart leaving two intact lines no longer connected to each other. The separated lines move away from each other. Each individual floating DNA now joins left hands with one of the sections of DNA in one of the two lines, thus forming a new rung. When all positions are filled, a new line is formed with the right hands of all the previously floating DNA members, connecting with the shoulders to their right. Now there are two DNA ladders completed.

*taken with permission from *First Steps in Teaching Creative Dance to Children* by Mary Joyce, Mayfield Publishing Company, 285 Hamilton Ave., Palo Alto, California 94301.

DNA ladder rungs

Earth Science

GUESS-WHO-I-AM
Rocks

Objective: To encourage observation and appreciaton of rock forms.

Getting Started: Ask participants to bring in favorite rocks to share. Include a variety of rocks, minerals, and crystals. Pass the rocks around, name and label them when possible. Talk about the rocks' qualities and characteristics and exchange data about their formation.

Warm-up: Have the group spread out evenly in the space.

Call out appropriate descriptive texture and shape words such as: straight, smooth, jagged, lumpy, crumbly, lined, spotted, pointed, heavy, light, square, round, and others that may specifically relate to the rock samples. As in the "Shapes" exercise, page 56 , ask participants to demonstrate descriptive qualities with body shapes. For example:

- Lumpy rock - form a humped over shape
- Smooth, flat rock - lie in a straight horizontal posture.

Activity: Ask each participant to study the rocks on display and silently choose one to portray with a body shape, remembering its name.

After an individual demonstrates the body shape of a rock, have others guess which rock was sculpted and state any further information about the rock that the group may have learned.

Extended Activity: After studying rocks, minerals and crystals, act out a story in which rocks play an important role. Some good examples are:

"The Stone in the Road" (see Language Arts Section in this book), grades 4-7

"Stone Soup", a traditional English tale, grades 3-7

"Sylvester and the Magic Pebble" by William Steig, Windmill Books, grades 2-4

"The Stone Cheese" from *Favorite Tales of Monsters and Trolls,* Random House, retold by George Jonsen, grades 2-4

"The Stone Cutter" (see Language Arts Section in this book), a Japanese tale told by Gerald McDermott, Viking Press 1975, grades 3-7

SUN, EARTH AND MOON ORBITS

Objective: To comprehend the movement of the sun, earth, and moon in relationship to one another.

Getting Started: Describe and draw diagram pictures of how the earth and moon travel in relationship to each other, or utilize demonstration models or rod props (cardboard circles or balls attached to sticks) for explanation.

Warm-up: Prepare to enact movements of the sun, earth and moon orbits with the following warm-ups:

Using a drum beat, have participants locomote with a variety of speeds, in a circle.

Have them:

- Run in slow motion
- Run at normal pace
- Run faster, yet controlled

Set up safe obstacles and ask participants to run around each object while progressing around the circle. Pieces of masking tape or books work well as "obstacles". Emphasize preciseness and control in moving evenly so that the action does not become sloppy.

Have participants try the same actions while continually keeping the *front* of their bodies facing each obstacle.

Challenge participants to try the following walks:

- Walk slowly across the floor with an even tempo (no noticeable pauses between steps).
- Progress forward slowly using many small steps.
- Walk and turn slowly, while walking.
- Side-slide or side-step across the room.

Activity: Divide the group into teams of three members each. Ask one participant to enact the sun by locomoting *very slowly* and steadily across the space. A second participant enacts the earth, making a slow orbit around the sun. A third participant enacts the moon by running quickly around the "earth" (as the earth revolves around the sun).

All of these movements can be conducted simultaneously as the group of three move together across the space. Practice will aid smooth interpretations.

Advance the activity further. Try adding the earth's rotation, *spinning,* while moving slowly around the "sun". Also, point out that the moon participant is to continually face *inward,* towards the earth while rotating around the earth.

Extended Activity: Add some additional planets using a larger space or playground area.

This would be an opportune time to include "mood" music. For creating a feeling of outer space, use selections from outer space or New Age sound tracks.

Sun, Earth and Moon orbits

ENVIRONMENTAL EDUCATION

Objective: To introduce ecological concepts and show how environmental systems work.

Getting Started: The following activities center around the earth's important operating principles that are grouped into seven categories: *energy flow, cycles, diversity, community, interrelationships, change,* and *adaptation.*

Discuss and compare these operating principles with the group to help them understand their differences and similarities. Simple activities such as the ones included below will help clarify the complex ideas.

Warm-up: Introduce the game "Share-the-Movement", page 32 , and adapt it to these activities by stating a theme useful in environmental enactments, such as: water, dying, sunshine, wind, growing, etc. and play the game with movements inspired by the theme words. As in the original game, each movement shared must be kept simple so that the movements can be accurately repeated.

Familiarity with body sculpting techniques and specifically "Instant Scenery", pages 56 and 61 , is very helpful for these activities. Also consider exploring "Guess-Who-I-Am", page 37 , adapted to focus on animals of different environments.

ENERGY FLOW

Concept: Solar energy is transferred in decreasing amounts from plants (food producers), which can capture it, to vegetarian and meat-eating animals (food consumers), which cannot capture it directly. This energy is taken in by plants and animals such as mold and fly maggots (food decomposers) which help the breakdown process enabling the energy to re-enter the soil and then, in turn, feed plants.

Activity: Divide the class into four groups to play the folowing roles:

>   Group one - play the sun or solar energy
>   Group two - the producers (edible plants)
>   Group three - the consumers (vegetarian and meat-eating animals including humans)
>   Group four - the decomposers (maggots, mold).

Guide the class to decide on a particular energy flow scenario so that each group has a specific character to enact which relates to the other groups involved. For example, two specific demonstrations of energy flow follow:

Example 1

- *Sunlight* travels down to,
- the *clover* which takes in sunlight (and produces carbohydrates). In turn,

- the clover is eaten by the *rabbits* which,
- die and are eaten by *fly maggots.*

Example 2
- *Sunlight* travels down to,
- an *apple tree* which takes the sunlight in (and produces carbohydrates), then,
- the *apples* are picked and eaten by *humans* who throw the cores away.
- These *apple cores* decompose and are eaten by *mold. (Participants may enjoy this role in the form of creepy mold-creatures slowly attacking the cores.)*

Discuss other energy flow scenarios with your class and have them choose one example to enact together. All the participants in each of the four groups will play their character in unison.

(For further study of energy flow refer to the activity "Photosynthesis" in this section.)

CYCLES

Concept: Water, air, energy, soil and the essential nutrients (sulphur, hydrogen, carbon, oxygen, nitrogen, and phosphorus) are continually recycling.

Activity: The water cycle includes four components: *water, sunlight, warm air,* and *cold air.*

Divide the class into these four groups. Ask each group to work in a corner of the room. Within each group movement ideas are to be tried and shared, culminating in one movement chosen to represent its part of the water cycle enactment (such as radiating arms for sunlight, shivering for cold water, etc.) Have each group share its movement with all the other groups.

Place the warm air group on one side of the room and cold air on the other. Practice moving the two groups toward each other and away from each other while each group repeats its characteristic movements.

What happens when they meet? Do the participants collide, intermingle, swirl round each other? There may be a variety of acceptable responses within an accurate enactment.

Now add the participants representing water. The warm air will carry along more moisture than the cold air. When the groups meet, the warm air will drop in temperature and lose the water being carried. The water group will continue to repeat a chosen movement individually, then in larger and larger numbers, while enacting rain, streams, rivers and finally, as all water merges together - the ocean!

Now, the warm and cold air will separate out to opposite sides of the room. The sunshine group will move toward the water with its chosen representa-tive movement. This leaves the water group to enact evaporation by slowly rising. The warm air joins and "carries" the water to its side of the room and the whole process repeats itself again.

Try enacting this concept several times giving each group a chance to play different parts. You may, for brevity, maintain the original movements for the groups or each new group may come up with new movements.

Another fascinating cycles activity, "The Rock Cycle", may be found in the Science/Earth section of this book.

Extended Activity: Through a study of cycles one may introduce recycling and action to counteract the trouble the planet is experiencing from unrecyclable man-made materials and their pollu-tion of air, earth and water.

DIVERSITY

Concept: The six essential nutrients of the earth form diverse eco-systems (environments plus related inhabiting communities) when coupled with varied climates. Some examples of environments are: mountain, foothill, plain, desert, swamp, ocean, coastal, etc. These environments promote varied plant and animal life.

Activity: Divide the class in half. Have one half, through "Instant Scenery", page 61 , create an environment. For example, a swamp that is com-posed of cypress trees, Spanish moss, water, mud, alligators, nutrias, mosquitos.

The other half of the class should create a con-trasting environment such as a desert with sand, cacti, lizards, hot sun and rocks.

This study on diversity can initiate an interesting thinking game. Varied environments support a rich assortment of plant and animal life, and within each distinct environment there is a great amount of diversity among its inhabitants.

Encourage group thinking about diversity using the examples below. Have small groups act out dif-ferences in plants and animals for others to guess in a pantomime guessing game. For example:
- A kingfisher kills and eats fish, a hawk kills and eats rodents, whereas a vulture eats only what is already dead (carrion).
- Some birds eat seeds (sparrows), some insects (swallows) and some meat (eagles).
- Some plants need full sun (corn, tomatoes, sunflowers), others do well in shade (impa-tiens, fungi, mosses).
- Some animals and insects are gregarious (humans, wolves, bees, horses, pigeons, pur-ple martins), others live basically alone, in

small family units or mother and offspring groups (moose, bear, fox, wrens).

COMMUNITY

Concept: Plant and animal life is grouped together in geographical areas where quantity and quality of sunlight and essential nutrients are compatible with their needs. Such a community group and its environment is called an eco-system. Within each eco-system are many communities.

Activity: As an extension of the study of diversity, have each group, using "Instant Scenery" techniques, explore a community of plant and animal life within the environment that it enacted while studying diversity. For example:

  • A stream habitat involving a community of water spiders, insect larvae, crayfish, fish, fresh water mussels, algae, etc.
  • A rotten log habitat involving pill bugs, centipedes, moth cocoon, worms, mold, fungus, etc.
  • A tidal pool involving crabs, mussels, barnacles, minnows, sea urchins, sea gulls, plankton, seed shrimp, etc.

Each group should discuss possible habitats and communities within its environment. Some participants can sculpt or enact environments, (the stream, rotten log, rocks, and water of the tidal pool) while others try mimicking as many animals and plants as they can come up with in a particular community. After exploration each group can share its enactment while other groups observe. Observers may then guess the habitat and its community

members, or the performing group can simply state their identity.

INTERRELATIONSHIPS

Concept: In the process of meeting their own needs, plants and animals within a community interact with one another. They are mutually useful or in some way effect one another.

Activity: Divide the group into teams of two to five members each. Ask each team to develop a short skit using movement and sound to show the interrelationships of the members of a specific community. You may wish to choose environmental settings, such as ocean, arctic, jungle, desert, forest, or enact the examples extracted from a class brainstorming session.

Forest example:
  • Nut *tree* produces *nuts,*
  • a *squirrel* uses the tree limbs and leaves for its home and eats and buries the nuts,
  • the lost buried nuts grow into trees.

Jungle example:
  • *Flower* attracts and feeds *insects,*
  • the insects pollinate the flower,
  • the flower forms *seeds,*
  • a *bird* eats the insects and seeds.

Ocean example:
  • *Plankton* is eaten by *small fish,*
  • the small fish are eaten by *medium sized fish* (group sculpture can be used here to fashion the big and medium sized fish),
  • the *big fish* are eaten by *man.*

Community — Forest environment
Nut, nut tree and squirrels

Ocean example:
- *Plankton* is eaten by *small fish,*
- the small fish are eaten by *medium sized fish* (group sculpture can be used here to fashion the big and medium sized fish),
- medium sized fish are eaten by *big fish*
- the big fish are eaten by *man.*

CHANGE

Concept: Because plants and animals are always in the process of being acted upon, or acting upon others, they remain in a state of change.

Activity: Divide the group into teams of two to five members each and ask each team to develop a short skit with motions and sounds depicting plants or animals in a state of change or transformation. Several examples follow:
- A meadow or field becomes overgrown with bushes, which in turn become overgrown with larger trees, which are chopped down, killed by blight or forest fire, leaving a meadow again.
- An egg changes into a caterpillar, cocoon or butterfly.
- An egg transforms into a tadpole, then a frog.
- An acorn grows into a tree, which is destroyed by a fire or by insects, and decomposes into soil.
- A seed sprouts and grows into a dandelion, which blooms then goes to seed. The seeds float off and plant themselves.
- An infant grows into a toddler, then a child, teen, adult, and finally an older adult.
- A specific local plant or animal shows change due to season such as leaf or hair growth and shedding.

ADAPTATION

Concept: All plants and animals need to adapt to their living conditions for survival.

Activity: Have participants work in teams of three or four members each to produce short skits centered around how certain plants or animals adapt. For example:
- Deciduous trees lose leaves in the winter and grow them back in the spring. Evergreens have an adapted leaf shape which withstands temperature and light changes.
- Birds build nests with string or telephone wire as well as with natural fibre.
- Giraffes have long necks enabling them to eat from treetops.
- Woodpeckers have beaks and skull bones to assist pecking out insects. A spoonbill has long legs and a bill allowing it to catch fish in shallow water.
- Insects build up resistance to the use of pesticides.

Extended Activity: Teams may invent new variations of adaptation for existing species. For example:
- Mice grow drill horns to drill into refrigerators to obtain food.

Interrelationships — Jungle environment
Trees, tree sloth, monkey and snakes

SHADOW SLEUTHING

Objective: To explore shadows and raise awareness about how they are cast by light.

Getting Started: Explain to the group that shadows are cast when light falls on an opaque object that blocks the light. The area where the light does not penetrate is dark. We call this dark area a shadow of the object. The object is always between the light source and the surface where the shadow is seen or cast. With the use of sunlight or a spotlight, demonstrate this concept on desk tops or the floor with various objects such as a ball, cardboard tube, or toy.

Have students share some of the smallest shadows they have seen (pebble, insect) and the largest (house, cloud, tall structure, mountain). Direct their attention to shadows and shade caused by clouds, buildings, and trees.

Warm-up: Indoors or outdoors, start your group with stretches such as simple head rolls or the "Bend and Stretch" and "Cat and Dog Back" exercises pages 18 and 19 .

Include a short session of the "Shapes" exercise, focusing on fingers and hands, followed by "Group Sculpting", page 61 .

Conduct "Characterization Locomotion", page 27 ,while moving at random around the space. Examples: a robot (stiff), scarecrow (loose), frightened or sneaky person, or in a classic Egyptian walk with angular wrists, elbows and knees.

Activity: Bring the group outside to the playground or parking lot on a sunny day to observe natural shadows such as those of a tree, cloud, building, car, flag and pole, preferably both in the morning and afternoon to observe the changing shadow shapes.

Note the placement of the sun in the sky, where and how the shadows fall and how the shadows are distorted at different times of the day.

Set boundaries for a locomotion activity. Arrange this activity so the shadows can be seen separately from one another. This will, of course, change at different times of the day.

Ask participants to line up and, as they locomote across the space, direct them to explore some of the walks, shapes, and poses of the characters they tried during warm-ups, this time casting shadows on the ground or against a wall.

Stop and discuss which shadows work well and which do not. Demonstrate how, when facing the light source, actions and gestures in back or in front of the body are blocked from view by the major body shadow. On the other hand, profile view and distinctive arm activities performed away from the body form the most complete shadow images.

Next, clearly reiterate the boundaries, then ask participants to spread out in the defined space and play around with some loosely improvised shadow dances - a free form exploration of improvised dances with *no bumping*. The addition of musical recordings would be enriching.

Have the group choose partners or form teams of three or four members each. The task now is to create group shape shadows. Be inventive! Some possibilities are:

- A shadow intersecting another shadow (an abstract design)
- Two-bodied, one-headed person
- Many-limbed Shiva of India
- Monster
- Flower
- Insect
- Stand-up letters forming a word
- Two or several interacting characters in a frozen pose
- An image related to something the class is studying.

Shadow Sleuthing

For an outdoor activity during mid-day, when the sun is directly overhead, experiment with hand shadows on the pavement or on a light sheet of colored paper laid on the ground or in the lap.

Extended Activity: Play around with hand shadow plays on a wall using a single light source. Each team of two to four persons should have a flashlight, overhead projector light, or other light source, and wall space in a darkened room. One person can hold the light while others experiment with shadows, taking turns improvising designs with hands and arms to discover shape in shadows. Young children may easily pursue the more traditional imageries such as a flying eagle or rabbit. Older participants can work alone or in teams of two (four hands can achieve exciting shapes) - an elephant, dinosaur, camel, giraffe, and flower, mythical beasts, or creatures from other planets.

Introduce full body shadow plays on more formal theatrical levels. There are two common approaches:

• *Actors stand in front* of a light source so that shadows are cast on a plain wall behind them. (This way actors can view their own shadows. Action occurs *away* from the wall.) Experiment with the amount of shadow captured by adjusting the height of the light.

• *Actors stand behind* a translucent white screen, white shower curtain, large bed sheet, or medium-weight Pellon stretched tautly across a frame with grommets on the corners secured to nails or hooks. The light source is a floodlight, overhead projector light, or strong lamp situated behind the actors and screen. Shadows are viewed by an audience and cannot be seen by the actors themselves. Action occurs close to the screen.

Either method is fun to try. The room must be dark for maximum effectiveness. Experiment with different lights, arrangements, and distances between subject, light, and surface for maximum success.

Begin either exercise informally with a locomotion exercise from Section One. Form participants in a single file semi-circle in the viewing area, enabling each person to pass, one at a time, behind the screen and/or between the light source and the viewing surface then back to the end of the line. Encourage participants to choose a locomotive movement to try behind the screen. Those in the semi-circle will be out front watching fellow classmates' shadows as they progress in one direction, passing one by one to cast a shadow, and then continue to the other end of the semi-circle line to watch others.

Have partners plan short skits to pantomime and present in shadow for the group. Emphasize large, distinct actions and the use of profile. Begin by concentrating on simple movement or frozen poses. Add props (a baseball bat, spoon, broom) and simple furnishings later to give added interest. Skits may evolve around situations such as:

- new dance rage
- detective searching for clues
- two robots meeting
- boxers, or action/reaction fight
- talent competition
- tug-of-war
- monster from outer space meeting an earth person
- two people tossing a ball
- two people sneaking in backwards and bumping into each other.

The addition of paper profile masks can give the shadows an added theatrical element. Refer to additional construction ideas in the back of this book.

Consider compiling a number of short skits into a full production or tackle the enactment of any story or play that would work well in pantomime narratives. The important factor is that the play progress through the action.

THE ELEMENTS
Earth, Air, Fire, and Water

Objective: To introduce and dramatize the four basic elements: earth, air, fire, and water.

Getting Started: Introduce the concept that all things are made up of one or more of the four basic elements.

Write the four categories down on the board and see if the group can name things that clearly belong to one element or another. Most things will be a combination of the elements. Challenge the group to name additional things and identify what elements they are made of.

Example: A tomato plant is a combination of all four elements and must have earth, water, air, and fire (the sun) to exist.

Discuss with the group each of the elements separately. List forms and variations of each particular element, with some possible crossovers such as:

Air:	Soft summer breeze, cold north wind, tornado, smog, intense heat waves, blast of air conditioning.
Earth:	Shifting sand, high peaked mountains, volcano, rock slide, swamp mud, earthquake, dust, garden.
Fire:	Candle, match, forest fire, smoky leaf fire, sparklers, fireworks, circular blue gas flame, camp fire.
Water:	Tap water, iceberg, rippling pond, hurricane, stormy sea, single drop, mud puddle, stream.

Warm-up: Interpret each element separately through an adaptation of the "Basic Scarves" exercise, page 51 .

Take time with each physical element for full exploration and involvement. . Call out some specific forms of earth, air, fire, and water as listed in "Getting Started" for the group members to express with scarves and movements.

Here are some suggestions to encourage variety through the use of the Basic Dance Elements as found in the introduction.

Levels:	High wispy clouds Low rolling fog
Dynamics:	Exploding volcano Dust slowly settling
Timing:	Pushing, white-water stream Single, suspended water drop
Size of movement and use of space:	Forest fire sweeping across land Small flame flickering
Body Parts:	Flames with feet and toes or fingers Back shaped as a mountain ridge that slowly erodes into a different shape
Group Formations:	Cloud, forest fire, ocean wave, mountain

Group sculpture of volcano — Earth and fire

Allow time for participants to try ideas simultaneously with bodies and the scarves and then share favorite interpretations with the group.

Encourage original movement by playing a simple musical instrument or some compelling recorded music. Search out the library as well as your own record and tape collection for appropriate or dynamically contrasting, musical selections. This can be a good opportunity to explose students to classical music.

Here are some suggestions, but it is often easiest to choose music from available resources:

Water: Handel: from *The Top 15 of 1750,* "Water Music" (Allegro)
"Concerto in B-flat Major for Harp and Orchestra Op 4, No. 7" (Andante-Allegro)
Beach Boys: *Sunflowers* "Cool, Cool Water"
Paul Winter: *Sun Singer* "Reflections in a Summer Pond" and "Dolphin Morning"
George Winston: *Winter into Spring* "Rain Dance"

Earth: Paul Winter: *Canyon,* "Canyon"
Linda Cohen: *Leda* "The Dust" and "Arroyo"

Air: Michael Hedges: *Aerial Boundaries* "Aerial Boundaries"
P.M. Hamel: *Nada* "Nada"

Fire: John Denver: "Sunshine on My Shoulder"
Paul Winter: *Sun Singer* "Sun Singer" and "Hymn to the Sun"
Bluegrass Banjos: "Fire on the Mountain"
Handel: "Royal Fireworks Music"

Activity: Let participants work in small groups using movement with scarves to express combined elements in nature. For example:
• Erosion of large boulder by wind and rain into an oddly shaped pillar of stone.
• A calm sea transformed into a treacherous tidal wave due to the effects of an earthquake.
• A calm hot day on the desert turning into a blinding, gusty sandstorm.

If time allows, have the small groups perform these enactments for the rest of the group. Ask the "audience" to guess what ideas are being portrayed. This ensures greater audience interest and involvement.

Extended Activity: Have participants dramatize stories involving elements using movement and scarves to create the environment, a character, or weather condition in the story. There are many stories that explain nature and personify the elements, thereby lending themselves to this type dramatization. Myths and legends in particular contain rich uses of the elements.

Fire: *The Fire Stealer,* Elizabeth Cleaver & William Toye
Earth: *The Stone Cutter,* G. McDermott
Air: *Shingebiss and the North Wind* as found in the story enactment segment of the Language Arts section of this book.
Water: *The Two Crabs,* Aesop's Fables

ELEMENTS DANCE
SCENARIO

The following dance scenario is included to give the reader an idea of what can be done to organize the movement of dancers on the stage (or other large space) to express an idea. This scenario, based on the four elements: earth, air, fire and water, can be used as a script or simply serve to provide a format for one's own original dance piece with the use of developing narration to guide the participants.

Note how the narrator provides cues for the dancers throughout the piece. This activity incorporates the use of repetition and the opportunity for individual expression.

Explore scarf movements beforehand with the participants and fill out the basic blocking in this scenario with scarf and body movements improvised by the participants themselves. "Shapes", "Dancing Words", "OK Bumping", and "Push/Pull", found in Section One make suitable warm-ups to the Element Dance ideas. For example: have the group members explore *shaking* and *freezing* while forming into interesting shapes. Use a rattle and call out different body parts, levels and emotional qualities to inspire the movement. Have the participants share their favorite interpretations and select shaking movements that would best express an earthquake and trembling actions that might represent the movement of the air.

Conduct similar exploration centered around each of the actions needed in the scenario: pushing, floating, rolling, etc. This improvisation familiarizes the participants with the movement needed to enact the scenario, helps the teacher observe and select participants to be cast in the various element groups, plus illustrates exciting movement to be highlighted in the scenario. The Science activity "The Elements - Earth, Air, Fire and Water", is also excellent preparation for this dance scenario.

Teach the participants the basic stage directions found below before attempting group blocking.

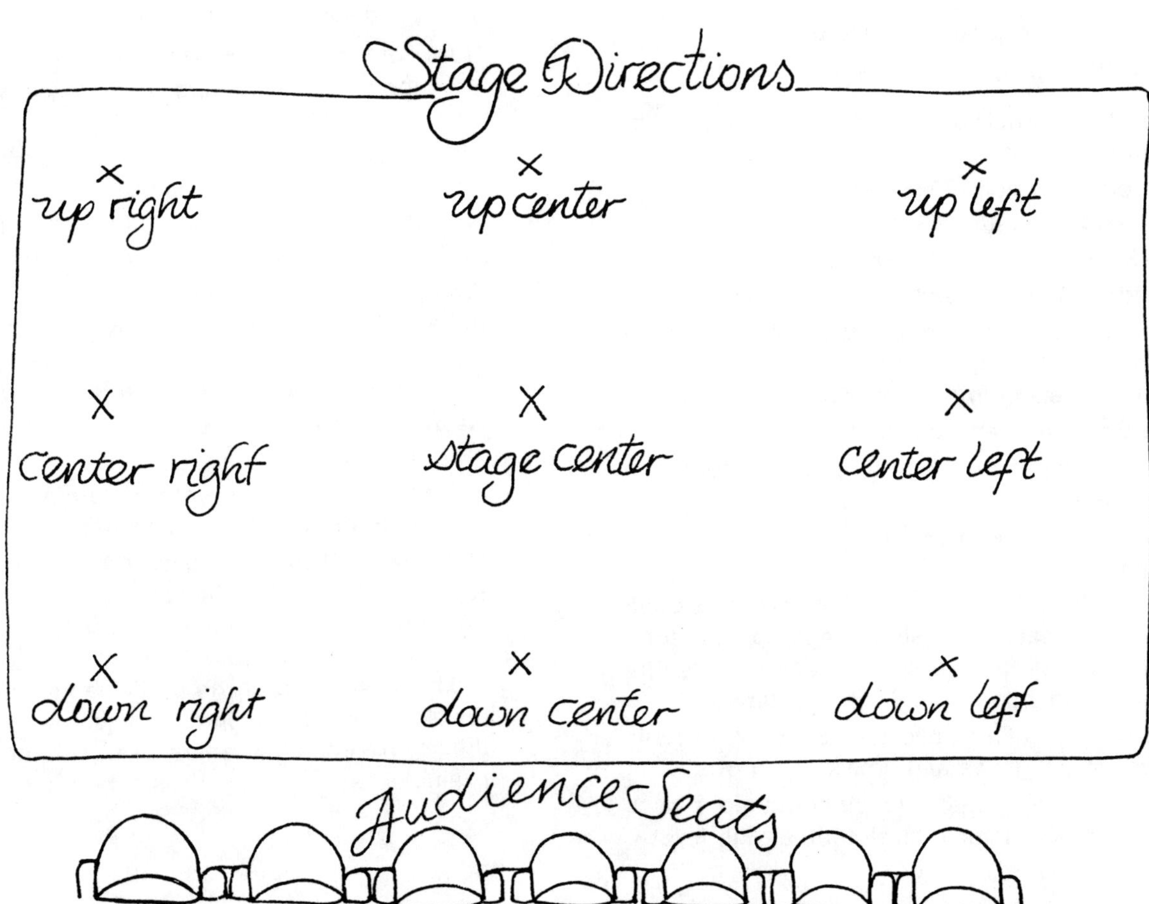

Explain to the group that the stages in early theaters were slanted; slightly higher at the back of the stage and lower near the front. That is why the back is called "upstage" and the front "downstage". This helped the audience, whose seats were all on the same level, to see better.

Emphasize that all stage directions are given from the point of view of the actor or dancer on stage, facing the audience. What is the left side of the stage for the audience is called *stage right* for those on stage, looking out at the audience.

The basic plot of the following elements scenario involves an earthquake, fissure, volcano, and lava flowing to the sea, creating clouds. Assign the parts of the characters – Earth, Air, Fire and Water. Each element should be represented by a number of participants with appropriately colored scarves.

- *Air* and *Water* members establish themselves at the periphery of the space.
- *Earth* and *Fire* members establish themselves stage center, on the diagonal, each participant in a still shape, facing a partner.

ELEMENTS SCENARIO

PHASE I – VOLCANO ERUPTION

Music begins: Paul Winter's *Canyon* "Canyon" (vibrating drum)

Narrator: "The molten lava deep down in the Earth heaves and shakes."

Fire: Moves for two drum phrases.

Narrator: "The air trembles."

Air and Water: Tremble and shake for two drum phrases moving toward the edge of the space and freezing in a low position.

Narrator: "The earth quakes."

Earth: Moves with sharp shapes for four drum phrases.

Narrator: "One stratum of rock pushes against another."

Earth and Earth, or Earth and Fire: Partners push against each other slowly regrouping to form a low level clump at center stage with the Fire in the middle of the volcano sculpture.

Narrator: "The Earth buckles. Slowly a volcanic mountain grows and grows and grows…"

Earth: Pushing against each other the group rises slowly to a middle level, then a high level.

(*Cymbals crash*)

Narrator: "The volcano explodes."

Fire: Leaps out from the center of the volcano structure, one or two participants at a time.

Then collapses and slowly rolls out from center toward the edges of the space.

Narrator: "The lava tumbles down the mountain sides. The mountain explodes!"

Earth: In various groupings these participants make explosive jumps, slowly collapse and roll stage right or stage left.

Narrator: "*Slowly* the lava tumbles and hardens making fantastic shapes as it rolls down to the sea."

Fire and Earth: Follow the narrator's description and freeze in unusual shapes on a low level at the edge of the space.

(*Music* changes to: P.M. Hamel *Nada* "Nada" or other airy, floating music selection.)

PHASE II – STEAM RISING

Narrator: "Steam swirls upward…"

Air: Slowly rises with light and floating movements, spins with circular arm movements.

Narrator: "Forming giant clouds…"

Water: Slowly rises with floating movements.

Narrator: "The warm wet clouds rise up, up, up; their wispy fingers curling outward and upward."

Air and Water: Rise with emphasis on arm and hand movements above heads.

Narrator: "The wind pushes at their middles creating swirls and spirals. It pushes them up into the upper atmosphere."

Air and Water: Move with swirling and turning movements to the back of the space, keeping movements light and floating.

Narrator: "As they rise their tops are blown this way and that."

Air and Water: Respond to narration with side to side arm and back movements.

Narrator: "They circle each other slowly."

Air and Water: Follow the narration using high, middle and low level variations with their circling movements.

The leader and/or the participants may wish to develop this further into a rainstorm or develop their own elements scenario using this format as an example.

THE THREE MAJOR CLASSIFICATIONS OF ROCK

Objective: To define igneous, sedimentary and metamorphic rock and demonstrate an understanding of these rock forms by enacting the processes by which they are formed.

IGNEOUS ROCKS

Getting Started: Discuss how the earth's composition forms igneous rocks. Igneous rocks are formed from molten rock (magma) deep within the earth. This magma forces its way to the earth's surface and exits by erupting through volcano fissures or other cracks in the earth's crust. This molten expulsion is termed *extrusive igneous rock* and is best known as lava. (Examples are pumice, obsidian, and scoria.)

On the other hand, when magma or molten rock forces its way between masses of rock below the earth's surface, then hardens slowly before it reaches the surface, it is called *intrusive igneous rock.* (Examples are granite, diabase, and gabbro.)

Warm-up: Practice some "Push and Pull" and "Group Sculpture", pages 63 and 61 .

Familiarity with the Science activity, "The Elements" can also be very helpful.

Activity: Divide the class into two groups (or if the class is large, consider working in smaller groups) to enact the formation of extrusive and intrusive igneous rock as follows:

Extrusive Rock – The first group creates an interlocking sculpture on a middle level to represent the earth's crust. One way this can be done is to have participants in a standing position with interlocking arms held at a middle level allowing room to raise arms upward when pushing from beneath.

The second group represents the magma. It starts on a *low level* (crouched low to the floor) positioned under the earth crust group. Slowly, with great show of effort and trembling, the magma group pushes up from underneath, while raising the "earth crust" sculpture, exploding out the top and center of its sculpture.

Intrusive Rock – Have the groups do a second enactment of the previous rock formation, this time, instead of then *exploding* out the top of the earth's crust, have the magma group slowly rise, then *freeze.* on cue, just before it (slowly rising) reaches the earth's upper crust, forming intrusive rock.

As a final action, have the "earth's crust" sculpture be washed away by erosion, (a third group or the leader can act out water and wind with scarves), leaving the intrusive rock fully exposed.

If you wish, improvise some narration during the slowly rising action segment to encourage unity. A drum beat or musical piece that builds up slowly in intensity also will help to propel the action and focus attention on the activity.

Reenact these actions, changing parts, so that participants playing the earth's crust have opportunity to play the magma.

SEDIMENTARY ROCK

Getting Started: Discuss with the group facts about sedimentary rocks:

Temperature changes, water and wind erosion cause these rocks to break down. Ask what other things besides rocks break down and accumulate at the edges of streams, lakes, and oceans. (Shells, bones, plant life, water soluble substances, and chemicals.)

• Sedimentary rocks are formed by the accumulation of these fragments. The fragments, called sediments, sliding down mountainsides, dragged away by glaciers, washed off by rains, rivers or waves, or blown into the air by winds, are often carried to places where they pile up in large quantities over millions of years.

• Once deposited, these different sized sediments - pebble, sands, silts, and clays - form layers sometimes hundreds of feet thick and harden, due to pressure, into rock. Fine materials such as clay and silt become compacted through pressure. The larger particles do not stick together unless cemented. Dissolved minerals in the ocean and lake waters such as silica and lime may be chemically deposited between fragments of sand and pebbles, cementing them into rock.

• Some sedimentary rocks can consist of large deposits of shells and coal. Coal is composed of ferns, mosses, and tree trunks buried in swamps. decayed and compressed for thousands of years.

Warm-up: Adapt "Basic Scarves" as in the science activity, "The Elements", page 161 , and concentrate on air and water. Have participants practice piling on top of each other gently and in small groups.

Activity: Choose a few of the actions involved in the formation of sedimentary rocks for small groups of partners to act out: For example:

• Wind blowing up dust. (Some participants represent wind, others dust being blown around) Add scarves if available to enhance expression.

• Water rolling sand particles along. (Some participants represent water, others sand particles .)

Dynamic Metamorphism — One rock plate pressing against another

• Layers of sediment piling on top of previous layers. (Participants find ways to pile up on each other, gently)

• Ferns falling and decaying, compressing into rocks. (Show with fingers and body-formation different types of plants.)

Ask the group to review, verbally, the different actions that create sedimentary rock formations.

Extended Activity: Divide the class into several groups, each assigned to enact the creation of a famous or fascinating rock formation in the United States. Colorful nature books would be inspiring for reference. The Grand Canyon, Badlands, buttes of the southwest, coastal cliffs of Big Sur are some intriguing material to try.

METAMORPHIC ROCK

Getting Started: Explain to the group that the term "meta" means change and "morph" means form. Metamorphic rocks are rocks that have changed form, from existing bedrock (sedimentary or igneous), because of the action of heat, pressure, and/or chemicals within the earth's crust.

Dynamic metamorphism is the result of pressure exerted on the rocks during mountain formation. *Thermal* or *contact metamorphism* results chiefly from contact with hot magmas (lava) and friction.

If possible, gather some examples of metamorphic rocks such as: marble, slate, and quartzite.

EXAMPLE # 1: QUARTZITE

Warm-up: Prepare the group with "Positive/Negative Sculpting", page 58 , and the preceding rock activities, before attempting this activity.

Activity: Illustrate dynamic metamorphism by having participants act out the formation of quartzite and/or anthracite coal:

Quartzite is metamorphosed quartz sandstone in which all the pores of the sandstone have been filled with crystalline quartz. It is among the most durable of rocks.

Ask half of the group to form a group sculpture with emphasis on body contact and the formation of many "holes" or open spaces such as found in "Positive/Negative Sculpting". This half represents the sandstone.

The other half of the group represents the quartz crystals and must move into the previously formed sandstone sculpture, "filling" the holes as described in the "Positive/Negative Sculpting" exercise. The aim here is for both groups to press together, forming a sculpture that is *without holes* and is thus strongly "cemented". Cue the group to freeze after completing each phase of this sculpture construction; the sandstone with holes; the crystals filling them; and then pressed together as one entire mass.

Repeat the entire process to reinforce the idea, reversing roles.

166

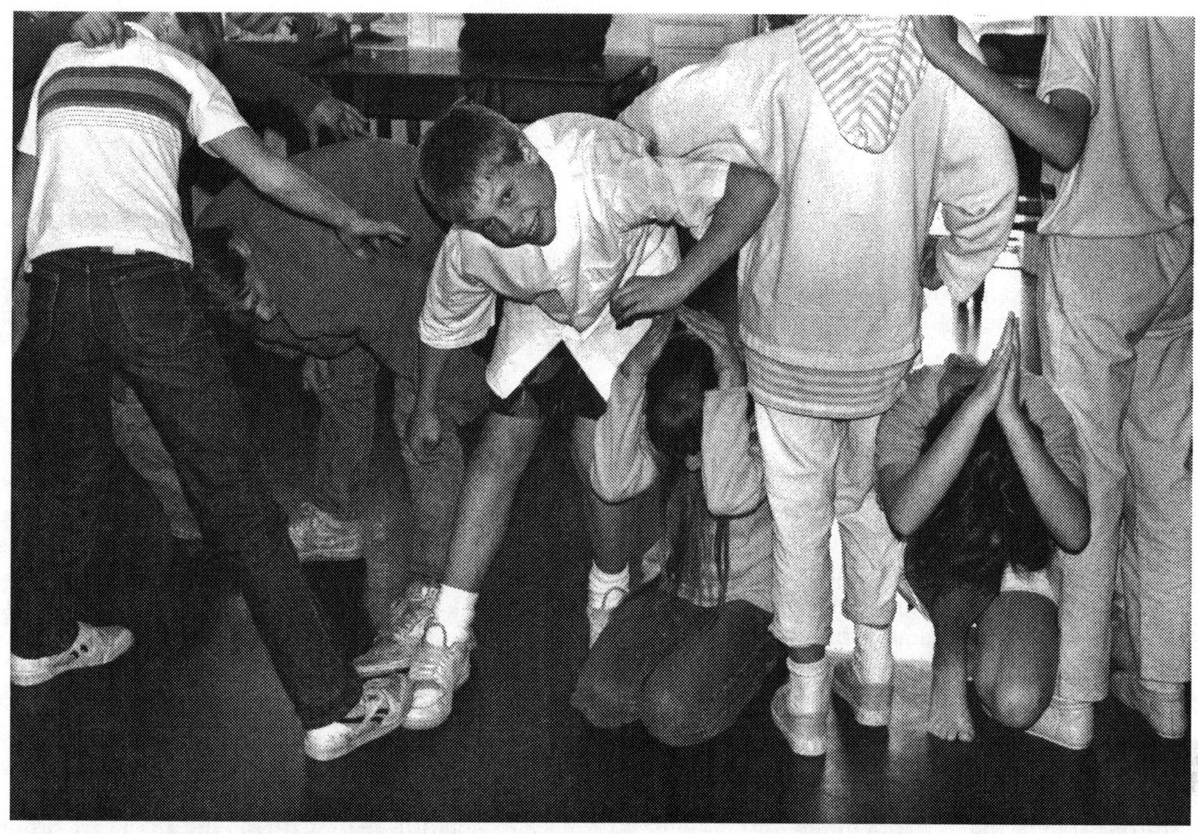

Quartzite rock formation — Crystals formed in sandstone pores

Encourage the group to verbalize what rock they are representing as soon as their formation is set and frozen. For example, some members might say: "We are sandstone." While others say, "We are quartz crystals." Together they could announce "We are metamorphosed quartz sandstone called quartzite." Or the teacher may recite the words for the group to repeat.

EXAMPLE #2: ANTHRACITE COAL

Anthracite coal is metamorphosed soft or bituminous coal. It is much harder and more lustrous than soft coal and splits with a conchoidal (shell-like) fracture. The rock containing soft coal is compressed and folded by pressure built up in mountains surrounding it. This pressure and folding results in a more dense coal called Anthracite.

Warm-up: The participants must be familiar with the medium and heavy aspects of the "Push and Pull" exercises , page 63 .

Activity: In this portrayal of rock activity, we will emphasize change in shape formation.

Divide the class into partners. One partner represents soft coal, and the other, the force folding and forming this coal and the earth's surface into a mountain.

The soft coal begins by lying flat on the floor or standing upright in a perfectly straight position.

The partner acting as the "force" must gently place constant pressure from one direction on the partner acting as "coal."

The coal responds by "folding" (such as doubling or bending over).

Have partners practice these actions in unison, changing roles to give each partner a chance to push and be pushed several times. Let teams share best examples.

Extended Activity: Illustrate another example of dynamic metamorphism and how this process involves bending and folding based on the previously practiced flat sedimentary rock formations while working in a large group.

Ask half of the participants to stand, one in front of another in a straight line, to represent layers of sedimentary rock.

The other half stands in a line shoulder to shoulder with the first line and applies gradual pressure against them as the first group resists. Because the participants will be of varying strengths, the once straight lines will become irregular and wavy just as occurs in the folding and forming of rocks. Done in very slow motion, the process of changing shape can be easily noted. Encourage action with a steady drum beat. Cue the group to freeze at various stages of the shape formation.

Compare the wavy line that the two groups have formed whenever the drum beat stops, to an illustration of an exposed rock formation with similar bends.

THE ROCK CYCLE

Objective: To illustrate how rocks evolve in a cycle over a long period of time and eventually become different rock forms.

Getting Started: It is necessary for participants to have explored the previous activity, "The Three Major Classifications of Rocks", to be prepared for this activity.

Discuss with the group the rock cycle as follows:

Igneous rocks, derived from magmas, are thought of as the primary or "parent" rocks of the crust. These rocks are transformed by erosion and deposited as sediments, which cement together and harden, creating layers of *sedimentary* rocks.

The cycle continues as mountain-making movements of the crust and chemical processes convert both igneous and sedimentary rocks into *metamorphic* rock forms.

The pressure and folding involved in the metamorphic processes may draw the rock deep under the earth's surface subjecting it to temperatures so high that it melts again into magma. This magma may be pushed up and solidify to form igneous rocks which completes the cycle.

Activity: Divide the class into groups of five to ten members each.

Ask each group to choose and enact the entire cycle of one rock form that is understood or has been researched, beginning with its igneous stage (if this is where it originates) or the accumulation of non-rock sediments (such as shells, trees, animal bones, debris, chemicals); into a sedimentary rock, then its transformation into a metamorphic form, then its return to an igneous form again using some of the techniques applied in earlier rock activities. Some examples of relations of sedimentary to metamorphic rock forms follow:

Sedimentary Material	Sedimentary Rock	Metamorphic Rock
Pebbles, gravel and sand	Conglomerate	Quartzite, gneiss
Sand, grains (usually quartz)	Sandstone	Quartzite
Clay, silt	Shale, mudstone	Slate, phyllite, hornfels, schist
Lime (shells)	Limestone	Marble
Peat	Bituminous coal	Anthracite coal

LIMESTONE ROCK CYCLE EXAMPLE

To enact this rock cycle the entire group divides into two teams. One half (Team A) represents the forces (water, pressure and heat). The other half (Team B) represents all the other participants in the cycle process, the animals, minerals and rock (calcite, lime, limestone, marble and igneous rock).

The Action Begins: The components of the rock cycle enacted by Teams A and B will continually change. For example, Team A starts as magma and next enacts the part of streams and oceans.

1. Magmas (A) push upward from inside the earth to form igneous rock (B). (A pushes B.) This rock (B) is washed by streams or oceans (A) which dissolves and carries calcite (B) and other minerals along in it.

2. Clams as well as other shellfish, coral, algae, etc. (B) extract calcite (originally from igneous rock) from the water (A). From this calcite they form lime from which they construct their shells.

3. When they (B) die the shells are ground by the waves (A) and accumulate on the ocean floor.

.4 Weight of the ocean (A) combined withe fine silt cements the ground shells together to form limestone (B).

5. Earth movements (A) compress the limestone (B) and transform limestone into marble (B).

6. Movement of magma (A) presses marble (B) deeper towards the earth's core and it melts from the heat and becomes magma again.

Repeat 1. Magma is pushed up again (A pushes B), cools and becomes igneous rock.

FORCE FUN
Friction

Objective: To introduce and experiment with mechanics or forces and the important part played by friction.

Getting Started: Introduce the class to the word "force" and ask for examples of illustrations. Pushing and pulling are examples of force. All machines need force in order to work.

Discuss everyday activities in which friction, or lack of friction, are key factors in performance. These activities may offer subjects for pantomime or small dramatic scenes. For example:

• *Hammering nails* - Nails are difficult to hammer into wood due to friction, but the same friction helps keep them in place, holding the materials together.

• *Ice skating* - Clear of snow, the ice is smooth, but add snow or bumps, or rust on the skates, and the friction slows you down.

• *Driving with snow tires* - The rough surface causes friction that stops the tire from sliding, enabling it to grip the snow and move the car forward.

• *Cooking with butter or oil* - A thin layer of a slippery substance stops the food from sticking to a pan.

Warm-Up: Conduct a tug-of-war game. After several minutes of pulling, stop and discuss the forces involved. In tug-of-war, the participants are pulling on the rope while, at the same time, pushing *against* the ground. (The ground is pushing back against their feet.) Whenever a person pushes something, that thing pushes or pulls back. This is a basic rule of force. Sometimes this rule is broken. If one team in tug-of-war stops pulling, the other team will fall down.

Another rule of push and pull action is that whenever a force does not have an equal force working against it, something will start to move.

Explore the "Push and Pull" exercise, page 63 , with a small, but crucial, adaptation that will work only if a smooth wooden or linoleum floor is available.

First, proceed with the "Push and Pull" exercise, working in partners, making sure everyone is barefoot or wearing non-slipping shoes. Emphasize the importance of the resistance that the floor makes to the pushing and pulling efforts.

Now try the same exercise requiring the partner that is being pushed or pulled to wear socks, and note how ineffective all resistant actions become. The friction between the person and the floor has been reduced because of the smooth surface.

Activity: Have participants work in small groups to present pantomimes of an activity affected by friction. For example, a skit on ice skating can involve participants gliding and skating over a slick, icy pond (with figure eights and other fancy patterns), then over a rough, bumpy surface of ice.

Push and Pull actions

WHEELS
Friction

Objective: To introduce the wheel as a major invention that overcomes friction to a large extent and thus is an important component of machines.

Getting Started: Discuss how machines use friction and overcome friction. On a skateboard, for example, one's foot pushes against the ground, or, when a person is skateboarding down a hill, the magnetic pull of gravity from the earth's core pulls the skater down the hill, closer to the earth's center.

Note that the wheels cannot push back against the foot that pushes off or against the pull of gravity. The wheels roll, so the board and the person on it move.

Warm-Up: Conduct the Push/Pull exercise, page 63 .

Activity: Discuss situations in which friction is necessary, such as moving a skateboard, bike, car, etc.

Separate the group into partners, A and B. A must push B while B lies on the floor in some flat or non-round shape. The object in this activity is to allow the natural friction to take place and resist any movement given.

In contrast, and to show what occurs when friction is minimized have B curl up in a ball or lie elongated, but ready to roll.

A is to push and B is to assist by rolling as easily as possible. Encourage a variety of rolling positions.

(Caution the B's to protect their heads and use gentle rolling motions. Demonstrate how best to do this.)

Allow the partners to change roles so that B pushes A, in both flat and rolling positions.

Activity: Rearrange the participants into larger groups and ask each group to improvise a short dramatization of the discovery, invention or use of the wheel. For example:

Assemble wheels onto the first automobile ever built, then drive it for the first time in history.

AIR PROPULSION
Friction

Objective: To explore and explain the force found in the compression of gases.

Getting Started: Discuss or show with a balloon how the compressed gas or air inside the balloon, when released, pushes against the outside air. The outside air, in turn, pushes back against the balloon. Explain that if there is nothing holding it down or opposing this pressure, the object propels *away* from the push (that is, the balloon flies around in the room, or a rocket goes up into space).

Warm-Up: Explore the gentle version of the "Push and Pull Exercise", page 63 . The partner being pushed must not apply inertia, but remain inactive, only responding to the direction, location, and amount of push being given by the other partner.

Activity: Read the story "Robert Fulton" (refer to the Social Studies Section) to the group. Have partners dramatize the entire story or concentrate solely on the invention of the steam engine in the latter part of the story.

Have the entire class work together in the end to create the successful steam engine following group sculpturing techniques as described in Section One.

SHAPE, SIZE AND DIRECTION
COMPARATORS

Objective: To learn the basic measuring tools, or comparators, as applied to science.

Getting Started: To compare is "to examine for likenesses and differences" and " to show different levels of quality, quantity or relation". After sharing these definitions with your group ask for examples of comparisons then identify the comparators used in each case. For example in the sentence "George is smaller than Jim" the comparator is *size*.

List and discuss with the group the comparators and how they can be used for measuring specific areas in scientific study. *Speed* can be used to measure lightning; *speed* and *direction* can measure velocity; *balance* and *force* can measure machinery, etc. Some general comparators follow:

direction	*time*	*force*
balance	*distance*	*color*
speed	*weight*	*texture*
temperature	*shape*	*size*

Each comparator can be explored on its own and then in conjunction with another comparator. In some cases, as with speed and direction which equal velocity, this study can help concretize scientific terms.

Warm-Up: Adapt the "Run, Skip, Jump" exercise, page 27 , to explore the comparators of *direction, speed, distance,* and *weight.* Include such concepts as "traveling as if weighing two tons or as if light as dandelion fluff".

Conduct "Shapes", page 56 , and use this exercise to compare contrasting shapes and sizes by exploring: big/little/; jagged/smooth; symmetrical/asymmetrical; round/square; horizontal/vertical and other comparators that members of the group suggest.

Activity: Build up a new word list, this time composed of words of opposite meaning applicable to measuring any of the comparator criteria, listed above, such as:

sink/float	*heavy/light*
hot/cold	*shallow/deep*
rough/smooth	*fast/slow*
balanced/unbalanced	*tiny/enormous*
thick/thin	*high/low*
curved/straight	

For older participants, consider developing an advanced word list that includes a more challenging vocabulary such as :

sinewy/flaccid
featherweight/heavyweight
accelerated/decelerated
high velocity/low velocity

Have participants work in pairs and develop one to two minute skits based upon the word list above. This may or may not include story content. For example:

Fast/Slow - Two brothers or sisters, one painfully slow, the other hyperactive, trying to get dressed or eat a meal before going out for a day's adventure.

Balanced/Unbalanced or *Symmetrical/Asymmetrical* - One partner makes all his or her movements balanced and symmetrical while the other shows contrast with unbalanced asymmetrical movements.

Have each pair present their skit to the group and follow this up with further discussion on the comparator used. In what areas of science can this same comparator term be used?

ARSENIC AND ALUMINUM:
What Do We Do With Them?

Objective: To define and identify some of the chemical elements and how we know them in everyday life.

Getting Started: Share information about elements with the group:

• There are fewer than 100 elements in nature.

• Elements are substances that contain only one kind of atom.

• Each element has a different number of protons in the nuclei of its atoms.

• Helium-4 (enacted in "Orbiting Atoms" in the Science Section) is one of these elements.

• Other examples of elements and their commonly known uses or sources are:

(H) *Hydrogen* - in water

(O) *Oxygen* - in water and air

(C) *Carbon* - in air, charcoal, and plant matter

(Cl) *Chlorine* - used in swimming pools

(Al) *Aluminum* - used in aluminum foil, house siding, etc.

(As) *Arsenic* - a poison.

(Cd) *Cadmium* - used to form Cadmium white oil paint

(Cu) *Copper* - a metal used for jewelry, pennies, pipes, wires

(Au) *Gold* - used in jewelry, basis of wealth backing the paper dollar

(He) *Helium* - used in helium balloons

(I) *Iodine* - used to disinfect cuts, abundant in fish

(Fe) *Iron* -used for bridge and building construction, iron pans

(Hg) *Mercury* - used in thermometers

(Ne) *Neon* - used in neon lights

(Ni) *Nickel* - used for nickel plating, coin money

(N) *Nitrogen* - used in explosives

(K) *Potassium* - abundant in potatoes and bananas; essential to health

(Ag) *Silver* - used for jewelry, money, teeth filling

(Na) *Sodium* - in salt

(S) *Sulfur* - inflammable; used in matches and gun powder

(Sn) *Tin* - used for cooking utensils, tin cans

(W) *Tungsten* - used in lightbulbs, glows when electricity passes through it

(U) *Uranium* - used in atomic fission, has a large atomic structure

Ask each participant to find some information, through research, about one or two of these most commonly known elements. Or, simply share information about these elements with the group and record on the chalkboard or a chart as a reference for the participants.

Warm-Up: Explore "The Magic Ball" game, page 50 . Create some of your own pantomime situations emphasizing clear and exaggerated action.

Explore the "Orbiting Atoms" activity, page 178 .

Activity: Play a drama game similar to "Guess Who I Am", page 37 , in which you whisper to each person the name of an element that has been discussed. Each person then acts out or pantomimes a use or property of the element for others to guess.

Sample Element Pantomimes:

Iodine: – A person:
whittles wood – cuts self – drops wood – winces with pain – sucks finger – looks at finger – walks to medicine cabinet and opens it – applies iodine – blows on finger – reacts as in pain

Helium - A person:
picks up a balloon – stretches it several ways – indicates with hands the helium tank's shape – attaches balloon to tank's nozzle – turns knob – reacts as balloon blows up quickly – turns off knob – ties end of balloon – shows with hands how big and round it is – ties string on balloon and lets it go – watches it float up – walks away looking up at balloon

Carbon - A person:
picks up sketchpad – shows how big it is by outlining with hands, sets it down – outlines campfire pit, warms hands and reacts to heat – picks up charcoal piece from fire – shows how big it is with fingers – shows it gets hands dirty by noticing black on fingers and wiping them on a garment or handkerchief – applies charcoal to paper and draws with it

CARBOHYDRATES SCULPTURES

Objective: To enact the formation of carbohydrates and oxygen through the use of sculpting.

If your group is advanced enough to know something of molecules and atoms here is another way to enact an aspect of photosynthesis.

Getting Started: Enact "Photosynthesis", page 147, or review the information with your group.

Warm-up: It helps if your group has had some experience with sculpting. "Shapes", "Partner Sculpting", and "Positive/Negative Sculpting" make a good foundation for this activity.

Spread the group out in the room. Ask everyone to sculpt themselves into the shape of an "O". Try a number of variations on this assignment by encouraging group members to use different body parts: whole bodies, their hands and fingers, legs and arms. Next have them form a "C" and then an "H" with their bodies, taking time for variations.

Activity: Divide the class into teams of three members each. Divide the teams into two groups. One half of the teams must create interlocking sculptures representing H_2O, with two persons each forming an H (or the two together form an H) and the third forms an O.

The other half of the threesomes must form sculptures representing CO_2 consisting of one C and two O's. These sculptures represent the molecules of water (H_2O) and carbon dioxide (CO_2). Each group can create its own sculpture making sure the letter shapes are fairly clear.

Next, each CO_2 team must find an H_2O team to combine with to form a carbohydrate, $C_m(H_2O)_n$.

The teacher or any unpaired threesome or participant can represent the sun. This person or group can create a movement to represent the energy of the sun. The sun makes a radiating movement towards each CO_2 and H_2O combination as the group members stand near each other in their sculptures. The energy from the sun enables tranformation. At this point the C breaks off from its two O team members, and forms a new link with the H_2O

The unused oxygen "O" escaping from a plant into the air

sculpture which leaves the two O participants free to float away separately or as a combined unit. Thus the formation of carbohydrates and the by-product of oxygen is enacted in a simplified manner.

Each CO_2/H_2O combination should:

1) Be radiated by the sun
2) Form a link and
3) Let go of two O's.

End the session with a discussion of what types of foods contain carbohydrates.

MOLECULAR FORMS
Solid, Liquid and Gaseous

Objective: To explain some of the differing properties of matter by enacting the three basic molecular forms: solid, liquid and gaseous.

Getting Started: Give an introductory explanation of atoms and molecules:

Everything we can scientifically test on earth is made up of matter. There are three categories of matter: solid, liquid and gas. Ask for examples of each:

> *Solid* – metal, wood, glass, rubber, ice
> *Liquid* – water, molasses, oil
> *Gas* – air, smoke, propane gas, steam

Each of these materials is made up of molecules which, in turn are made up of atoms. There are about one hundred kinds of atoms. Each atom contains protons and neutrons in its center, or nucleus, and electrons which travel in orbits around its nucleus, like planets going around the sun. (See "Orbiting Atoms", page 178.)

Under a powerful microscope, we can see that these tiny specks called molecules shake and jiggle in all different directions. They dart and bump into other molecules in the material.

Warm-up: Adapt the extended activity in the exercise "Jump/Freeze", page 23, to this activity by concentrating on tiny jumps up and down, side to side, backward and forward. Also have participants try jiggling and shaking different parts of the body in rhythm to music (fingers, arms, shoulders, legs, hips, head, etc.).

Explore "OK Bumping", page 23. If necessary, separate the group into "heavy bumpers" and "light bumpers" or pull out those participants who are not gentle enough, allowing them to re-enter after they have watched how this exercise can work when bumping is done with *even* energy.

Activity: Explore the different material types through movement:

Solid Materials. Using group sculpting techniques, have the group form a giant ice cube. Direct them to press very close together as if *stuck* to each other. Starting with very small movements, have participants begin small gentle bumping and jumping actions. Members should strive to stay tightly stuck together and always be in contact with adjoining members as they continue to jiggle, shake, and bump.

Cue the group to freeze then relax in place and listen as you instruct. Explain that this previous movement activity is an enactment of molecules in a hard or solid state such as ice. The molecules that compose ice and all other solid materials are *always* in motion. But, they are also tightly stuck together due to strong forces between the atoms and molecules.

Liquid Materials. Tell the group to re-form their pressed together ice cube and repeat the gentle bumping motion. Pretend to turn on a giant stove with exaggerated movements and guide the enactment as follows: "As I add heat, the outside of your ice cube is beginning to melt. As this happens the outside molecules move a bit faster. The bonds between the molecules slowly loosen. In expressing this idea of expansion, the outside molecule participants should begin to slide past each other as all the molecules move faster and farther apart while *still staying in contact* with the others in the group at all times."

Once the entire group ice cube formation has expanded, loosening from the outside towards the inside, and outer participants begun to slide past each other, have participants freeze, sit down right where they are and discuss what worked and what did not. Re-enact the entire expansion and melting process if some aspect of the enactment was not done correctly or if ideas for better enactment are suggested.

Gaseous Materials. Have participants regroup as they were when enacting the liquid state: all in loose physical contact (not in close contact). At this stage they are to jump and bump gently at arms length from one another.

Announce that the heat is now being turned up to a high temperature under the water and that this heat is turning the molecules that they represent into steam. In this condition, the members move (jiggle and jump, shake and bump) faster and faster until they jump clear out of the water group and fly off into the air. (Stress caution and control of movements so that participants do not crash into each other.)

As the molecules spread out and move faster cue them to imagine that they are bumping into other random steam and air molecules, above, below and all around them, so that they move fast but for relatively short distances. (In gasses the forces holding the molecules together are weak. They do not stay in contact with one another or stay arranged in a particular way.)

Extended Activity #1: Repeat the water cycle in scenario form. Example narration:

"The group will now start as water. That means you must be in contact with those around you and constantly be in motion sliding past each other. Begin!

I'm now turning up the heat. You are moving faster and also are moving away from each other. You are at arms length but are still in contact with each other. The heat under you is getting hotter and hotter and you are starting to boil. Jump up without bumping into other molecules too heavily. Now you are evaporating into steam. Jump out of the water and into the air around the pan of water. Now you are flying for short distances into the air, darting this way and that.

You move to the sides of the room and come into contact with a cold window or wall. Still jumping this way and that, the cold window or wall makes you slow down. Your movements do not carry you very far and you clump together with other water molecules. In these small groups you are drops of water that slide by each other and move even slower. It's getting colder and colder as I open the door. Now move even closer together within each drop of water. Your movements are slower and smaller until each water droplet freezes. Freeze!"

Afterwards, have participants sit down in a circle and share what happened. What worked well, first, and then what did not work well and how it could be improved.

Extended Activity #2: Brainstorm with the class what materials are able to change categories, or molecule states such as liquid to solid metals, solid wood to ash and smoke, liquid to solid glass, etc.

Divide the class into smaller groups. Have each group create a scenario in which the narrator for the group describes the changes of a substance from one state to another. The rest of the group should enact the action of the substance's molecules and possibly the heating and cooling elements involved.

Example narration: "We are starting with sand which is in a solid state therefore containing tightly bonded molecules. This sand is then put in a special oven and heated to a very high temperature. The molecules expand and move faster. The bonds between them loosen and they begin to slide by each other as the sand becomes liquid. The liquid is then blown into a vase by a glass blower and cooled. Note how the molecules slow down and move closer together but still maintain tiny movements in their solid state."

After some exploration have each group share its narration and enactment as the rest of the class watches.

MAGNETISM

Objective: To explain and demonstrate the principles of magnetism through directional movement exercises.

Getting Started: With the use of magnets and metal, or metal filings, demonstrate the basic principles of magnetism to the group. Explain how an object becomes magnetized when brought into contact with a magnet or source of magnetism causing the molecules to line up side-by-side, all facing north or south.

Warm-up: Carry out the "Push and Pull" and "No Bumping" exercises, pages 63 and 23.

With participants lying on the floor, practice and explore various ways of spinning and turning around (on knees, stomach, bottom, hip), calling out different places in the room for participants to direct either heads or feet. Emphasize no bumping.

Announce that participants' feet will represent the *south* pole and their heads the *north* pole. The leader or a chosen participant will represent the magnet and all participants on the floor will represent metal objects.

The magnet should approach individual participants with his or her north (head) or south (feet). The person approached must spin to show his or her opposite end (head or feet) is being attracted to the "magnet".

Activity: • *Enact how metal objects become magnetized.* Announce that the majority of the participants will represent the molecules in a metal object. Have them lie down randomly on the floor. As in the previous exercise, everyone's head will represent the north pole, and feet the south pole, but before the molecules are magnetized, they are lying every which way inside the metal object. The leader, or several participants together, will represent the magnet (head - north pole, feet -south pole).

The "magnet" locates at one end of the room and approaches the "molecules", feet first. (This may be done by scooting or doing a walking bridge.) The magnet touches the molecules with its south pole (feet) and all the molecules must react by rearranging themselves side-by-side, all heads (north poles) facing toward the magnet.

Repeat this idea a number of times with the magnet going to different locations in the room, touching different molecules with one pole or the other. Each time, the molecules must react and realign themselves accordingly.

Extended Activity: Explore personal magnets. Divide the group into partners. Have one partner represent a magnet and the other a metal object that is attracted to the magnet. Hands or feet contact can be emphasized initially.

Have the partners lie on the floor at random, approximately eight feet away form each other. Explain that the magnetic field is only strong within an arm's length of the magnet.

Tell participants that you have the power to turn on and off the "magnetic field". (Provide a signal such as turning the lights on and off, or clapping hands.)

Use the signal to turn on the magnetic field. Tell the "metal objects" that they are to be *very slowly* attracted to their magnet partners. Challenge the objects to move very slowly until they are within the magnetic field (within arm's length) of the magnets. Then they will move quickly as the magnetic force becomes much greater, until they *abruptly* stick to the magnet.

Challenge the magnets to move about with their objects attached.

Repeat the procedure as though the partners were magnets with *like* poles coming toward each other. Instead of being attracted to one another and coming within the magnetic field, they will fiercely repel one another.

Repeat the procedure focusing on various points of attraction. Try shoulders, head, knees, back as the focal point of the magnetic pull.

WHY IS THE SKY BLUE?

Objective: To better understand light, and how light waves cause the colors we see.

Getting Started: Discuss with the group: What is light? What is color? What is pigment?

Light is a form of energy. Experiments have proven that light behaves both as particles and as waves. Therefore, there is no final decision on what light is. It can affect matter and be affected by matter – as the particles in the air "scatter" various bands of light. White light is a mixture of all colors of light. When these colors or varying wave lengths of light are separated this is called the "spectrum" and can be seen in a rainbow or when light goes through a prism.

Color is not in the objects we see. It is in the light by which we *see* the object. A piece of green paper appears green because it absorbs all the colors of the spectrum in the white light except the green, which it reflects back to our eyes.

Warm-Up: Practice "No Bumping" and "OK Bumping" page 23 . Line the group up on one side of the room as in "Run, Jump, Skip" locomotion exercise, page 27 , and explore two types of wave motion: the first being a quick, zigzag side-to-side jump; the second, a smoother, longer wave-like motion from side-to-side across the space.

You may wish to use these predetermined movements or proceed to have the participants explore their own versions of quick, short and longer smoother wave movements.

Divide the group into two parts, one half to represent *violet and blue light.* This group must travel across the space with the quick , short wave movement characteristic of this kind of light.

The other half represents *red and orange light.* This half must enact the sweeping, longer wave-like pattern across the floor as described above.

The goal is for both groups to cover the same amount of ground within the same amount of time, while each group adheres to its movement pattern.

Activity: Divide the class in half again. This time, the members in the first group the members will be subdivided, one half will represent *blue/violet light,* and the other half *red/orange,* while the second group will now be *air molecules, dust and water vapor* (as well as other impurities and pollutants).

Participants representing air molecules, dust and water vapor are to spread out in the space. The blue/violet light and red/orange light members gather at one end of the space which represents the location of the sun.

At a given signal, members in the the two light groups start the wave motion characteristic of their type of light, as practiced earlier, as they travel away from the sun and across the space.

The members representing red/orange light will weave in and out *around* the particles in the air members and end up on the other side of the space. While the violet/blue light will gently bump into the particle members and be scattered, going off their paths in all different directions, *away* from the sun.

At this point explain further the phenomens of light to the gorup: In actuality, blue and violet light waves are scattered by our atmosphere with ten times more frequency than the red light waves. This means that more red rays go straight through our atmosphere while blue rays are scattered and therefore *seen.* When the sun is low, the light travels through more atmosphere before reaching us. This causes the red light waves to bump into additional molecules. When there is lingering pollution or dust in the air this also causes the red light waves to be scattered and therefore seen. We then have the phenomenon of a reddish sunrise or sunset.

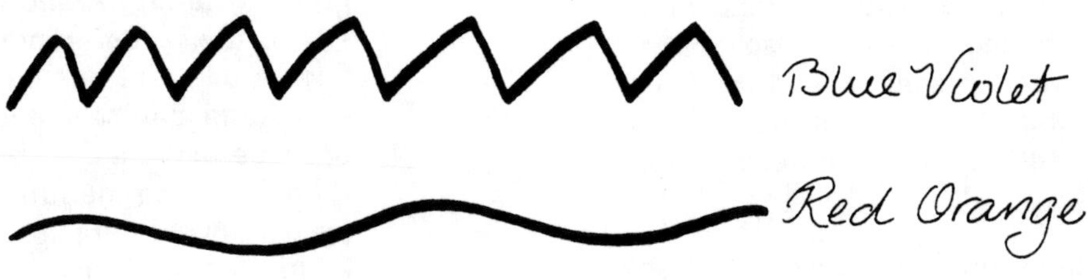

THE LITTLE RED CAR

Objective: To enact the reflection and absorption of the bands of the light spectrum that result in the colors we *see*.

Getting Started: Explain to the participants that the colors we see are a reflection of that same color in the light spectrum. All other wave lengths of the spectrum are absorbed by the object and therefore not visible to our eyes. For example, a yellow flower reflects the yellow part of the light spectrum.

Enact "Why Is The Sky Blue?", or discuss before trying this activity.

Warm-up: Conduct "Dancing Words", page 44 , to prepare the participants with increased movement vocabulary.

Familiarize the class with "Shapes", page 56 , and "Group Sculpting", "Positive/Negative Sculpting," pages 61 and 58 .

Divide the class into two groups. One group will represent, through group sculpture, an object of a single color: a red car, a blue sweater, field of green grass, etc. This group must huddle together and secretly decide what object and what color they will be in preparation for group sculpting. Emphasize that their planned sculpture must be large enough to "absorb" the majority of the second group. Absorption may be accomplished by leaving an open middle in the sculpture, or by instructing the second group representing colors of the spectrum to fit into the open spaces of the object group sculpture as in "Positive/Negative Sculpture", page 58 .

As the object group works on this decision and on forming the shape, participants in the other half of the class should divide into six groups, each representing a color in the light spectrum, (red, orange, yellow, green, blue, and violet). Each of these color groups work separately in a section of the room to create a wave-like or vibrational movement to represent its color as in the activity "Why Is The Sky Blue?"

To help the group invent movements, encourage the use of different body parts; fingers, arms, shoulders, backs, hips, legs and feet. Also mention the use of levels, varying speeds, and rhythms. Emphasize simple but distinctive movement that can be done in locomotion to represent each color.

Activity: When all groups are ready, have each color group state its color and demonstrate its characteristic movement. At the same time, the members of the object sculpture group observe carefully the color group that they will be reflecting (the color they have chosen for their object). For instance, if the object is a red car then they must take careful note of all members in the red color group. The goal will be for the object group to push away all members of the red group while absorbing all members of other color groups into their sculpture.

To start the enactment have all the color groups mix together and gather at one end of the room representing the location of the sun. The object sculpture is formed at the other end of the room.

The entire light spectrum travels from the sun toward the object while clearly displaying the different characteristic color movements. The members of each group, though mixed together, must keep repeating their distinctive color movements. It may help to have each color group quietly say their color as they move to help reinforce the movements. When the members of the color groups reach the object sculpture they are to be absorbed into the sculpture unless they represent the same color as the object. In that case they are "reflected" or pushed away by the members of the sculpture group and continue moving away from the object while still repeating their characteristic movement. A quiet steady drumbeat can serve as accompaniment to this enactment.

Afterwards, sit and discuss with the class what happened, then switch roles so that the object group can enact the colors of the light spectrum and vice versa.

ORBITING ATOMS

Objective: To explain and enact the structure of a basic atom and create the structure of a Helium-4 atom.

Getting Started: Discuss atoms with the group:

- Atoms are made of three basic particles - protons, neutrons, and electrons.
- One atom is different from another if it contains a different number of these particles.
- An atom may have a large or small number of these particles.
- Protons and neutrons form the nucleus (center) of the atomic unit.
- The electrons run in an orbit or circle around the nucleus.
- When not electrically charged, atoms have the same number of electrons as protons.
- The number of neutrons may vary in an atom.

Warm-up: Conduct "Shapes" or "Positive/Negative Sculpture" exercises as found on pages 56 and 58 . Have partners form their interpretation of an atom's nucleus. Encourage the use of shapes that are angular, rounded, side-by-side, interlocking and on varying levels.

Ask each participant to find a partner and a space in the room. One partner represents the proton and the other the neutron (together they compose a nucleus).

After exploring this basic nucleus forming activity, ask partners to share a favorite nucleus sculpture with the group.

Activity: As an advanced activity, recreate the structure of a Helium-4 atom.

(Helium-4)

• Coordinate three sets of partners (six participants total) to enact a single atom. Assign roles: one pair will represent the protons; the second, the neutrons; and the third, the electrons.

• The proton and neutron pairs must create a combined group sculpture to represent the nucleus (following techniques described in the warm-up).

• As this is happening and in a separate part of the room, encourage the electron pairs to explore different locomotor means of orbiting, such as skipping, sliding, crawling, vibrating, etc.

• The electron pairs wait until the nucleus is fully sculpted then run or otherwise locomote in a circular pattern (orbit) around the nucleus.

• Re-enact this activity three times so that each pair has opportunity to play all three atom parts.

• Have each group share its favorite interpretation with the class. If the class contains an odd number of participants, consider designing some atoms of diverse composition. For example:

Five Participants	two protons
(helium-3)	one neutron
	two electrons
Four Participants	one proton
(tritium or	two neutrons
hydrogen-3)	one electron
Three Participants	one protron
(deuterium or	one neutron
hydrogen-2)	one electron

Two Participants	
(ordinary hydrogen or	*one proton*
hydrogen-1)	*one electron*

Extended Activity: Complete the project by having the class create one colossal atom mobilizing all the participants. The rules are that the protons must equal the number of electrons; and the electrons may form one or two paths of orbit surrounding the atom's nucleus.

SPLITTING ATOMS
NUCLEAR FISSION

Objective: To understand how nuclear fission works.

Getting Started: Introduce the principles of the atom to the group:

To our knowledge, all material substances are made up of small units called atoms. These atoms, in turn, are composed of smaller particles called protons, neutrons, and electrons.

There are about 100 kinds of atoms. Some are small, involving a few particles, and others are large, involving many particles. Radium is one of the largest atoms, containing 88 protons, 138 neutrons, and 88 electrons. When an atom is big, such as this, it may break apart and shoot out pieces of the nucleus (protons and neutrons) like exploding kernels of popcorn in a heated pan. In nature, nothing specific initiates this breakdown and nothing stops it. It is a natural occurrence, inherent in a big atom such as radium. Once exploded, it becomes several different atoms.

The glow-in-the-dark paint on clock arms and numbers contains small amounts of radium. (Bring in such a clock for participants to observe.) Viewing this paint with a magnifying glass in the dark, the sparks of energy shooting out can be seen as they are released from the breaking radium atoms.

Usually these shooting pieces of nucleus do not hit the tiny nuclei of other atoms. Many thousands miss for every one that hits another atom's nucleus. But occasionally they hit another atom and are absorbed by this atom's nucleus, or hit another atom and split it.

Warm-up: A controlled enactment of "OK Bumping" and "No Bumping" exercises, pages 23 and 23 will help prepare the group for the action involved in atom splitting.

Divide the group into two halves:

Have participants in the first half spread out

evenly in the space. Provide a steady drum beat as participants in the second half move slowly to the beat *through* the first half *without* bumping anyone. Freeze action.

Next, change the rules and require that the second half of the participants intentionally, but gently, bump into individuals in the first half.

Switch roles and repeat the process.

Activity: Arrange paired participants at random throughout the space, spreading them out evenly. Each pair represents the nucleus of a single large atom, so these pairs are to stand closely together, as if one unit.

One beginning pair, when given a cue, *pops* apart; each partner shoots off in a different and random direction. Each of these two beginning persons now represents a shooting particle and must:

- Locomote in a *straight* line and *by-pass* all other atoms; or
- *Bump into* and be **absorbed** (enclosed or enveloped somehow) by another atom;
- Or *bump into* and *cause* the other atom's nucleus to *split apart.*

Repeat this activity several times encouraging varied occurrences.

Extended Activity: Proceed to the next activity, dramatizing a chain reaction of an atom.

CHAIN REACTION
Atoms

Objective: To describe and enact the process of a cyclotron or a chain reaction.

Getting Started: Open up discussion on atomic energy. Ask, "What is the powerful energy that comes from splitting atoms called?"

Explain that in the atom enactment (refer to previous activity) many particles may have hit other atoms, but in reality many thousands miss for every one that hits.

In order to increase the numbers of atoms actually hit, and to harness the energy released by the splitting action, scientists invented a machine called a *cyclotron.* This machine gathers particles or pieces of nucleus and whirls them around faster and faster, then hurls them at a target of atoms.

While experimenting, scientists used a metal called *uranium* which contains one of the biggest atoms. The uranium nucleus splits into two big pieces plus a few neutrons. Remarkably, this split-

ting of the uranium atom lets loose hundreds of times more energy than does splitting the nucleus of most other materials.

As each atom splits, it shoots out a few neutrons that dart off and hit other atoms. These, in turn, make more uranium atoms split and additional neutrons shoot off, which in turn hit and split more atoms. This is what is known as a "chain reaction". If nothing stops this chain reaction, the acceleration is so quick that all the atoms explode in a flash. This is the working principle of an atomic bomb exploding.

Warm-up: Divide the group into pairs. Each pair decides which member will be called "A" and which "B". (Members might wear something color coded.)

"A" then sculpts "B" (see "Positive/Negative Sculpturing," page 58) and him or herself into an inter-locking sculpture representing a nucleus of an atom. Once this is achieved, they practice "splitting" apart, then "exploding" apart (with control).

Switch roles.

Have each pair, one at a time, share with the class its sculptures and explosions.

Activity: Combine two sets of partners to create new groups comprised of four members each. Spread these groups of four out evenly around the room, leaving space around the perimeter.

Each group represents a uranium nucleus. Two members represent the two large halves of the uranium atom; the other two represent the random neutrons that dart off to hit other uranium atom nuclei. Each group of four should sculpt itself into a new shape. This four person group sculpture represents the nucleus of the atom. Have an additional participant represent a "particle" in the cyclotron.

Begin by having the particle run around the perimeter of the space faster and faster. With care, and of course, in slow motion, this particle bumps into only one of the four-membered nucleus teams.

Two members of the hit nucleus team respond by exploding away from each other and moving out of the action, to the side of the room (becoming inactive).

The other two members representing the neutrons dart off and hit each uranium nuclei, which in turn explode and repeat the actions. This process continues in a chain reaction fashion until all groups are exploded. Pacing and practice will aid smooth interpretation.

Switch parts and re-enact, giving each person a chance to play both roles, halves and neutrons.

LEAPING LIGHTNING

Objective: To explain the action of lightning.

Getting Started: Prior to this activity, to introduce positive and negative charge concepts, explore "Orbiting Atoms", page   , with the group.

Discuss the principles of lightning. Lightning is a huge electrical spark caused by a build up of opposing positive and negative charges of electricity in a cloud. It forms in the following manner:

• Within a cloud, water droplets are carried upwards by strong currents of rising air. As these droplets break up, they become positively charged by losing electrons; the surrounding air becomes negatively charged by gaining electrons. Thus, a large positive charge builds up near the *top* of the cloud.

• In the highest and coldest parts of the cloud, the water freezes and forms ice crystals. These may become negatively charged due to friction that occurs in the process. The weight of these ice crystals causes them to fall to the **lower** part of the cloud, making the lower and rear of the cloud negatively charged.

• These charges build up so that there may be a difference of 100 to 1000 million volts between the positive and negative charges. The air insulates and separates these charges from one another. But when the charges become too great and the air, saturated with water, has lost its insulating ability, a giant spark of electrons leaps to restore the electrical balance back to neutral. These huge sparks are what is known as lightning and can travel within a cloud, from cloud to cloud, or from cloud to earth.

• In other words, lightning is caused by hot air rising rapidly (becoming positively charged) and hitting the water in the cloud (negatively charged). When rising air collides with falling drops of water or ice crystals, an electrical charge is formed by friction. If this buildup of energy difference is great enough (and the air is wet enough), the air becomes a conductor and the result is a flash of current we call lightning.

• Some of the spark's energy is used up in heating the air. When heated, the air molecules expand and spread out. This happens so fast that the air expands violently, then it quickly contracts to its normal state. In doing so, it creates the sound we know as thunder as the molecules crash into one another upon contracting.

Warm-up: Have the group spread out in the space and explore shapes to represent neutral, positive and negative charges. Explain that you will call out a shape directive and beat the drum (or

count) five times. At the count of "five" all participants should find a still shape, individually or with a partner, that fulfills the directive. Call out the key shapes for this activity, "rounded", "straight" and "crossed" a number of times in different order. Encourage the use of levels and body parts. Work towards a variety of rounded "O" shapes to represent neutral charges, straight "–" shapes to represent negative charges and crossed "+" shapes to represent positive charges.

Explore "Staccato/Legato Locomotion", page 29 . In addition have participants enact through movement appropriate images such as rain (gentle rain, driving rain, mist, etc.), ice crystals falling, clouds (light and heavy), lightning, etc. Emphasize the use of different body parts (elbow, head, back, eyelashes, toes and fingers), and varying dynamics and body shapes (angular, limp, rounded, etc.) to depict the actions involved in a lightning storm.

Develop one or several of the following locomotive warm-up activities into an exercise centered on different *levels*. First ask the group to move across the floor while changing levels. For example, begin with a low level and move to a high level.

Next, challenge the group by calling out transitions as movement is in progress. For example, to move across the room making sharp ice crystal shapes that start on a high level (arms up while leaping and jumping straight up), move to a middle level, and end on a low level (crawling, rolling, scooting on bellies or backs). Encourage participants to keep the quality of movement consistent.

Activity: Divide the class into three groups to compose a cloud:

Group 1 - Rising hot air (arrange in front on a low level)

Group 2 - Falling water and ice crystals (arrange in back on a high level)

Group 3 - Insulating or "lightning" air (arrange in the middle on a medium level)

Decide which direction the wind is blowing your cloud. Have the entire cloud/group move in that direction while performing the following actions:

Remind the group that round shapes will represent a neutral charge, straight shapes will represent a negative charge and crossed shapes a positive charge and participants should continue to form these shapes individually or with partners within the group formation as it changes.

• The **hot air group** starts on a low level and slowly begins to rise, changing from a neutral (rounded) shape to a positively charged (crossed) shape, as it rises.

All areas of cloud mass move forward
showing neutral electric charge

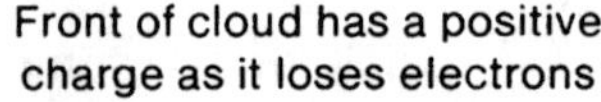

Front of cloud has a positive
charge as it loses electrons

Negative charge on
tail end of cloud

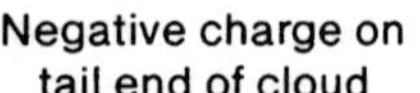
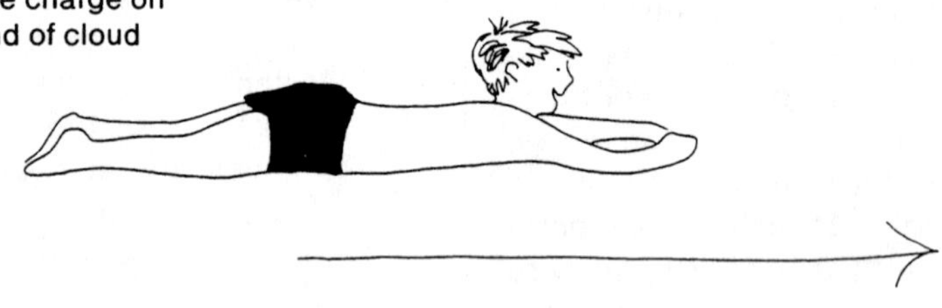

• The **insulating air,** or **lightning group** begins in a neutral (rounded) shape on a middle level. They act first as insulators, then on cue explode into lightning, either as individuals or in a chain-reaction pattern. This represents the exchange of electrons (lightning) when the air's insulating ability breaks down, making it a conductor of electrical charges.

• The **falling water** or **ice crystal group** begins in a neutral (rounded) shape on a high level. These shapes gently bump into one another, causing friction. In reality, this friction causes them to gather electrons and therefore they become negatively charged (straight) shapes as they fall to a low level behind the insulators and hot air. All three groups should end up in neutral (rounded) shapes. The front is now high, the middle remains on the middle level, and the back ends on a low level.

Practice these three major changing actions (locomotor, level and shape) several times, to achieve smooth sequencing, first in slow motion, then more quickly. Give participants a chance to exchange parts.

Extended Activity: Dramatize and integrate the element of lightning with a story or poem using a simplified expression of lightning (leaps, pulsing movements, etc.).

"Once There Was A Tree" by Natalia Ramania is a story about a tree that is split by lightning then felled by woodsmen so only the stump remains. A new tree grows in its place. Two children can take on the parts of the split tree, the lightning, the woodsmen and the new tree.

Other stories involving lightning are Greek myths in which Zeus is said to hurl thunderbolts and Norse myths in which the god, Thor, pounds his hammer to cause thunder and lightning.

You may also wish to discuss lightning and safety tips.

THUNDER

Objective: To learn what causes thunder by acting out the movement of molecules, affected by heat and expansion.

Getting Started: Open up discussion with the group about the fact that heat, a form of energy release, causes movement in molecules. When head increases the molecules move faster and move away from each other. Thus heat causes expansion.

In the case of thunder, heat generated by lightning causes air molecules to expand; then contract back to normal positions.

The waves in the air caused by this expansion/contraction are picked up by our ears as sound, known as thunder.

Warm-Up: Have the participants practice vibrating movements with the whole body.

Using the image of a balloon, have participants practice expanding and contracting movements to a drum beat or verbal cue.

Activity: Direct the participants to spread out in the space. Tell each person to dramatize an air molecule as follows:

• Wrap up into a tiny shape, the tightest, tiniest shape possible.

• Slowly expand. Slowly, very slowly, get bigger and bigger.

• Then quickly snap back into a tiny shape again.

• Come close together with the rest of the molecules in the middle of the room. Form the tiniest tucked-in molecule shape and huddle as closely together as possible, in a group formation.

• As the leader beats a drum or other instrument, grow bigger and bigger, expand and move, *gently* bumping into other molecules and move outwards in all directions. (Not only is each molecule shape growing bigger but the whole group's shape is expanding as well, spreading out and filling the entire space as much as possible.)

• When the drum sounds a big bang, *rush* back to the center to form your original small shape.

For additional enhancement, increase the tension of the movement activity with a little drum roll or small rapid beats as the shapes or molecules vibrate and expand.

As a more advanced activity, have individuals or a group enact the flashing lightning (refer to the previous "Leaping Lightning" activity) that heats the air, while others act out the expansion and contraction of air.

Extended Activity: Dramatize these same concepts while improvising narration and or dialogue about lightning, thunder, and molecules' actions. This could be factual information or fiction/fantasy based on myths, poetry, or other. Refer to the "Leaping Lightning" activity in the Science Section for story and myth suggestions.

MATH

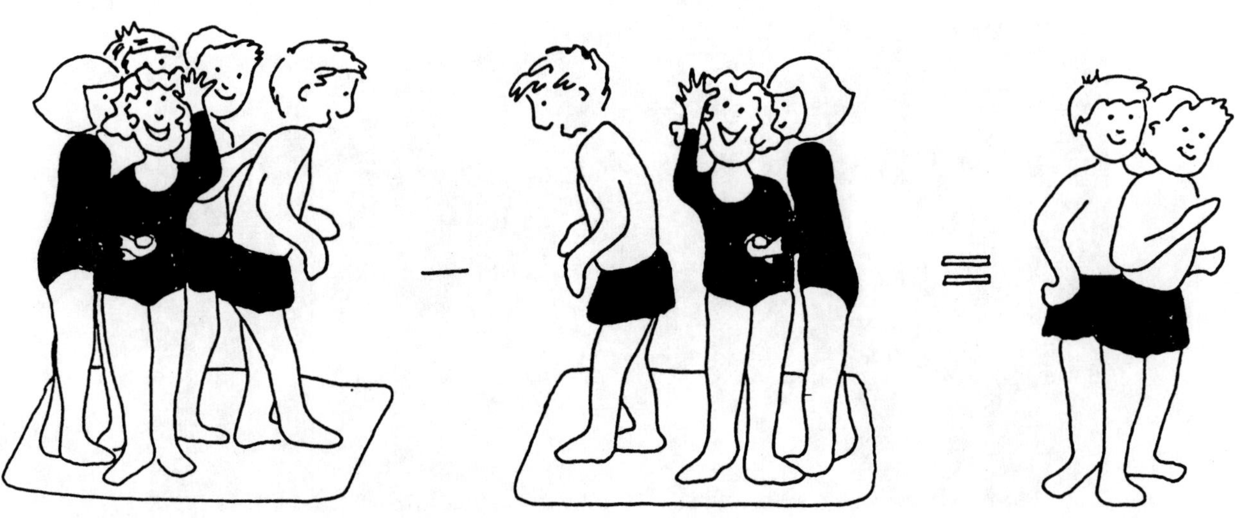

"Minus is a careless gnome, he loses what he should bring,
His ragged bag is empty for he subtracts everything."
From Gnomes and Jewels activity

MATH INTRODUCTION

There is a natural affiliation between basic math and movement. The lessons in this section offer a smattering of ideas to open thinking and demonstrate the possibilities.

The authors of this book were graciously given permission to use a number of Waldorf education activities from the book *Math Lessons for the Elementary Grades* by Dorothy Harrer. The Waldorf approach to education is known to be the largest private school system in the world. The founder of this system, Rudolf Steiner, states: "What lies at the root of arithmetic is consciously willed movement. Counting combined with movement will have the effect of bringing the child's arithmetical powers to life" (*Course on Pedagogy,* by Rudolf Steiner).

Touching the body as in the movement song "Head, Shoulders, Knees and Toes", as well as moving in time to a rhythm and stopping on cue, are examples of Steiner's "consciously willed movement". Moving an object such as a beanbag from in front of the body to behind the body, while counting to three so that it arrives on the count of three, is another helpful example.

These simple concentration exercises in movement activate the will and stimulate thinking so that class members will be alert and able to focus on academic math tasks.

The teaching of math is greatly aided by the use of rhythmic movement combined with counting as in the activities "Deadly Silence" and "Rhythmic Multiplication". A firm foundation for math studies is also formed when the participants actively take on the roles of digits or characters involved in the actual math problems as in the activities "Add and Subtract With Us" and "Negative Numbers". Such active involvement incorporating body movement alleviates stress that can block progress towards learning basic math concepts.

Other math activities encourage participants to become a physical component of a math problem as illustrated in the story "The Giant's Pie" found in this section. This activity demonstrates fractions by incorporating the children into the story as pieces of a pie that a hungry giant wishes to eat.

It is hoped that the diverse sampling of math activities that follow will inspire both teacher and participant to venture into new territory, enhancing mathematical comprehension.

ARE YOU "2"
Body Sculpting Numerals

Objective: To help participants gain familiarity with the numerals and provide a different approach for those with reversal problems.

Activity: Adapt the activity "Body Letters" on page 84 in the Language Arts Section.

Challenge the participants to body sculpt numerals and geometric shapes, first individually and then in pairs.

In the pairs, ask one partner to create a numeral such as a nine and have the other partner check the direction of the numeral and correct this if necessary. Have those with directional difficulty view their partners in a correctly formed numeral and trace the outline of the sculpture with large arm movements, inscribing the giant numeral in the air in front of the body sculpture.

Body sculpted number "2"

ADD AND SUBTRACT WITH US

Objective: To practice beginning addition and subtraction using the participants as numerical symbols.

Getting Started: Use the participants: the whole class, one-half the class, or some portion of the class, as your unit. Add and subtract members of the unit using them as *active* participants in math problems. Explain to the group that they will be active participants in the problems. When members of the group are added or subtracted from each other all the participants will calculate the total. When a participant knows the solution to a problem he or she will give a signal (place hand on the elbow, finger to the nose, fold arms, hold the ear lobe, hop on one foot, or any signal the leader selects for that activity). As soon as all participants are signaling, the leader chooses one participant to divulge the answer out loud.

Warm-up: Conduct the "Jump/Freeze" exercise, page 23 , to assist in the occasional stillness needed in this activity. "Are You 2?", page 187 , is an optional warm-up.

Addition Example #1: Add boys and girls; Have the boys line up in a number sequence and each call out (or body sculpt) in sequential order his number to discover the total number of boys. In a line on the opposite side of the room, have the girls follow the same procedure. Then call on the girls in groups of two, three or four, to skip, hop or run to the line of boys. As each group of girls is added, and integrated, into the boys line, the class calculates the total number in the line, concluding with the total number of children in the whole class. Reverse the process so boys integrate into the girls line.

Addition Example #2: With the same locomotor format as above add children with one color socks to children with another color socks to get the total. For example: Add children with pink socks to children with gray socks. Ask a volunteer to announce the total number of children with pink or gray socks: 2 children with pink socks and 8 with gray socks make 10 children. Additional colored socks can be added for a final total.

Subtraction Example #1: From the total of all children in the class of, say 27, have those with sneakers on (for example, 24 participants) sit down to discover how many are left wearing a different kind of shoe, in this case, 3.

Activity: *Add and subtract story excursion* – Make up a story in which all the children go on a picnic/exploration day. First, direct the participants to spread out in the space. Then call out for various numbers of participants in small groups to gather, one group at a time, at a designated spot in the room. Direct the action through a narrative such as "Three boys from the Tree House Club; Bobbie, Jacob and Ted, showed up at the gathering spot. How many have gathered so far?" As each group arrives, have the participants add up the total number gathered increasing the sum of the whole until the total number of participants has been figured.

Now the entire class sets out together on the hike. Announce different activities as you go along. Those choosing to enact a specific activity break off from the whole to do that activity such as: fishing, fort building, bird watching, picnicking, resting, story telling, swimming, etc.

Note the number leaving at each activity point and the number still remaining in the group with appropriate narration: "27 children set out and 8 went fishing. How many children were left to go on?" Have the participants signal when they know the answer. Call on one to share the answer.

As the sum begins to shrink, the leader or last group to do an activity retrace their steps and add each smaller group on again until the whole is reunited.

Extended Activity: Encourage children to bring in and make up addition and subtraction jokes or stories and riddles. For example:

> "On the road to St. Ives
> I met a man with seven wives
> The seven wives had seven sacks
> In each sack was seven cats
> Each of the cats had seven kittens
> Kits, cats, sacks, wives
> How many were going to St. Ives?"
> > *Answer:* One, the man telling the story.

> "How many beans make 5?"
> > *Traditional answer:* 2 in each hand and one in the mouth.
> > *Another answer:* One on each hand, one on each foot and one on the head.

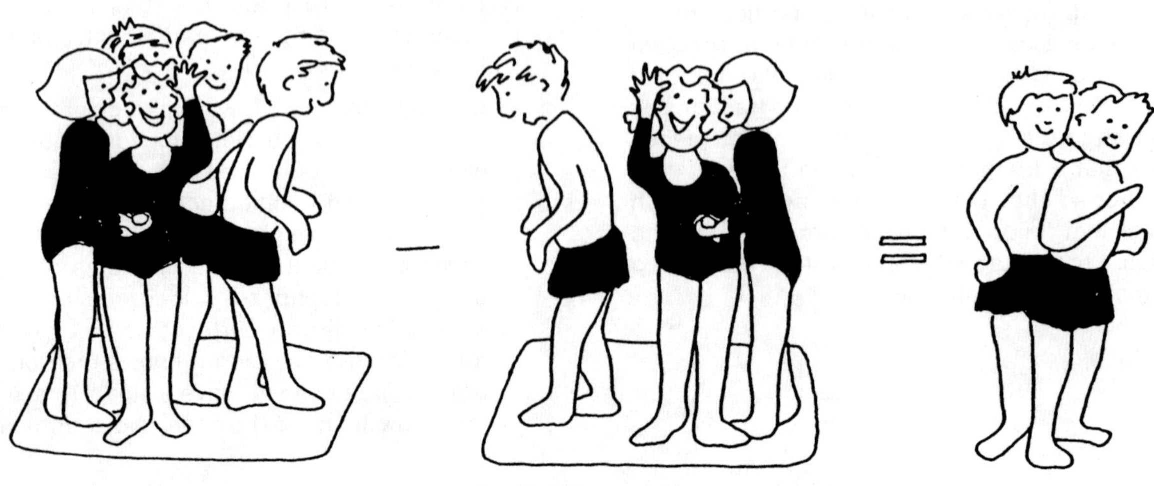

A subtraction example

WE ARE ALL ONE WHOLE CLASS

Objective: To demonstrate through rhythm and geometric pathways simple examples of the triangle, square and star inscribed within a circle.

Warm-up: Conduct the "Round the Circle" exercise, page 26 . Practice locomotion in a circle and the rules of staying in place in a circle. Have participants practice two quick steps, followed by one slower step which takes the same amount of time as the two quick steps together. Use a clap or drum beat to make this rhythm clear.

In the following way, have participants practice the transition from a single file circle to a circle consisting of partners: Start with a circle formation and face the participants so that they are all traveling in one direction. Choose one participant in the circle and have him move forward to join the person in front of him who becomes his partner. Then proceed around the circle of participants in this manner until every other person has stepped forward to join with a partner. Have all participants skip around the circle with their partners.

Activity: Have participants return to the single file circle. Read the poem before proceeding, then follow the activities accompanying the poem. In the first line of the poem, participants will stamp out two quick (short) steps forward in the circle, and then take one slower (long) step. Each line of the poem is stepped out in this same rhythm.

"We Are All One Whole Class"
from *Math Lessons for the Elementary Grades*
by Dorothy Harrer
(acted out in circle)

POEM	ACTIONS
We are all one whole class One by one see us pass While our feet sing the song, Two short steps and one long.	In a single file circle, step to the rhythm of two quick steps and one slower step, for each three words.
	Have every other person step forward to form partners.
Now we walk two by two In a ring round and true While our feet sing the song, Two short steps and one long.	In partners continue with the rhythm as in the previous section.
	Leader chooses three children equi-distant in the circle, giving them the number names One, Two and Three.
In we run, merrily, One to Two, Two to Three.	First, number One runs to Two's place. Two then runs to Three, and Three runs to One's former place.
While our feet sing the song Two short steps and one long.	Return to single file circle again, continuing rhythm.
Run a square and count four – One - -, two - -, three - -, And one more - -.	Leader chooses four children in the same way as before to run a square.
While our feet sing the song, Two short steps and one long.	All travel single file.
We are stars full of light With five rays shining bright In the dark sky at night.	All stand facing the center of the circle, with arms and legs out-stretched.
	All hold hands.
While our feet sing the song, Two short steps and one long.	All move hand in hand around the circle with the previous rhythmical steps.

RHYTHMIC MULTIPLICATION

Objective: To practice counting by two's (three's, four's, etc.), and to reinforce the times tables through body rhythm.

Warm-up: Conduct the "Round the Circle" exercise, page 26, practicing locomotion in a circle and the *rules of staying* in place in the circle formation.

Activity: Have participants walk in a circle, counting "1", as they step on one foot, and "2" as they step on the other. They should emphasize the number "2" with a louder voice and a stronger stamp of the foot.

Proceed in the lesson by continuing to count and stamp out numbers emphasizing all the *even* numbers from one to twenty-four. At the same time have participants practice saying the odd numbers more and more softly until the numbers completely fade away and only the even numbers are distinctly heard.

When number twenty-four is reached, have participants *turn around* in the circle and proceed to walk in the opposite direction while counting backwards, by two's, until they again reach the number 2.

When the participants feel secure about the sequence of even numbers have them recite only the even numbers in correct sequence around the circle: that is, the first participant says "2", the next "4", and so on until the number "24" is reached.

Then repeat the procedure backwards again from "24" to "2".

Extended Activity: In teaching the multiplication tables adapt the above activity emphasizing any number up to twelve, or to the ability level of the participants. Have participants silently step and count the in-between numbers then stamp and call out the multiples of the number which is being studied. For instance counting, 1 -2-**3**, 4-5-**6**, 7-8-**9**, etc., helps participants learn the three times table.

DEADLY SILENCE

Objective: To wake up the participants through a concentration exercise which serves to focus thought in preparation for further math or other academic activities.

Getting Started: Stand with the participants in a circle formation. Explain the exercise as follows: The class members will turn to the right and *walk forward* in the circle while counting 8 steps. Immediately repeat the same action but go forward only 7 steps and then backward 1 step. Each time complete 8 steps in total, but one less step will go forward and one more step will go backward. In the end all 8 steps go backward.

Warm-up: Practice the forward and backward steps, as described above while everyone counts out the forward steps loudly and whispers the backward steps.

Activity: For the actual activity the forward steps are called out loudly and in unison by all participants, while the backward steps are counted *silently*.

The pattern is as follows:

Steps forward counted loudly	Steps backward performed in silence
8	0
7	1
6	2
5	3
4	4
3	5
2	6
1	7
0	8

NEGATIVE NUMBERS

Objective: To help conceptualize and visualize negative numbers.

Getting Started: In order to visualize negative numbers, line the class members up in one long line. Tell participants that each represents a number in an infinite, unending line of numbers. As the leader, stand to represent the zero, or have one participant stand as the zero in the middle of the line. Ask participants to imagine that the lines on either side of the zero go on forever in both directions. Everyone from the left hand side of zero represents a *positive* number, while everyone from the right hand side represents a *negative* number such as —1. Explain that negative numbers are needed to indicate concepts such as air temperature that is colder then the temperature at which water freezes. The freezing point of water on the Fahrenheit scale is zero and every degree of temperature below that is —1, —2, —3. etc.

Warm-up: Conduct the pantomime song "When I Wake Up in the Morning", page 49 . It simply goes "When I get up in the morning, I jump right out of bed." Have participants stand in a circle formation and jump. Ask the participants for movement or pantomime suggestions to replace the words "jump right out of bed". For this particular activity you may ask for suggestions of things people do in cold weather or warm weather. For instance, "When I get up in the morning I shovel and shovel the snow", or "I walk and pick the flowers".

Activity: Have one person stand as zero in the middle of the space or place a chair there to represent zero. Have participants sit down so that there are an even number of them lined up on each side of zero. They will represent positive numbers on zero's left and negative numbers on zero's right in ordered succession. Have the participants call out their numbers from left of zero to the right and from right of zero to the left so each knows what number or negative number he or she represents.

Call out a temperature below or above freezing. The persons representing those degrees in temperature must stand up. They are counted and then they sit down again.

For example: "Minus 11": the eleven people at stage right of zero stand up, are counted, then sit down. (See "Stage Directions" in Science/Earth "The Elements".)

After five consecutive temperatures below zero have been called out, all the participants representing negative numbers may pantomime ice skating or another appropriate cold weather activity for 10-

15 seconds upon which the leader beats the drum and they quickly return to their line. After five consecutive temperatures above freezing, the positive numbers can all plant peas, skateboard or do some other chosen spring activity.

THE GIANT'S PIE
Fractions

Objective: To introduce fractions through story creation and enactment.

Getting Started: This activity is composed for the fraction 1/12th involving twenty-four or more participants but can be adapted to suit any group of eight or more participants using different fractions. For example, given eight participants, four would form the pie, two would enact the children, one the giant and one the giant's wife. The fraction would be 1/4.

Warm-up: Make sure participants have had some experience with pantomime exercises as in "The Magic Ball", page 50 , and with sculpting as in "Group Sculpture", page 61 .

Conduct "Characterization Locomotion", page 27 to help create interesting characters for the enactments.

Activity: Tell the following story, then assign parts. For an enactment involving the fraction 1/12th, twelve participants can sit in a circle, with their toes in the middle to form the giant's pie. One participant can enact the giant and another, his wife, or to involve an extra number of participants, have several form a group sculpture to depict the giant and/or his wife. Ten participants can act out the children in the story. If necessary adjust the number of pie pieces and participants enacting children to fit the class size.

Repeat the following story as participants act out parts.

THE GIANT'S PIE
By Kristen Bissinger

Ten children knocked on the giant's door. The giant's wife answered and the children begged for some food for they were very hungry. The giant's wife told the children to go away for there was only one pie in the house and that was for the giant's supper. "It is plain to see that one is not enough for all 10 of you and the giant, too."

The children said, "If you let us in we will show you how there can be pie for the giant, all of us and you, too."

"Alright," said the giant's wife, "if you are able to do this you may have pie, but if you fail you will be made into my husband's next pie."

Cutting The Giant's Pie

The children came in, cut the pie evenly in half (the children may make a large pantomime gesture of cutting over the pie) as six participants in the pie formation scoot to the left, six to the right. The children cut it in half again across the other way. They sliced each quarter (1/4) into three pieces (separating each of the twelve participants in the pie as a slice). The giant's wife counted the pieces and found 12 pieces, one for the giant, one for each of the 10 children and one for herself. She was totally surprised and delighted. She called the giant in and they each ate 1/12th of the pie.

Extended Activity # 1: Continue "the Giant's Pie" story emphasizing the division of the whole into a variety of fractions and an introduction to ratios.

The Story. The next time the children came to visit, the giant's wife welcomed them in. "You were very clever last time you came," she said, " but there is a problem. When you left, my husband complained he had not had enough to eat. If you stay for dinner this time, he must have half the pie and I must have at least a quarter of the pie." The children began to think: "If the giant gets one half the pie and his wife gets one quarter, how much is left for all of us children?"

"This is impossible to figure out," said one child. "Last time we divided evenly, but one half and one quarter and what's left is not even division."

They all sat down in a circle around the pie (composed, again, of twelve participants).

One child cut the pie in half (six participants in each half). Leaving one half of the pie for the giant, they cut the other half in half to make two quarters (with three participants in each quarter of the pie). The children could see that there are four quarters in each whole pie and two quarters in each half pie.

"Very good so far," said the giant's wife, " but only one of you has something to eat."

"There are twelve of us," said the children, "so we must cut this quarter into twelve pieces." First they cut the quarter into three even pieces (separate the three participants in this quarter of the pie). Then they cut each of these into four even pieces (an arm or leg of a pie-participant in each piece).

The giant's wife called her husband to come to dinner. Being a greedy giant, he said, "I would like to know how much more pie I am getting than each of you."

The children looked at the pie: the giant's portion was one half (1/2) of the whole pie. It was also equal to two quarters (2/4) of the whole pie. The quarter pie that had been divided for the children had been cut into twelve even pieces. The giant's half of the pie contained two quarters. Two times twelve pieces equals twenty-four pieces (2 X 12 = 24). The giant's half of the pie was twenty-four times as much as each child's piece (1/2 = 2/4 =

12/24 = 24/48). These fractions express the same ratio. There are 48 slices the size of each child's slice in the whole pie; 24 such slices in the giant's 1/2 of the pie.

This satisfied the giant and they all sat down and ate heartily.

Note: The leader may pose the above paragraph concerning fractions in the form of questions such as, "What fraction of the whole pie was the giant's portion?" The participants would be required to give a signal (as suggested in the "Add and Subtract With Us" activity) when they know the answers.

Extended Activity #2: Brainstorm with the group ways in which fractions are useful. Divide the class into small groups. Ask each group to make up a story or skit involving a fraction or fractions. Give the groups approximately ten to fifteen minutes to think up their story and practice its enactment. Then have each group share its skit with the others, followed by a brief discussion.

RATIONAL NUMBERS
(Integers)

Objective: To illustrate integers through short skit enactments.

Getting Started: Explain to participants that rational numbers are numbers used to describe the relationship (the ratio) between one whole number and another. An integer is one kind of rational number. Some examples of integers written as ratios are:

$$\frac{4}{2} = 2 \qquad \frac{3}{1} = 3 \qquad \frac{24}{2} = 12$$

Warm-up: Create a warm-up appropriate to the activity examples you wish to use. For example, the first activity involves fighting so warming up with "Partner Sculpting", page 56 , and "Mock Battle", page 64 , would be appropriate. For the skit about the children and the flowers, conduct "Shapes", page 56 and adapt it to the needs of the activity by calling out words such as "flower", "sun", and "grass", to inspire body shapes as in "Instant Scenery", page 61 .

Activity: Ask volunteers to act out each skit as it is told. Adjust the numbers involved to suit the number of participants within your group. For example, decrease the numbers of flowers in example #2 if you do not have 27 participants in the group.

Story Example #1: (Begin with all volunteers in seated position.) Two gangs were fighting. One gang had eight members and lived on the second floor of the apartment house. (Eight participants stand up to represent the upstairs gang.) The gang on the first floor had four members. (Four more participants stand up.) When the first floor gang went upstairs to fight, the second floor gang divided up evenly to fight them.

The participants proceed with a mock battle, as described.

When the skit has been enacted ask the question "How many second floor members fought with each of the first floor gang?" Then write the problem on the board:

$$\frac{8}{4} = 2$$

The answer is that there were two second floor gang members fighting against each one of the first floor gangs. The odds were two to every one, or a ratio of two to one.

Story Example #2: There were three children who wanted to pick wildflowers for their mother for Mother's Day. (Three participants stand.) When they climbed to the top of the hill they agreed to share evenly the twenty-four flowers that they found. (Twenty-four participants spread out in the room and shape themselves to represent flowers.) Each of the three children "gather up" his or her share of the flowers.

When the skit has been enacted check to see if each child has gathered the same number of flowers and ask "How many flowers did each child gather?"

Write on the board:

$$\frac{24 \text{ flowers}}{3 \text{ children}} = 8 \text{ flowers}$$

for each child, a ratio of eight to one.

Extended Activity: Note that the stories always have the smaller number *come up* and divide the larger number.

Challenge the participants to make their own skits involving ratios and integers for the entire group to enact.

Forming the number "8"

GNOMES AND JEWELS
Mathematical Processes

Objective: To familiarize the participants with the four mathematical processes: addition, subtraction, multiplication and division.

Getting Started: Have on hand a large number (at least twelve per participant) of small stones, shells, beans or pieces of paper to represent jewels.

Warm-up: Lead the participants in the exercise, "If You're Happy and You Know It", page 35 , including the emotions needed for the story enactment (joyful, greedy, sad and kind).

Practice "No Bumping," page 23 , while the participants travel at different speeds about the room.

Conduct the basic locomotion exercise, "Run, Skip, Jump", including a: slow "fat man walk" to represent *Plus;* slow, sad, backwards walk to represent *Minus;* fast run-leap done several times to represent *Times;* and tiptoe backwards in a variety of directions, to represent *Division.*

First have the participants stand in a circle and introduce the four mathematical processes with the following body poses and poems. Ask the participants to copy the verse, line by line, after the teacher recites it.

• *Division.* Stand with participants in a circle formation. Divide the participants in the circle into pairs. One member in each pair represents Subtraction and kneels with outstretched hands (palms upward) while the other member represents Division and stands facing the first member with one fist above and one fist below Subtraction's outstretched hands. Have the participants repeat the verse copying the teacher, one or two lines at a time.

"Division is a kind old gnome,
With each one he will share,
The jewels which he gathers,
He divides with greatest care."

When the participants enact the "Gnomes and Jewels" story, Division will drop jewels into Subtraction's outstretched hands.

• *Plus or Addition.* Have the students copy the verse, line by line after the teacher, as all stand facing the center of the circle, feet together and arms straight out to both sides at shoulder height.

"Plus keeps whatever he can find.
Each hand holds quite a heap.
He adds the jewels together
And says, 'They're mine to keep!'"

• *Minus or Subtraction:* Have all participants lean forward with one fist near the shoulder (as though holding a sack over the back), and one open hand straight back. Everyone repeats the verse while walking forward into the center of the circle in this pose, and walks out again, backwards:

"Minus is such a careless gnome.
He loses what he should bring.
His ragged bag is empty
For he subtracts everything."

• *Times or Multiplication.* Participants stand again in a circle with arms at sides and up above shoulder height with legs placed wide apart. All repeat after the teacher:

"Multiplication knows quite well
That two times two is four.
He always likes to multiply
So that he'll have much more."

Activity: Proceed by having the participants sit down to listen. Read or recite the story 'Gnomes and Jewels", by Dorothy Harrer. Have the participants distribute the "jewels" throughout the room in places where they can be seen but are not in the way of the action.

Divide the participants into groups containing five members each, to enact the story. One member of each group will play the King while the other four will each play one of the four math processes represented as gnomes in the story. If there are participants left over couple them up so that two participants play one part within a group.

Have all those playing the role of the King sit on their "thrones" and call their gnomes into the "throne room" one at a time. As each gnome is called, the persons playing that gnome approach their king with their prescribed characteristic movement as practiced in warm-ups, then stand before the King in a characteristic stance. For example, when the kings call "Multiplication" all those playing the role of the gnome called Multiplication run and leap back and forth several times until they arrive in front of their King and stand in their characteristic pose; arms up and legs wide.

When all the gnomes have arrived the Kings announce together that each gnome is to bring to their King twelve jewels a day, then sends all the gnomes out to look for jewels.

Those members playing Multiplication go very fast and gather two times twelve (or twenty-four jewels). The Plus members *slowly* gather "three and three and three and three" to obtain twelve jewels. The Minus members gather and lose jewels, then look sad at their empty bags, while those playing Division gather and then divide a portion of their jewels with the Minus in their group.

Finally, they all return to the King and present their jewels which the King counts. Because Minus and Division will have varying amounts the total may differ from one group to the next. Specific assignments may be given if the teacher wishes,

such as :"Minus gather twelve and lose eight jewels."

Exended Activity: Have each group of five sit together on the floor. Start with twelve jewels per gnome and a pile containing an indefinite number for the King. Call out different problems such as the one given below as the participants work out the problem together in each team of five with their jewels.

Example problem:

If each gnome has twelve jewels and –
• Minus loses 8 thus has 4 left, and –
• Plus picks up those 8 which he adds to his 12, and —
• Division divides his jewels in half giving 6 to Minus and keeping 6 for himself, and –
• Times gathers 2 times 12 (12 from the King's pile) how many jewels do they bring together to the King? (60)

GNOMES AND JEWELS
Poems and Story by Dorothy Harrer

Deep, underground, the gnomes are always busy working to gather jewels for the Gnome King's Treasure House. Every gnome has to bring in exactly 12 jewels every day, no more, no less, for most of them can only count to 12; but there are four gnomes who can count both more, and less, and this makes them act differently. They even look different from their ordinary companions! Two of these fellows usually come home with more than 12 jewels and the other two with less.

Times is the name of the first gnome. Yellow as a candle flame, he lights up hidden places so as to find more treasure, at least 2 times more than 12 jewels a day. And he has to make two trips, instead of one, to be able to show off before all the others, bragging, "Twice as much I bring to please my King!"

Plus is the second gnome, fat, green and greedy. He loves to think, "3 and 3 and 3 and 3 are twelve" and as he adds up what he finds, he wants more and more not only for the King but for himself. He fills his hands and stuffs his pants so that they rattle as he approaches the King. When he gives the king only 12 of his pretty stones, the King hears his rattling pants and turns *Plus* upside-down to get all the rest. Says *Plus*, "My pants I pad with all I add."

Minus, the third gnome, is blue and ragged. He has holes in his suit and holes in the sack which he carries. The jewels he gathers fall out through the holes as he wails, "Raggedy-blue, what will I do?" He always has less than he should have, even when he meets one who is willing to share what he has found and consequently, also has less.

Gnomes counting jewels

"Times is the first gnome's name, yellow as a candle flame"

Division, the fourth gnome is warm-hearted and red as the heart's blood. When he hears the wailing of blue *Minus,* he hurries up to him saying, "With you I'll share the jewels I bear."

Now the Gnome King knows all about these four gnomes. He knows that *Minus* will always be losing his jewels but that *Plus* will find them and add them to his pile. The King knows that *Division* will have less because he is kind enough to divide up his jewels and give a share to *Minus,* and that although *Division* brings in only a part of what he is supposed to, *Times* will bring in more than he should so that in the end nothing is lost but something is gained.

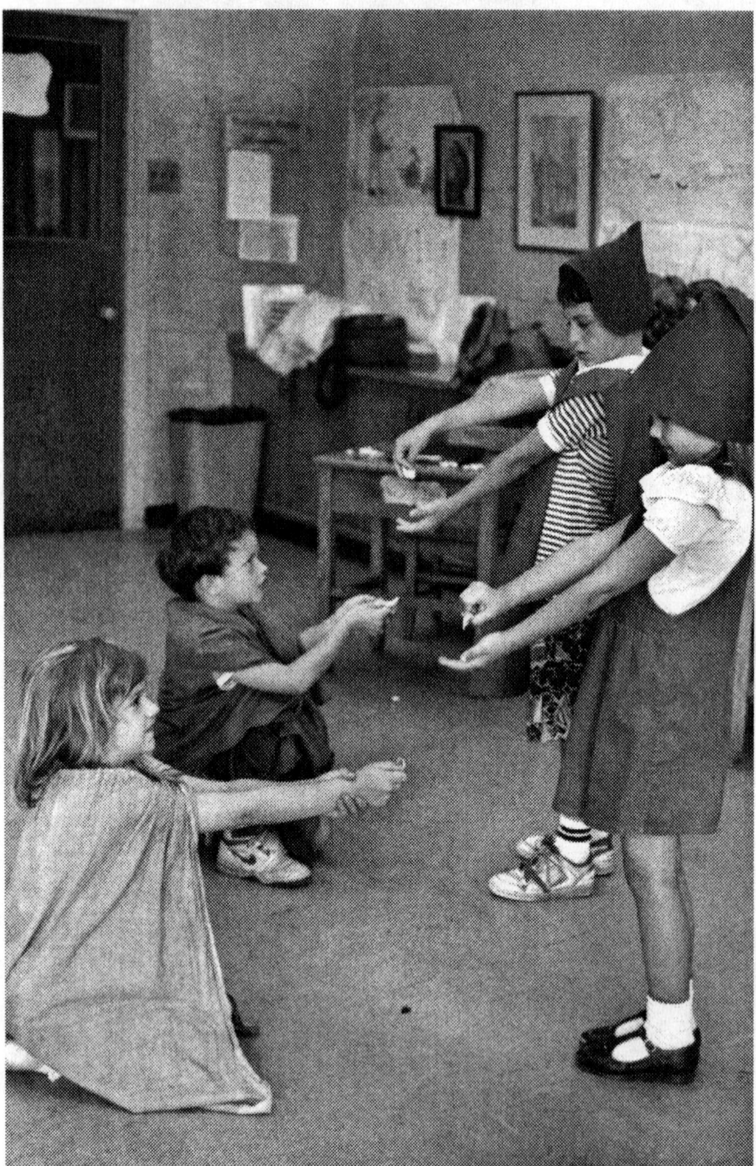

Division says "With you I'll share the jewels I bear."

RESOURCES

Creative Drama & Mime

Curtain I: A Guide to Create Drama for Children 5 to 8 Years Old. Trillium Press, Inc. Contains 75 stories, fairy tales, poems, and drama kernels for students to enact.

Dorian, Margery and Frances Gulland. **Telling Stories Through Movement.** Fearon Publishers. A Fearon Teacher-Aid Book with abbreviated story selections along with movement theme suggestions.

Hamlin, Kay. **Mime, a Playbook of Silent Fantasy.** Doubleday & Co., 1941. A beautiful book with many black and white photographs to inspire the reader with basic mime concepts.

Keysell, Pat. **Mime, Themes & Motifs.** Plays, Inc., 1975. A great little book of simple games and stories to pantomime, including a section for deaf students.

McCaslin, Nellie. **Creative Drama in the Classroom.** Longman, 1984. A comprehensive text that incorporates creative drama in the classroom and provides excellent companion material for **Leap Into Learning!**

Nobleman, Roberta. **Mime and Masks.** New Plays, Inc., 1979. Masks and mime merge to form a rich variety of animal and human characters to explore, including skits for middle and upper level students. Write the publisher for other books by Ms. Nobleman and other authors.

Stolzenberg, Mark. **Clown for Circus and Stage.** Sterling Publishing Co., Inc. A highly pictorial and in-depth look into the clown character from makeup and developing character to skit situations.

Torbert, Marianne. **Follow Me, A Handbook of Movement Games.** Prentice-Hall, 1980. Building skills through movement games is the thrust of this book.

Ward, Winnifred. **Playmaking with Children.** Prentice-Hall, Inc., 1957. Here is one of the basic well known texts on Creative Dramatics with instructions for teachers who wish to share dramatic experiences with children and present plays as well. It includes an extensive bibliography, story and record list appendices.

Ward, Winnifred. **Stories to Dramatize.** Anchorage Press, 1952. A very helpful collection of stories for dramatization by children, including age categories from 5-14 years.

Way, Brian. **Development through Drama. Humanities Press, 1967. A comprehensive text written by a renowned author in this field. One of the primary source books for Creative Dramatics.**

Wilson, Robina Beckles. **Creative Drama and Musical Activities for Children.** Plays Co., Inc., 1979. A charming little book of improvised movement, action songs, games, rhymes and playlets. Of particular interest in the section on fashioning homemade rhythm instruments from household objects.

Dance

Baba Hari Dass. **A Child's Garden of Yoga.** Sri Rama Publishing. A fine book to introduce stretches and yoga concepts to children. P.O. Box 1569, Santa Cruz, CA 95061.

Benzwie, Teresa, Ed.D. **A Moving Experience: Dance for Lovers of Children and the Child Within.** Zephyr Press, 1988. This exceptional best seller provides new insights to learning through creative movement. It includes over 100 exercises on communication skills, self-knowledge, cognitive principles and much more.

Goodbody, Slim. **The Force Inside You.** Coward-McCann, Inc., 1983. A highly recommended book by a popular mime performer in schools, nationwide. Centers around discovering the child's inner forces through balance, body and sensory exploration.

Joyce, Mary. **First Steps in Teaching Creative Dance to Children.** Mayfield Publishing, 1984. This clear and comprehensive book is highly recommended for the novice and advanced teacher wishing to pursue further dance techniques, as explained in **Leap Into Learning!**

Morgenroth, Joyce. **Dance Improvisations.** University of Pittsburgh Press, 1987. An excellent collection of dance improvisation structures aimed for a teen to adult group but with many structures adaptable to younger groups.

Makeup, Masks and Costumes

Bruun-Rasmussen, Ole and Grete Pebersen. **Makeup, Costumes and Masks for the Stage.** Sterling Publishing Co., 1981. Shows imaginative use of paper, paper bags and suggestions for costuming that can be found around the house.

Emery, Joy Spanabel. **Stage Costume Techniques.** Prentice-Hall, Inc., 1981.

Corson, Richard. **Stage Makeup.** Prentice Hall, Inc., 1981.

Education

Barton, Bob. **Tell Me Another.** Pembroke Publishers Limited Heinemann Educational Books, 1986. An excellent short book by one of Canada's foremost educators and storytellers on how to tell stories aloud and using storytelling effectively in the classroom, including choral dramatization, a story list and much more.

Benzwie, Teresa, Ed.D. **Math: A Moving Experience.** Zephyr Press, 1988, 430 S. Essex Lane, Tucson, Arizona 85711. An inspiring 30 minute color and sound video documentary on a Kindergarten learning math concepts and vocabulary through movement.

Berends, Polly Berrien. **Whole Child/Whole Parent.** Harper's Magazine Press, 1975. With humor and understanding, the author presents the sound spiritual bases of love and authority in the parental years; includes nearly 500 book titles for children under four.

Caduto, Michael J. and Josepth Bruchae. **Keepers of the Earth, Native American Stories and Environmental Activities for Children.** Fulcrum, Inc., 1988. A large beautifully written and illustrated volume of lessons in environmental education presented through the teaching of Native American stories.

Dewey, John. **Experience and Education.** The Macmillan Co., 1938. An authoritative book on the vital place of experience in education.

Furth, Hans G. and Harry Wachs. **Thinking Goes to School (***Piaget's Theory in Practice***).** Oxford University Press, 1975. An excellent educational book containing theory, information on how this theory has been put to use to nourish the normal developing process of thinking in the primary school, and a third section containing a large variety of thinking games.

Mearns, Hughes. **Creative Youth. / Creative Power. / The Creative Adult.** Doubleday and Co., 1940. Inspiring books on creative education. Though concerned specifically with developing writing skills these books are also valuable for teachers in any other field.

Miller, Olive Beaupre'. **My Book House.** The United Educators, Inc. An excellent anthology of literature for education and enactment with a superb cross-referenced index. These twelve volumes contain stories for pre-school through young adults.

Pearce, Joseph Chilton. **Crack in the Cosmic Egg. / The Magical Child. / The Magical Child Matures.** E.P. Dutton, Inc. 1985. Pearce is an eloquent spokesman for the link between academia and art or the intuitive. His scientific understanding of the brain and the human child strongly verifies the need for storytelling, enactment and this drama/dance approach to education.

Other Useful Sources

New Plays, Inc. Box 273, Rowayton, CT 06853. Write for this well established publisher's catalog of plays and excellent drama books.

Theater, Drama & Communication Arts. Write for catalog by Contemporary Drama Service, Box 452-PL, Downers Grove, IL 60516. A fine source specializing in a wide selection of how-to books and plays in this field.

PUBLISHERS ACKNOWLEDGEMENTS FOR REPRINTS

"All About Columbus", "The Boyhood of Robert Fulton", "Johnny and the Three Goats", "The Lion and the Mouse", "The Little Snow Maiden", "The Right Time to Laugh", and *"Shingebiss and the North Wind",* adapted from Olive Beaupre' Miller's **My Book House** and *"In Columbus' Time"* by Annette Wynne in the same book. The United Educators, Inc., Tangley Oaks Education Center, Lake Bluff, IL 60044.

"Chip-Chop" by I. Tupaj and *"Snowflakes whirl through winter night"* (titled *Hunter and Hare* in **Leap Into Learning!**) by M. Meyerkort from the book **Winter.** Wynstones Press, Brookthorpe, Gloucester GL4OUW UK.

"Fire Stealer, The" by William Toye, illustrations by Elizabeth Cleaner, Oxford University Press, 1979.

First Steps in Teaching Creative Dance to Children by Mary Joyce. Mayfield Publishing Co., 285 Hamilton Avenue, Palo Alto, CA 94301.

"Golden Egg Book, The" by Margaret Wise Brown. Western Pub. Co., Inc. (1947, 1971), 1220 Mound Avenue, Racine, WI 53404.

"How the Rhinoceros Got His Skin" from **Just So Stories** by Rudyard Kipling. Doubleday and Co., Inc. (1974) 277 Park Avenue, New York, NY 10017.

"Hugin and the Turnip" from **Seven-Year-Wonder Book** by Isabel Wyatt. Rudolf Steiner College Publications, 9200 Fair Oaks Blvd., Fair Oaks, CA 95628.

"Jabberwocky" from **Through the Looking Glass** by Lewis Carroll in **The Annotated Alice** with introduction and notes by Martin Gardener. Bramhall House, a division of Clarkson N. Potter, Inc., 419 Park Avenue South, New York, NY 10016.

"Row" by Ralph Pomeroy from **Sound and Sense, An Introduction to Poetry** by Laurence Perrine. Harcourt, Brace, Jovanovich, 1987, Orlando, FL 32887.

"Seal" by William Jay Smith from **Laughing Time.** Farrar, Straus and Giroux, Inc., 19 Union Square West, New York, NY 10003.

"Silver" by Walter de la Mare. Faber and Faber, the Society of Authors Representing the Literary Trustees of Walter de la Mare, 84 Drayton Gardens, London SW109SB UK.

Stonecutter, The A Japanese folk tale by Gerald McDermott. Viking Press, New York, 1975. 625 Madison Avenue, New York, NY 10022.

Very Hungry Caterpillar, The by Eric Carle. William Collins Publishers, Inc. 2080 West 117th Street, Cleveland, OH 44111.

"We Are All One Whole Class", "Rhythmic Multiplication" and *"Gnomes and Jewels"* from **Math Lessons for Elementary Grades** by Dorothy Harrer. The Association of Waldorf Schools of North America, 1985. Mercury Press, Fellowship Community, 241 Hungry Hollow Road, Spring Valley, NY 10977.

"Who Has Seen the Wind?" by Christina Rossetti from **The Complete Poems of Christina Rossetti.** Louisiana State University Press, Baton Rouge, LA 70893-5461.

NANCY RENFRO STUDIOS
"Quality Puppetry Products"

BOOKS In Paperback & Hardcover

For adults who work with children:

Puppetry in Early Childhood Education by Tamara Hunt and Nancy Renfro. Comprehensive resource for "Puppetization" of hundreds of new learning activities.

Celebrate! Holidays, Puppets, and Creative Drama by Tamara Hunt and Nancy Renfro. A treasury of storytelling and puppetry activities, as well as creative drama for use in the classroom or group. This encompassing book includes both major and minor holidays.

Imagination! At Play with Puppets and Creative Drama by Nancy Frazier and Nancy Renfro. Twenty-four projects designed to help children expand their "imagining powers", includes a variety of puppetmaking, play, and creative drama. Special emphasis on developing team cooperation, thinking on one's feet, integrating classroom material, and introducing works of fine art.

Storytelling with Puppets by Nancy Renfro and Connie Champlin. Traditional and contemporary literature are treated to an exciting lift through this complete guide to the use of puppets in storytelling. Includes extensive practical information on story adaptation, puppet selection and construction, as well as child participation techniques.

For children:

Bags are Big! by Nancy Renfro. Shows how even the lowly paper bag can be transformed by the wizardry of our imagination into something marvelous or magical. Grades 1-6.

Puppet Shows Made Easy! by Nancy Renfro. A wonderful book that explains how to put together a complete puppet show from script to final performance.

Make Amazing Puppets by Nancy Renfro and Beverly Armstrong. Jam-packed with exciting ideas for making puppets from paper products and recycled junk.

An exciting series

Pocketful of Puppets: Activities for the Special Child by Debbie Sullivan, illustrated by Nancy Renfro.

Pocketful of Puppets: Mother Goose Rhymes by Tamara Hunt and Nancy Renfro.

Pocketful of Puppets: Three Plump Fish by Yvonne Winer, illustrated by Nancy Renfro.

Pocketful of Puppets: Poems for the Church School by Lynn Irving, illustrated by Nancy Renfro.

WRITE FOR FREE CATALOG:
Over 200 Puppet Characters • Curriculum Kits • Show Kits • Cassettes • Books

NANCY RENFRO STUDIOS, Inc. P.O. Box 164226 Austin, Texas 78716 (512) 327-9588 800-933-5511